D1453795

Inside Graduate Admissions

INSIDE GRADUATE ADMISSIONS

Merit, Diversity, and Faculty Gatekeeping

JULIE R. POSSELT

Harvard University Press

Cambridge, Massachusetts
London, England
2016

First printing

Library of Congress Cataloging-in-Publication Data
Posselt, Julie R.
Inside graduate admissions : merit, diversity, and faculty gatekeeping /
Julie R. Posselt.
pages   cm
Includes bibliographical references and index.
ISBN 978-0-674-08869-6 (hardcover : alk. paper)
1. Universities and colleges—United States—Graduate work—Admission.
2. Discrimination in higher education—United States.   3. Minorities—Education
(Higher)—United States.   4. Universities and colleges—United States—Faculty.
5. Teacher participation in administration—United States.   I. Title.
LB2371.4.P67   2015
378.1'55—dc23   2015015782

To Derek and Daniel

Contents

Preface

It has been about twelve years since I first imagined conducting research on graduate admissions, and almost exactly five years since I began designing and conducting the study described in this book. In this time span, I have transitioned from being a college administrator and lecturer, to a doctoral student, to an assistant professor on the tenure track. My interest in understanding doctoral admissions from the faculty point of view originated in a problem of practice—a simple question from an advisee that, at the time, I was ill equipped to answer. I was new to my job with the McNair Scholars Program, and she had just decided to apply to graduate school. She wanted to learn what reviewers would be looking for in her application, and I had little more for her than a boilerplate response about strong GRE scores, letters of recommendation, research experience, and fit. I promised to get back to her after reviewing the literature.

It surprised me to discover that the research literature offered little more detail than I had offered my student. Scholars have been examining undergraduate admissions from the institutional point of view since the early 1970s, but until this project there had been only one study—a chapter in Robert Klitgaard's 1985 text *Choosing Elites*—that offered an empirically grounded explanation of what was important to admissions decision makers at the graduate level and why. The seed for a research study on faculty evaluation in graduate admissions was planted for me that day in 2003, and it has been a privilege and pleasure to see it come to fruition through the support, high standards, and academic freedom extended to me by my mentors.

Today, when I advise students about graduate admissions, I have a better-informed answer about what admissions committees in leading doctoral programs are looking for in applicants. At one of the conferences where I shared some findings of this project with faculty members, the discussant started her remarks by admitting how vulnerable she felt while reading the paper—how she squirmed to read the provocative quotes from scholars in disciplines far afield from her own, only to realize the squirming was because she herself had held similar thoughts or made similar comments. She was uncomfortable, she said, but she couldn't put down the paper (which has since developed into Chapter 5 of this book) because it helped her see assumptions that she didn't even realize she had been holding. I received these comments positively, for one of my principal aims with this work has been the classic sociological task of "seeing the strange in the familiar." It can be hard to see our own assumptions, and harder still to let them go in favor of new ways of thinking. Aside from the intellectual contribution this book makes to the literature, I hope it will help faculty members see familiar admissions work with fresh eyes.

My own moments of vulnerability have come recently, as the tables have turned and I have participated in admissions, not as an outside observer, but as one of the faculty decision makers. As a member of my department's master's admissions committee and a participant in the late stages of reviewing applications for the PhD program, I came to empathize in new ways with my research participants. I saw for myself the complexity of comparing applicants' relative admissibility when they have diverse strengths. I felt the pangs of saying no to highly qualified applicants due to budget constraints, the fatigue brought on by constantly checking myself for cognitive and other biases, and the tension of choosing carefully the moments to speak up in committee meetings. This empathy hasn't changed my findings or the way I describe them. It has, however, redoubled my own commitment to approaching admissions work as an area worthy of professional development—one that can't be separated from improving how we recruit and mentor the students whom we *do* admit. I hope readers of this book will join me in committing to ongoing learning about how we can select and serve graduate students more effectively and equitably.

INSIDE GRADUATE ADMISSIONS

Introduction

Gatekeeping Reconsidered

F OR THREE HOURS the philosophy admissions committee had been working in a cramped storage room that doubled as their meeting space. They had been discussing applicants on their short list, one by one, but had reached a point of deadlock over who should ultimately receive offers. Breaking a long silence that betrayed the group's exhaustion, their administrative assistant, Leon,[1] spoke up for the first time. He noted that agreeing to admit everyone who received an average rating of 1.8 or higher would give them their desired cohort size: the lucky 13. Their work would be done. No one jumped at the idea, but the committee chair, Liana, and a senior professor, Olivia, expressed their support. Another senior professor, Gerald, wasn't so sure.

"People seem to be very confident about the line where admissible leaves off and inadmissible picks up," he said. "I have a hard time drawing lines because wherever we draw it, it's going to look arbitrary."

Olivia emphatically responded, "Well, it *is* an artificial line!"

Continuing to push, Leon noted that drawing the line at a rating of 2.4 would finish the job even more quickly by giving them the optimal number of admitted *and* wait-listed students. A long pause and a few sighs and shoulder shrugs later, they agreed to use this threshold and started packing up.[2]

There is a story behind every statistic—including the lucky 13, the 2.4 rating, and the 18 percent of applicants admitted to research doctoral programs nationally.[3] This book tells the story of how faculty in ten top-ranked doctoral programs draw the almost imperceptibly fine line between those whom they admit and those whom they reject. Two years of observing and interviewing graduate admissions committees in core academic disciplines—astrophysics, biology, classics, economics, linguistics, philosophy, physics, political science, sociology—gave me a unique window into the evaluation and selection processes that go into graduate admissions. My research revealed faculty members' nebulous, shifting ideals about student quality; how departmental, disciplinary, and personal priorities are woven into judgments of admissibility; and the implications of it all for equity and the health of the academy.

Changes in society, the applicant pool, and the labor market have fundamentally altered the markets for graduate education and for people with graduate degrees, yet the criteria associated with admission to degree programs have changed little. Of the three strongest determinants of access to graduate education—college grades, Graduate Record Examination (GRE) scores, and the reputation of a student's undergraduate institution—the latter two are part of a conventional notion of student quality that fails on at least two counts.[4] GRE scores and college prestige fail to reliably predict whether a student will complete the PhD, and disproportionately exclude some of the very groups whom our mission statements and websites claim we wish to attract. What is more, the structure of the academy in the twenty-first century will not sustain many of the positions that admissions decision makers themselves hold. If faculty do not adapt their mindsets to meet changes in the academy, labor market, and society, they will select and train students for jobs that do not exist. For graduate education to fulfill its promise of developing leaders for today's knowledge economy and diverse democracy, many faculty will need to rethink how they evaluate prospective students and draw the line in admissions. Let's consider these dynamics in greater detail.

Doctoral Students and Their Professional Pathways

Worldwide, pursuit of the PhD continues to grow. The PhD is not only the central prerequisite for faculty careers; credential inflation has also rendered graduate degrees necessary for access and promotion in many professions that once required only a bachelor's degree.[5] Economic and technological development outside the United States has also sparked interest in graduate education from international students, whose share of doctorates awarded in the United States has more than doubled in the last forty years.[6]

Overall, the proportion of adult women (thirty to sixty years old) in the United States with graduate degrees grew almost tenfold from 1965 to 2005, from 1.1 percent to 9.68 percent.[7] And from 2000 to 2010 alone, the number of master's degrees earned by African American and Latino/a students more than doubled.[8]

Yet aggregate statistics like these conceal considerable complexity about the state of equity in graduate education. Gender and racial inequities are persistent and pervasive in doctoral education, for example, despite the progress in closing gaps in master's degrees awarded. Women and U.S. residents of color remain less likely than men and whites to attend research universities, and they continue to receive fewer doctorates than we would expect given their shares of both the overall population and the population of baccalaureates awarded.[9] African Americans and Latinos comprised 13 percent and 16 percent, respectively, of the U.S. population in the 2010 Census, but received just 6 percent and 7 percent of the doctorates awarded that year—numbers that reflect little change from the previous decade. Meanwhile, Native American doctoral attainment has fallen to its lowest point in twenty years.[10]

Gender and racial/ethnic representation also varies by academic field of study.[11] The well-known disparities in science, technology, engineering, and math (STEM) disciplines are evident in many humanities and social science fields as well. In the humanities, for example, only 3 percent of PhDs in 2009 were awarded to African American students and only 5 percent were awarded to Latino students.[12] Table 1 displays data from the Survey of Earned Doctorates (SED) about the number of PhDs awarded in 2012, by gender and race, for a selection of fields. Philosophy, which is not represented in SED data, awarded only 29 percent of their PhDs to women in 2009. It is notable that fields of study with continued racial and gender inequities also have some of the lowest admission rates, nationally.[13]

Like the population of graduate students, the range of careers pursued by persons who have earned a PhD has diversified.[14] As a result, most graduate programs are preparing, ad hoc, a much broader group of professionals than the next generation of faculty researchers. For example, applied intellectual and technical expertise is instrumental in today's economy, and the diffusion of public research into industry has created a whole sector of PhD-level researchers outside the academy. Less than half of engineering doctoral students now expect to enter academia.[15] Specialized intellectual inquiry is the heart of doctoral education, but viable alternatives to the academic track are necessary because there are far fewer tenure-track faculty positions than PhDs looking for jobs. Just one academic track faculty position is posted for every twelve PhDs produced in science, technology,

Table 1 Doctoral Degree Attainment by Gender and Race in Selected Disciplines, 2012

Academic Discipline	Gender	African Amer./Black	Amer. Indian/Alaska Native	Hispanic/Latino	White	Asian Amer.	Native Hawaiian/Pacific Island.	Other	Total
Astronomy	Male	***	***	***	137	***	***	10	190
	Female	***	***	***	52	***	***	8	85
	Subtotal	***	***	***	189	53	***	18	275
Physics	Male	***	***	***	805	464	***	132	1,504
	Female	***	***	***	163	134	***	45	363
	No answer	***	***	***	***	***	***	4	4
	Subtotal	35	***	87	968	598	***	181	1,871
Biological Sciences	Male	119	***	231	2,171	1,083	***	324	3,936
	Female	195	***	269	2,385	1,268	***	353	4,494
	No answer	***	***	***	***	2	***	8	10
	Subtotal	314	15	500	4,556	2,353	17	685	8,440
Economics	Male	***	***	86	416	276	***	90	897
	Female	***	***	26	179	184	***	29	433
	No answer	***	***	***	***	***	***	1	1
	Subtotal	***	***	112	595	460	***	120	1,331
Political Science/Public Admin.	Male	***	***	45	443	90	***	65	696
	Female	***	***	39	330	81	***	57	549
	No answer	***	***	***	***	***	***	1	1
	Subtotal	90	***	84	773	171	***	123	1,246
Sociology	Male	***	***	21	147	26	***	26	235
	Female	40	***	45	244	55	***	28	412
	No answer	***	***	***	***	***	***	1	1
	Subtotal	***	***	66	391	81	***	55	648
Linguistics	Male	***	***	9	64	21	***	18	117
	Female	***	***	10	77	39	***	13	143
	Subtotal	***	***	19	141	60	***	31	260

Note: *** = suppressed to avoid disclosure of confidential information.
Source: NSF/NIH/USED/USDA/NEH/NASA 2012 Survey of Earned Doctorates.

engineering, and mathematics. And in the humanities, where the glut of PhDs relative to academic jobs regularly makes the news, many graduates end up working in positions that do not require the PhD at all, much less in the narrow specializations for which they received training.[16]

The professoriate itself is changing in ways that compel a fresh look at recruitment, selection, and broader ideals of what makes an excellent scholar. Adjunct, clinical, and other nontenured appointments, not tenure-track positions, now constitute the majority of faculty positions listed. In response to these trends, a few PhD programs are shifting or broadening their focus and degree requirements. Some institutions are scaling back the size of their doctoral cohorts, while others are reevaluating their qualifying exams and the structure of the dissertation.[17] Largely absent, however, has been a conversation about what the changes inside and outside the gates of graduate school mean for who gets in.

Gatekeeping Reconsidered

Reform in doctoral education today must better align notions of student quality with the diverse students and varied career pathways that doctoral students pursue. Tenured faculty have both the influence and the responsibility to respond to changes in student trajectories. Some, though, are uncomfortable with students' increasingly diverse identities and career paths or feel stymied by political dimensions of the change process. Most professors in research universities, after all, are products of a system that gauges program excellence by placing graduate students in faculty positions at research universities, and that privileges theory over applied research. Rising demand from a diversified population is leading some within academia to circle the wagons around the PhD, striving to preserve its purity as a badge of honor that signifies individuals with special aptitude to advance theory.

The urgency to reconsider gatekeeping is greater than ever, but these issues have been building for more than a century. In his famous essay "The Ph.D. Octopus," Harvard philosopher and psychologist William James called his colleagues to task. Worried that rising demand for the PhD as a college teaching credential was degrading its character as a stimulus for scholarship, James denounced "the increasing hold of the Ph.D. Octopus upon American life" and graduate education's development into "a tyrannical Machine with unforeseen powers of exclusion and corruption." He wrote:

America is thus as a nation rapidly drifting towards a state of things in which no man of science or letters will be accounted respectable unless some kind of badge or diploma is stamped upon him, and in which bare personality will be a mark of outcast estate. It seems to me high time to rouse ourselves to consciousness, and to cast a critical eye upon this decidedly grotesque tendency.

He charged that faculty and universities had been complicit in these trends, allowing the patina of prestige and the vanity of titles to distract them from the university's educational mission. Elite doctoral programs had responded to rising student demand by raising standards rather than expanding enrollments, he concluded, which preserved their status but heightened competition and created a mismatch between the degree requirements they publicized and those they put into practice. James wrote:

> We advertise our "schools" and send out our degree-requirements, knowing well that aspirants of all sorts will be attracted, and at the same time we set a standard which intends to pass no man who has not native intellectual distinction . . . We dangle our three magic letters before the eyes of these pre-destined victims, and they swarm to us like moths to an electric light.[18]

The competitive trends James identified—among doctoral programs for status and among prospective students for admission to top programs—continue in the twenty-first century.[19]

Among the barriers to expanding access are the strong incentives doctoral programs have to limit their size. Selectivity goes hand-in-hand with prestige.[20] Today, "proportion of applicants admitted" is one factor used to calculate program rankings, such as those published by the National Research Council and *U.S. News and World Report*. And as has already been mentioned, fiscal concerns and uncertain employment prospects after graduation are driving some departments to cut the number of students they admit.[21]

Together, increasing demand and a stagnant supply of spaces have raised the competitiveness of admissions to many doctoral programs. Access has become what economists Robert Frank and Philip Cook call a "winner-take-all" market—a type in which "barely perceptible quality margins spell the difference between success and failure."[22] This type of market frustrates both those trying to break into it and those who want to understand it, because the margins between acceptance, rejection, and the wait-list are difficult to perceive. Further, what counts as quality is a moving target. Necessary credentials for admission to graduate programs are just as subject to inflation as those required for jobs, and faculty judge applicants not according to a fixed standard but relative to others in the applicant pool that year.[23] Therefore, like undergraduate admissions and other forms of faculty decision making, doctoral admissions is a process cloaked in secrecy.

Defining Merit

People are also anxious about how admission is carried out because it is thought to provide a barometer for how selective educational institutions are fulfilling the ideal of allocating opportunities equitably and on the basis of "merit." In the United Kingdom, these twin standards constitute what is known as fair access to higher education. Merit is always a conditional, not an absolute, assessment. No one inherently merits admission. They do so because they are judged to possess attributes that decision makers have deemed legitimate grounds for drawing the line between the many who would like to enroll and the few who should be given the opportunity. In the United States, potential for strong academic performance is one such attribute, but as this book will show, it is hardly the only one.

As in other academic competitions, the conditions under which someone is judged to merit admission to graduate school are bound up with ideals of individual or organizational quality. What does and should count as merit is therefore deeply contested. Is there a single, proper standard we should be working to define and defend? Is it legitimate if different academic disciplines use different standards? Why should we elevate individual academic performance over qualities that may contribute to the common good? Is merit open to reinterpretation as times and conditions change?[24] Personal opinions and conventional wisdom about these and other questions abound, but the current research record offers little in the way of clear answers. Graduate education may play an increasingly important role in shaping professional opportunities, but we suffer from a relatively one-dimensional research literature about graduate admissions, especially compared to the well-developed literature on selective undergraduate admissions.

By examining graduate admissions in practice, from the perspective of those who make the decisions, I see merit differently than most previous scholars of graduate admissions. The vast majority of previous research has tried to statistically model whether applicant characteristics, especially scores on the GRE and TOEFL, predict various indicators of student success.[25] Some scholars have been motivated by concern about decision makers' use of "explicit cutoffs or tacit minima" when weighing standardized test scores.[26] They want to understand just how risky that practice may be in excluding students with lower mean test scores, who nonetheless might be academically successful. Others want to determine whether test scores can be counted upon to deliver satisfactory returns on the investment that admission represents.[27]

Whether focused on a single field or a range of disciplines, results of predictive validity analyses have been mixed. Maria Pennock-Roman described the assumptions of this body of research and a fundamental problem with it:

> There is one unidimensional [variable] Y, such as college grade-point average, that measures "success" . . . A predictor X exists, which can be a linear combination of variables that has demonstrable validity for estimating Y in advance . . . Since the relationship between predictors and Y is far from perfect, some selection decisions will turn out to be correct pre-classifications of candidates, and others will turn out to be errors.[28]

The difficulty of reliably predicting long-term outcomes from any information in an application is understandable, for "success" and "failure" are complex concepts with multiple dimensions and debatable definitions. Further, most existing research has limited generalizability due to their samples, the restricted range of observed GRE scores in most studies, and significant changes to the GRE in 2011.[29] The most recent study, published by psychologist Nathan Kuncel and colleagues in 2007, found correlations between GRE scores and first-year graduate school grades at levels that testing proponents could hold up as statistically significant, but that skeptics could dismiss as practically insignificant.[30] Neither a student's application nor a model developed from information in the application will work very well as a crystal ball in predicting the probability of a given student's success. Even the Educational Testing Service, which administers the GRE, recommends that the test be used as just one factor among many in a holistic review process.[31]

My observations of admissions committees support previous research in demonstrating that for better or worse, a few key criteria, including GRE scores, go a long way in shaping a student's odds of making the short list. Very high GRE scores and attending a prestigious college or university were clearly among the revealed preferences of faculty in the programs that I studied. However, my research also suggests that previous research has misrepresented merit as overly narrow, monolithic, and stable across disciplines.

As I show in the chapters to follow, what faculty construct as merit in highly selective graduate programs is complex and dynamic. Faculty use academic achievements to narrow the pool, so those criteria pattern the outcomes, but they bring a host of other factors into the conversation to make their final choices. They do this in part because many students meet the bar of conventional academic achievement,[32] and in part because they see admissions as an opportunity to enact a variety of values and create the futures of their departments and disciplines. What counts as a quality applicant varies by reviewer, committee, department, discipline, and university, and involves layers of inferences made from seemingly minor details in the application. Although statistical methods would be unlikely to pick up on these details because they are idiosyncratic to individual cases, they are crucial to evaluative cultures of the disciplines and specific academic programs.

Whether in research or in practice, conflating the quality of an applicant with a narrow set of academic achievements thus misses some of the most interesting parts of the story about graduate admissions. However, this definition of merit has other important limitations that also bear mentioning. For example, assuming the most accomplished applicants are the best candidates reduces doctoral education from a developmental process to a scholarly finishing school, and implies that mentoring relationships and learning environments matter little to students' success.[33] Focusing attention solely on student qualities also misses the broader context of who is defining what is desirable in applicants, how and why they determine this, and what the consequences are of those choices. Finally, the tendency to focus on the validity of common admissions criteria ignores important reviewer effects that also affect the fairness of the admissions process, such as susceptibility to fatigue and to cognitive and implicit biases.

Reconsidering merit may seem like a radical proposal. By glimpsing the deliberations of the committees in this book, however, it will become clear that, already, faculty operate on a more expansive notion of merit than that of simple academic achievement and academic potential. I found that admissions may start with the official goal of identifying applicants who are likely to succeed, but organizational interests such as prestige, diversity, collegiality, efficiency, and fiscal responsibility also drive the process and endow it with legitimacy in the eyes of important stakeholders.[34] Revealed preferences therefore vary across time and place in response to changes in applicant pools, the political environment, the mission of the program, and who is making the decisions. Program and disciplinary priorities, the balance of student characteristics in an emerging cohort, as well as other preferences that are idiosyncratic to specific committees and reviewers, all frame judgments of who the "best" or "most qualified" student prospects are.[35]

For example, under a purely student-centered view of merit and academic view of quality, one might admit the students who rate highest on criteria that best predict first-year grades in graduate school. Under this standard, however, the proportion of students from China in many American doctoral programs would skyrocket to levels that, to some, would appear unacceptable. Cohorts that contain very large or small numbers of any one population are often seen as undesirable by faculty and students alike because they send the message that the program has skewed interests. Diverse student bodies, on the other hand, are thought to reflect balanced interests and the richness of our society. A political scientist nicely summarized the tension between assessing quality in terms of student characteristics versus cohort characteristics:

> I think from practically everybody's viewpoint getting talented, motivated people is the top priority . . . But we want to have some balance. I would say *[Pause]* my guess is—no, no it *was* explicit. We had a whole bunch of top Chinese. And *[Pause]* we decided we don't want to admit a class consisting of one-third Chinese and so we didn't. And it was clearly not because of bias *against* Chinese, it was just—we wanted balance.

In practice, merit in graduate admissions is not an absolute assessment of achievements to date and perceived potential for good grades or a great dissertation. It is an assessment of admissibility relative to a specific applicant pool, by a set of specific decision makers with specific personal preferences. These preferences include potential and achievements, but an applicant might also be judged preferable if her admission will appease a difficult colleague or if it improves the balance of students across departmental concentrations. A solid student from Malaysia or Mongolia, countries that produce few applicants to U.S. doctoral programs, might be judged more admissible than a very strong one from China, India, or Korea, which produce many. A student who grew up in foster care and overcame extraordinary personal challenges might be judged more admissible than a student with a similar academic record who grew up in a well-known college town. There is not a single hierarchy of admissions priorities as can be implied by tables of coefficients in quantitative studies. Rather, because faculty use admissions to pursue a variety of interests, multiple hierarchies of priorities (which sociologists call a heterarchy) simultaneously and interactively shape an applicant's odds of being admitted.[36]

What is more, because quality takes many forms in graduate admissions, no single applicant could possibly personify all that the institution and its various stakeholders value. Rather, collective cultural priorities are more likely to be reflected in groups of students than in individual applicants. In this context, the best that decision makers can hope for is to cobble together a cohort that, together, represents what is important to them.

FOR THESE REASONS, I argue that we need to rethink how we talk about merit in graduate admissions. Discussions about merit can't be one-sided. How we understand and recognize merit makes sense only in light of the larger organizational challenges, goals, and missions that faculty face. Therefore, we can't talk about student achievement and potential unless we also talk about the organizational context that determines how achievement and potential will be defined. Further, we shouldn't treat "merit" as if it is merely the sum total of an applicant's "deservingness" based on what the applicant has done already or how easily he or she will thrive in our graduate programs as they are currently designed. What it means to warrant access to graduate education is more complicated than that, and more programs would do well to embrace it as such. Professors can use admissions and other student review situations as an opportunity to think critically about their own professional practice and how their departments and graduate programs might better realize their educational mission for a changing labor market and population. In short, those of us with a stake in graduate education need to broaden the conversation about merit to encourage collective responsibility for student learning.[37]

A conversation about what we value in admissions, and why, thus provides a natural entry point into questions at the crux of the current debate over graduate education's future, or as Leonard Cassuto calls it with regard to the humanities, "the graduate school mess." This conversation beckons faculty to align admissions work with program mission and, in so doing, to consider the professional system and social contexts of which graduate education is part. For example, Harvard Law professor Lani Guinier has urged admissions policymakers and decision makers to ask themselves whether privileging test scores *or* the first-year grades with which they are modestly associated will help higher education fulfill its democratic mission. Her idea of democratic merit advises admissions be conducted with an eye to selecting students who demonstrate capacity for leadership in a racially and ethnically diverse democracy.[38]

To summarize, merit and quality are subjectively assessed and socially constructed. Although students' GRE scores and college reputations undeniably shape the profile of short list, and therefore of admitted cohorts, what counts as merit is complex and dynamic, and varies by context. Where faculty draw the line between admitted and rejected students, it turns out, is as much a reflection of who is doing the evaluating as who is being evaluated. Although this insight is new for analysis of graduate admissions, it has propelled research on undergraduate admissions research since the 1970s, when historian Howard Wechsler declared, "The essence of selective admissions is the subjective judgment of the admissions officer."[39]

Untangling a Paradox of Admissions

I designed this research to untangle an apparent paradox in the research literature on higher education. On the one hand, diversity[40] is a well-institutionalized value in higher education today, and recruiting applicants from underrepresented groups is common practice in areas from undergraduate admissions to faculty hiring.[41] However, two of the three strongest predictors of admission to graduate programs, GRE scores and attending a selective undergraduate institution, privilege populations that already enjoy an enrollment advantage.[42] Male, white, and Asian American students remain overrepresented in the most selective colleges and universities and, on average, earn higher scores on the GRE.[43]

Therein is the paradox. If diversity is valued and concerns about inequality are widely known, why do faculty continue to rely upon criteria that undermine equity and diversity? One can imagine a range of possible explanations. Perhaps professors actively resist admissions reform they way they tend to resist change in general. It could be that they are deeply invested in the entrenched standard and, thus, unwilling to rethink their reliance on specific criteria or vision of ideal applicants. Maybe this paradox is simply a product of myopia to the implications of current practice. Or maybe the reasons are more sinister. Are there informal efforts to limit diversity beneath public images of inclusiveness? Are they overtly racist or sexist behind closed doors?

Recent experiments have found evidence that we should not discount these last possibilities—that faculty judgment in selection situations is marked by informal discrimination and unconscious (that is, implicit) biases. A randomized double-blind study by Corinne Moss-Racusin and colleagues focused on hiring for a laboratory manager position, found that faculty rated applications headlined by male names as significantly more competent and hireable than identical applications headlined by a female name.[44] And in a field experiment with a large sample of 6,500 faculty, Katherine Milkman, Modupe Akinola, and Dolly Chugh found that participants ignored email inquiries from prospective students with female, Indian, Chinese, black, and Latino-sounding names at higher rates than they ignored those with traditionally Caucasian male names. These findings held across institutional types and disciplines, but were particularly acute in higher-paying disciplines and private universities.[45] If faculty are discriminating against women and people of color in the informal interactions that precede application and admission, it is important to take a closer look at how they are interpreting and evaluating the applications they do receive.

My research into the admissions process did not find evidence of overt discrimination,[46] but it did find that a "colorblind" approach to admissions—the dominant model in all ten of these programs—also creates conditions that sustain inequalities. We have reached a point where policy need not formally exclude or segregate on the basis of race or gender, because inequalities can also become locked in (or institutionalized) as organizations operate according to shared understandings and informal rules that may look neutral but have a disproportionate, or disparate, impact on some groups.[47] For example, I found that through their use of shared, discipline-based assumptions to define which applicants were better, more competent, or deserving, faculty members often accepted inequitable admissions outcomes as logical or necessary. What disciplinary outsiders might have challenged as discriminatory, unjust, or simply wrong could be deemed perfectly legitimate from an insider's perspective.

By getting inside the faculty perspective, this book thus uncovers the common mental pathways scholars use to legitimize a system whose rules look neutral and by some standards fair, but that nonetheless is marked by what Charles Tilly called durable inequalities.[48] In a society where overtly racist and sexist behaviors are socially unacceptable and where diversity is something to celebrate, the institutionalization perspective makes it clear that durable inequalities are neither inevitable nor natural, but instead are the result of a process *we* have created.[49] This perspective is also useful in identifying common perceptions that are out of step with current research, and in bringing to the surface assumptions that are so deeply held as to be taken for granted.

I therefore portray the current system of admissions from professors' own point of view while making clear that the system has cracks—ones through which students from already underrepresented groups continue disproportionately to fall. Working with faculty throughout an entire admissions cycle, I gained real sympathy for the magnitude and difficulty of reviewing files and selecting applicants in these programs. I came to see that there are unintended consequences for equity from the organizational apparatus that programs establish to deal with a pile of 800 applications in total, or 250 from China alone. I observed how ambiguities inherent in the review process prime faculty to defer to stereotypes, such as when they judge applicants from China. These findings help reveal why it is so difficult and complex to make diversity, as one participant put it, "more than a platitude."

However, I also found racism and sexism subtly institutionalized in misguided perceptions about what common admissions criteria signal, in deference to "fit" with the status quo as a core determinant of admissibility, and in reluctance to take on students from underrepresented backgrounds whose profiles suggest they may benefit from more intensive mentoring. Orienting toward traditional ideas of prestige also set up these graduate programs to reproduce inequalities as they recreate themselves—as William James noted more than a hundred years ago.

Notes on the Research Design

In this section I provide a general overview of my research design; readers interested in greater detail may be interested in the methodological appendix. I conducted 86 interviews with 62 faculty and 6 graduate students, the vast majority of whom were sitting on admissions committees at the time. The heart of my study, though, was the time I spent observing admissions committee meetings and recruitment events in six of the ten programs. My perspective in these meetings as an outsider-turned-insider enabled me to capture routine details of the review process that committee members may take for granted and to compare the principles and preferences that faculty espoused with those that they put into practice.

Due to my agreements with the Institutional Review Boards (IRBs) and participants, I refrain from naming or describing the universities where I collected data. What is important for readers to know, and which I can share, is that two universities were public and one was private, that they were in two different regions of the country, and that all three are well-known research institutions. Also of note: Each university had a graduate school that coordinated the admissions process and offered resources to help increase the enrollment of women and students of color, such as diversity-focused fellowships and trainings for faculty engaged in admissions work.

My sample of highly ranked doctoral programs in pure disciplines is not intended to be representative of American doctoral education or the full range of fields of study, but it provides insight into the intellectual core of the academy. It covers the humanities, social sciences, and natural sciences and, within each, intentionally includes fields known for being relatively centralized, hierarchical, and paradigmatic (such as economics, physics, and philosophy) and others with less intellectual consensus (such as political science, biology, and linguistics). This variety allows for comparisons on multiple dimensions.

Focusing on programs ranked in the top fifteen for their discipline also has benefits. Most importantly, in highly selective programs like these, the many demands and sociocultural dynamics of selection come into sharper focus. Dynamics of elite organizations are also important to understand because, as sociologists have noted, their practices and priorities often set a standard that others adopt to improve their standing. A better understanding of elite organizations—and of efforts within those organizations to resist prevailing trends—offers a glimpse into the direction that the system, as a whole, may be headed.[50]

I have masked and/or changed information about applicants and faculty that might be personally identifiable, starting with their names. In referring to colleges and universities, I tried to balance ensuring anonymity with conveying a real-world sense of the institutional strata in which these programs are located. Therefore, when quoting participants who named specific universities, including their own, I replaced those names with the results of random draws from fifteen universities in the same tier of program rankings for the speaker's discipline. This approach means that the actual universities in which data were collected could be named due to chance, but it ensures that readers should be no more able to recognize the data collection sites than other, similarly ranked institutions.

People commonly ask me how I gained access to the programs, and although I will never be certain about the answer, my typical response is that it was likely a combination of factors. As a white female student from a respected university, the faculty with whom I interacted may have seen me as a member of their community and as relatively nonthreatening. I also attribute my unusual access to making clear in early communications what the study's confidentiality protections were, the genuine desire many faculty have to improve admissions, and a dose of divine intervention. There was also a respondent who agreed to participate out of "karmic obligation to the many who had participated in [his] own research over the years."

Most participants were current members of the admissions committees, and their demographic characteristics are summarized in Table 2. Just 18 percent of the sample were women and only 3 percent were U.S.-born scholars of color—a decidedly skewed composition that can be thought of as a limitation and a strength of the book. On the one hand, the sample is broadly representative of tenured faculty in elite universities, making my research findings a more trustworthy picture of admissions in highly ranked graduate programs. On the other hand, my data lacks the voices of women and scholars of color. The imbalanced sample makes plain the need for research on inequity in graduate education and, more importantly, for recruiting and retaining more diverse cohorts of doctoral students.

Reading This Book

I wrote this book with three audiences in mind: faculty across the disciplines who are engaged in graduate admissions work, scholars of higher education and sociology, and administrators with whom faculty coordinate to facilitate admissions. Prospective graduate school applicants will also no doubt be curious to learn how faculty evaluate files and deliberate behind

Table 2 Sample Demographic Characteristics by Program and Subject Area

Programs	N	% Female	% International	% Scholars of Color	% Domestic Scholars of Color	# Graduate students on Committee
Humanities						
Classics	5	40	40	0	0	0
Linguistics	7	29	29	14	0	2
Philosophy (University 1)	6	33	33	0	0	0
Philosophy (University 2)	7	29	14	14	14	0
Subtotal	25	33	26	7	4	2
Social Sciences						
Economics	6	0	33	0	0	0
Political Science	8	25	38	13	0	3
Sociology	10	20	33	34	10	0
Subtotal	24	15	35	16	4	3
Natural Sciences						
Astrophysics	6	0	33	33	0	1
Biology	6	17	33	17	0	0
Physics	7	0	71	14	0	1
Subtotal	19	6	46	21	0	1
Total/Average	68	1	36	15	3	6

closed doors. They may be encouraged or dismayed, for example, to learn that credentials, connections, and effort can propel an application to the short list, but beyond that, outcomes are almost impossible to predict and subject to myriad factors that are outside the applicant's control.

My hope in writing this text was to encourage reflection and dialogue among those with a stake in graduate education, especially about aspects of admissions that persist mainly because they are the way things have always been done. The data do not generalize to admissions everywhere, but readers who have participated in the process are likely to see some of their own assumptions and tensions reflected back to them in partici-pants' narratives and deliberations.[51] Reading how others struggle with admissions—the tough calls they make, the questionable assumptions they hold, the displays of inertia or courage—can validate one's own struggles. It can also provide positive and negative examples from which to learn. And as cultural sociologists have demonstrated, "thick description" of cases and episodes can uncover social mechanisms and concepts that are present or may apply outside of the samples from which they were derived.[52] Con-cepts emerging from this study include deliberative bureaucracy, disciplinary logics, and counterscripts.

To build upon the existing sociocultural literature on academic evalua-tion, I set out to analyze three major issues: the decision-making process in graduate admissions, the meanings faculty attributed to common evalua-tion criteria, and disciplinary variation in faculty approaches to admissions. Those themes are the anchors of Chapters 1 through 3, respectively, and are helpful in documenting central elements of graduate admissions prac-tice. However, because I took an inductive approach to analysis and re-mained open to learning what was important to faculty participants, other important findings emerged from the data, including several that relate to the social psychology of faculty identity and judgment. For example, I had expected that faculty would prefer applicants who shared their elite academic pedigrees, but I did not expect to see some other dimensions of preference for students like themselves (such as experiences overcoming poverty and presenting oneself as cool or hip) (Chapter 4). I had not anticipated that faculty would circle around to intelligence over and over again as one of their central concerns (Chapter 5). Finally, committees very rarely men-tioned the race or ethnicity of domestic students, but they were vocal with their assumptions about Asian international students, especially those from China (Chapter 6).

Consistent with constructivist qualitative research, each chapter begins by presenting faculty participants' perspectives without supportive or crit-ical commentary so that readers can immerse themselves in the ways participants think and deliberate. Each chapter takes up the consequences of current practice, and examines the extent to which the prevailing mindsets of faculty participants are consistent with current research. Some chapters also include results of my searches for disconfirming evidence or alternative explanations. I will admit: knowing the risk of confirmation bias—the tendency for people to listen mainly to ideas that support their preconceptions— there are perspectives I hesitated to put in print out of concern that it would lead readers to become entrenched in ruts they are already in. I think, for example, about some faculty narratives around intelligence and belonging within academe. But I have included it all, both to provide the most honest portrayal of admissions' good, bad, and ugly, and in trust that readers will engage participants' comments and interactions with the same critical thinking they bring to their own scholarship.

Conclusion

This is, in part, a story about the impact of a system motivated by good intentions. A common thread in the findings is that faculty enter the admissions process intending to hold firm on their ideals, but that they compromise again and again to get the job done. Faculty experience admissions work as politically, cognitively, and procedurally difficult because it positions them between impulses, principles, and pragmatism. At the level of *process,* they are caught between attractions to a collegial ideal of deliberative democracy and the efficiencies of bureaucratic decision making. At the level of *evaluative criteria,* they feel that conventional achievements and pedigree are critical, even as many feel obligated to and see opportunities afforded by holistic review and a more inclusive notion of excellence. They struggle with the prospect of rejecting African American, Native American, and Latino students whose applications receive full committee review, but they worry about considering diversity as one of their initial criteria. In the end they exclude many who could be successful and admit some about whom they feel ambivalent.

More fundamentally, faculty feel caught between satisfying their own consciences, respecting their colleagues' values and priorities, and the aims of the program and discipline whose futures they are trying to shape. Determining who should be admitted often becomes an elaborate, ad hoc compromise rather than an application of specific values and priorities. In that compromise, good intentions and principles often fall prey to pragmatic interests, and faculty frequently default to the safety of self-reproduction. In this political pressure cooker, it is no wonder that change comes slowly, if it comes at all.

I wrote this book because faculty often draw the fine line between admitted and rejected students without a sense of how their program's approach compares to others', without consciousness of the many tacit values that drive the process, and without clarity on viable alternatives to the status quo. My hope is to encourage greater awareness on all of these dimensions by documenting how they play out in departments representing a range of disciplines. I hope this book puts graduate admissions work into perspective, encourages mindfulness about the premises and consequences of gatekeeping at this level, and builds decision makers' capacity to bring about change where it is needed.

CHAPTER ONE

Decision Making as Deliberative Bureaucracy

This is hard work. We are all intelligent, competent people trying to do our best.

—Chair of philosophy admissions committee

How should admissions decisions be made? How are they made in practice? Judgments of admissibility may seem to be the heart of admissions work, and indeed most sociological research on this topic emphasizes how reliance on certain selection *criteria* reproduces inequities. My observations suggest, however, that one explanation for overreliance on those criteria involves the review *process* used in these programs to manage the scores or hundreds of applications received. Before delving in subsequent chapters into the nature of faculty judgment in graduate admissions, I therefore start by outlining key dynamics of decision making.

In general, faculty believe that decisions should be the product of an open debate among equals in which all members have an equal opportunity to be heard. Following political philosophers Amy Gutmann and Dennis Thompson, we could call the model of decision making to which faculty aspired a deliberative democracy. Such a model makes explicit and accessible the reasons for decisions,[1] which is thought to legitimize the outcomes and to encourage mutual respect and collegiality. Under deliberative democracy, governance itself can become an educative process in which individuals learn, through the give-and-take of ideas, to look beyond their own perspectives.[2] Yet despite faculty allegiance to ideals of deliberative democracy, in practice they settled for a model that I characterize as deliberative bureaucracy.

Deliberative bureaucracy is an organizational adaptation to rising numbers of applications and associated demands on faculty time and attention, through which they strive to maximize efficiency while upholding the deliberative, democratic norms that lend legitimacy to their work. Norms of collegiality, shared governance, peer review, and consensus seeking have long been reflected in the processes surrounding faculty hiring, tenure, and promotion.[3] However, as the volume of graduate applications has risen, faculty have come to feel that there is simply not enough time to involve the entire faculty in open discussions of every file.

Unlike deliberative democracy, bureaucratic decision making delegates individuals to serve as group representatives, and because they are not personally invested in outcomes, they can prioritize efficiency and technical expertise.[4] Max Weber famously argued for the technical superiority of bureaucratic administration relative to collegiate administration. He argued that the need to find compromises among competing interests in the collegiate model delays decisions and makes the process less reliable and precise.[5] By contrast, bureaucracy's procedural rules and standard operating procedures downplay personal interests such that "official business is discharged precisely and efficiently with as much speed as possible."[6] Under a logic of formal rationality, bureaucracy also tries to minimize ambiguity by applying quantifiable standards, which are thought to suppress individual values and ensure more consistent outcomes.[7]

And indeed, I found that bureaucratic practices such as delegating file review and quantifying judgment increased efficiency by reducing the time that the admissions process required. Many were uncomfortable with these apparent shortcuts, however, and tried to preserve a spirit of deliberation by discussing a smaller set of borderline files. Yet even in those conversations, the tendency was to focus on procedural matters rather than on the potentially controversial reasons for their judgments of applicants. By doing so, they minimized conflict while protecting democratic values such as collegiality and consensus seeking.

The efficiencies introduced by deliberative bureaucracy came with costs, however. Compromising on holistic review produced decontextualized interpretations of information in the application, making it more difficult for reviewers to identify, value, and recruit promising students with unconventional profiles. Bureaucratic processes also obscured the considerations on which applicant ratings and admissions decisions depended. To insiders, sacrificing a discussion of the reason for one's rating or decision may have facilitated a more orderly, legitimate process because disagreements were fewer. However, it also masked the use of unseemly considerations and allowed misperceptions about common criteria to go unchecked. It too often made the basis for admission and rejection opaque rather than transparent.

Each chapter in this book is aimed at explaining why faculty in highly ranked doctoral programs rely on admissions criteria that undermine their equity and diversity aims. This chapter offers a distinctly organizational explanation: faculty members' preference for efficient, collegial decision making made it easier for them to fall back on bureaucratic processes than engage in the more difficult conversations that may be needed to encourage greater equity and diversity. In the first section of this chapter, I provide an introduction to doctoral admissions for readers who may be unfamiliar with its procedures, timeline, or the way that evaluation work is delegated. I then summarize two other characteristics of deliberative bureaucracy—quantifying judgment and efforts to uphold collegiality and deliberation—before assessing the costs of this model. Finally I present a provocative episode from linguistics, a program whose deliberations were marked by both vigorous debate and clear collegiality.

An Overview of Admissions Procedures

Before discussing the details of deliberative bureaucracy, some readers may appreciate a bird's-eye view of the admissions process. Admissions has an annual cycle in most universities, beginning with faculty, graduate programs, schools/colleges, and universities persuading students to submit applications. There would be no need for decision making without a surplus of applicants, and faculty develop the applicant pool through the image they present, their reputations in the field, organized outreach and recruitment efforts, and early interactions with prospective applicants. After applications are received, reviewed, rated, and debated, committees make their admission determinations. In the programs I studied,[8] faculty made these decisions with an eye to building a cohort, but elsewhere in higher education the goal is also one of hiring apprentices to support faculty research and/or teach undergraduate courses. At the point of admission, decision making shifts back into the hands of admitted students. Faculty move into a posture of recruitment once again, sometimes using financial aid awards as a way to signal interest in a student and often inviting admitted students for a campus visit. One by one, students file their intent to enroll—or their plans to enroll elsewhere. This book focuses on faculty gatekeeping as a window into graduate programs as organizations, but the lengthy dance between selective institutions and prospective students ends not with institutions choosing or rejecting students, but with students choosing or rejecting institutions.

Table 3 provides some basic information about admissions in the programs represented in this research, such as the number of applications received, which varied by an order of magnitude, from 80 in classics to 800 in economics. The admission rates ranged from 5 percent in one philosophy program to about 20 percent in physics, with a median admissions rate of 9.5 percent. Rather than involving all faculty in selecting doctoral students or delegating the admissions process entirely to administrative professionals, as is common in many masters programs, departments entrusted the work of processing these applications and selecting students to a faculty committee, sometimes aided by an administrative assistant and/or a few outside readers or graduate student members. Admissions chair was in most cases a rotating position, but two programs strove for continuity of leadership, and there, the same individuals served as chair for twenty-five and nine years, respectively. One jokingly called himself the "admissions czar" in describing the power he had wielded over the years to shape the program.

Indeed, at the graduate level, the decision to admit or reject is negotiated not in a central campus office, but rather by individuals and committees representing academic programs. One strand of higher education's history concerns the transfer of authority over graduate education from university presidents to departments and programs. Early in the twentieth century, scholars' role shifted from polymath to specialist, disciplines consolidated around common research interests, and departments and programs became independent—if not autonomous—administrative units.[9] Each of these changes supported department authority over graduate admissions. Recently, leading research universities have reasserted a coordinating role in graduate education over enrollment management activities such as admissions, financial aid, and diversity recruitment work. Typically, their oversight serves to rubber-stamp academic departments' work and decisions, build capacity for challenges that are common across disciplines, and make explicit the connection between doctoral education and sponsored research. As sociologist Burton Clark noted, disciplines and universities converge in department activities, and because those activities are so vital to universities' broader institutional mission, departments are relatively resistant to external pressures.[10]

Some admissions committees' autonomy is limited by institutional policy or formal law, such as the bans on race-conscious admissions that are currently in place in eight states. And in programs where admission is as much about hiring research assistants for specific grants as it is about selecting students for a cohort, the committee may consult with other faculty.

Table 3 Comparison of Admissions Process across Programs

Department	Committee Size	Number of Committee Meetings	Number who Applied/Were admitted/Enrolled	Rounds of Review	Key Evaluation Criteria	Admissions Chair's Gender & Nativity	Interview (of whom & how)	Notes
Biology	5	~8	150–200/20–35/14	2–3	Research experience	Male, domestic	Short list, via video conference	3 admissions processes used: standard, via interdisciplinary program, & in rare cases direct admit. Numbers reflect standard admissions process. Initial review of applications by a subset of the committee; full committee reads files on short list. 2/3 of admitted are international students.
Astrophysics	5	4	150/20/7	3	Physics GRE, research experience, coursework/grades	Male, international	Short list, via video conference	Initial review of applications by full committee. All-male committee. 1 graduate student on committee. Extensive consultation among committee members via email.
Physics	10	1	450/90/26	1–4	Physics GRE, research experience, coursework	Male, international	Non-native English speakers on the short list, via video conference	Rolling review; initial review of applications by committee chair & 2 members. Number of rounds of review depends on consistency of initial ratings.

Classics	5	1	80/9/4	Language training, grades, Verbal GRE	Male, international	Very short list, during recruitment weekend	Committee members required to provide narrative with their ratings. Subsets of committee may meet to discuss a few specific cases. Chair has strong managerial role. Department administrator conducts initial review of applications, then full committee reads files on short list. Committee includes department chair.
Philosophy 1	5	3	200/7 + wait list/7	Writing sample, letters of recommendation, GRE	Female, domestic	No interviews	Initial review of each application by two committee members; then, full committee reads files on short list. Wait list used extensively to ensure the desired size of cohort. Chair has strong facilitator role. Committee appoints diversity officer. 5-point rating scale used.

(*continued*)

Table 3 (Continued)

Department	Committee Size	Number of Committee Meetings	Number who Applied/Were admitted/ Enrolled	Rounds of Review	Key Evaluation Criteria	Admissions Chair's Gender & Nativity	Interview (of whom & how)	Notes
Philosophy 2	5	2	225/20/5	1–2	Writing sample, letters of recommendation	Male, domestic	No interviews	Initial review by admissions chair; any applicant accepted or put on wait list will have application read by at least 4 people. 4-point rating scale used.
Linguistics	6	5	105/8/4	4	Grades/ coursework, college reputation, alignment of research interests with department vision	Male, international	Very short list, via recruitment weekend	Initial review of each application by 2 committee members; then, full committee reads applications on short list. 3 meetings of committee only; 2 meetings with full faculty deliberation of short list (~30) & very short list (~12). Last round of review occurs after the recruitment weekend. 2 graduate students on committee. Committee includes department chair. Reviewers each give each applicant a yes/no vote, then number of yes/no votes used as proxy for energy behind the applicant.

Sociology	5	2	225/22/10	1–3	Committee members free to use their own criteria	Male, domestic	No interviews	Number of rounds of review determined by initial ratings. Initial review of each complete application by two committee members. Minimal deliberation about files. Strong reliance on average ratings. Chair has a strong manager role.
Political Science	8	2	350/25/16	2–4	Committee discouraged from heavy reliance on GRE	Male, international	Rarely, usually intl. students via video conference	1 meeting to set process; 1 to discuss files. Initial review by 2 committee members; then full committee reads all applications on short list (~80). 3 graduate students on committee.
Economics	6	2	800/65/25	3 or more	Quant GRE, math coursework	Male, domestic	No interviews	Additional consultation occurs outside of committee meetings. 10-point rating scale. Program chair adjudicates final decisions. Admissions chair cuts 50% of pool before committee review & has a strong manager role.

Nevertheless, in each of the ten programs I studied, a committee mediates the individual and collective wills of a department's faculty. Analytically, I found that focusing on academic departments and programs allowed me to analyze up to the levels of the university and disciplines, whose futures are shaped *by* admissions, and down to the levels of the committee and individuals who *make* the admissions decisions. These committees represent a vital locus of power in admissions, but their work has rarely been the focus of empirical analysis.[11]

My participants were well-aware that forming admissions committees is a somewhat political task; they noted that members are often the first to see the pool of prospective advisees and that their decisions affect the entire department. Most committees included faculty at all three ranks—assistant, associate, and full—and the astrophysics, linguistics, and political science programs included graduate students. Only two of the ten chairs mentioned diversity as a factor in their committee formation decisions, which may help explain why white males predominated in nearly all of the programs' committees.[12] As a relatively labor-intensive service appointment, membership rotated year to year in most programs, although those who gained a reputation for thorough, thoughtful, timely review found themselves tapped more frequently.

Leaders also made appointments to admissions committees to downplay internal conflicts, protect specific program interests, or buffer the process from program faculty with outlying perspectives or difficult personalities. In a humanities program with a new strategic plan, the admissions and program chairs appointed committee members whom they knew to be supportive of the program's new direction. Two of three committee chairs in the social sciences were careful to ensure the committee represented the full suite of program concentrations. Such strategic committee appointments are consistent with findings of previous research. James Wilson's classic analysis of bureaucracy argued that organizations use bureaucratic practice to balance multiple interests and manage untrustworthy subordinates,[13] while sociologists John Meyer and Brian Rowan found that delegating work can serve to institutionalize specific interests and manage uncertainty.[14]

To enhance efficiency, the admissions chair or an administrative assistant in most programs conducted the initial screening of the applicant pool. In a humanities program with 200 applicants, for example, the chair described her objective for the first round of review as "select[ing] out the top quarter" before the committee "takes a serious, collective look at fifty [applications] in the second round." The chair of a social sciences program encouraged self-selection by publicizing the range of GRE scores among recently admitted students, and then relied predominantly on GRE and TOEFL scores to cut the pool—still hundreds strong—in half. After this first screening, in all but the two programs with the smallest pools each applicant's file would be assigned to two or three committee readers again, to reduce the time commitment and encourage a close reading. Only if there was a large discrepancy in reviewer ratings would other committee members review the application or weigh in on whether it should be advanced to full committee review.

Interestingly, in the course of delegating admissions work, effort and expertise were often decoupled from decision-making authority. In all ten programs, a member of the department's administrative staff typically organized files for review, scheduled meetings, and provided institutional memory. Often, he or she was familiar with all of the files, attended committee meetings, and was the only person in the room to have had personal contact with an applicant. This individual was a professional who committed large numbers of hours to admissions work, yet was the only member of the committee without a vote. By contrast, when committees included graduate student members, they had full voting rights, regardless of prior experience with application file review or decision making.

Perhaps in part because I was a graduate student myself at the time, I was intrigued to observe differences in how graduate student committee members handled their role and how often it reflected conventional status hierarchies. Whereas a white male graduate student in political science contributed with the outspoken self-assurance of tenured faculty on the committee, a white female graduate student spoke only when spoken to, and a male student from an underrepresented ethnic background did not speak at all. In linguistics, an international graduate student member worried about senior faculty seeing and disagreeing with his ratings, whereas a white male graduate student on the same committee actively challenged senior professors' interpretations of files. In this way, committees operated as microcosms, small worlds that reflected common department and academic politics.

Sometimes, leaders involved outside reviewers with specialized research expertise or knowledge of a country's educational system. Eight of the ten admissions chairs consulted with program faculty or doctoral students from China, for example, in the hope that an additional set of eyes would clarify ambiguities and ensure a fairer review of those applicants. As Chapter 6 will detail, efforts to improve the quality of review for international applicants were well warranted. Yet in several departments, the role of "China expert" fell to one or two individuals year after year and appeared to be neither voluntary nor accompanied by compensation, recognition of service, or authority to make admissions recommendations. Similarly, programs that required writing samples assigned them to be reviewed by colleagues with subject area expertise, and sometimes this required tapping faculty colleagues outside the committee. Especially in the humanities, the writing sample was very important to overall judgments of applications, but committee leaders recognized that there are idiosyncrasies in, for example, how a Kantian ethicist versus a philosopher of language would judge what counts as quality writing in philosophy. One faculty member relayed the process to me:

> We send it out to the experts and then we get the reports. But sometimes there is disagreement with the experts too. The experts who read the paper haven't seen the whole pool, so there has to be some balance too . . . Unless the experts totally, you know, dismissed it and couldn't find any value in the paper.

Committees were thus often entrusted to connect outsiders' judgments of select cases with their own knowledge of the entire pool. Finally, in eight programs, the admissions committee also consulted with the department or program chair,[15] either in recognition of the department chair's authority or as a source of accountability for the representation of key student constituencies (such as women, international students, and students of color) among the admitted students.

In two programs, the chair's approach to delegating work backfired, and faculty outside the committee actively challenged its decisions. In one program, faculty from a particular concentration were upset that students in the concentration seemed underrepresented in the incoming cohort. In the other case, a senior scholar complained to the department chair that he had not "received any good students in several years" and suspected admissions committee members had been "cherry-picking the best students." After agreeing to admit an additional student for the next year who would work with this professor, the admissions chair invited him to participate in the admissions committee the following year to see for himself whether the concerns about cherry-picking were warranted. Delegation thus can save time, but by excluding some stakeholders from the process, it can also create tension between appointed decision makers and those who feel negatively affected by decisions in which they were not involved.[16]

Quantifying Judgment

Another bureaucratic practice involved putting numbers to judgments in order to simplify comparisons among applicants. Quantification in admissions is a foundation of American meritocracy. The movement to incorporate numbers into admissions began with the optimistic, democratic intention that standardized aptitude tests might ensure that talented college applicants from less privileged backgrounds would be judged by the same standard as their wealthy peers. Henry Chauncey, who founded the Educational Testing Service, reacted in amazement to the congruence between his first aptitude test and student grades. Historian Nicholas Lemann wrote,

> Chauncey was bowled over. It was magical . . . Testing touched upon the deepest mythic themes: the ability to see the invisible (what was inside people's heads), the oracular ability to predict the future (what someone's grades would be in courses he hadn't even chosen yet).[17]

In admissions and elsewhere in education and social life, quantifying quality is a key indicator of deeper trends toward bureaucratization and positivism. When we want quick and convenient knowledge about student achievement, college quality, or teaching effectiveness, we turn to numbers.[18]

Quantification is central to graduate admissions review, in spite of widespread doubts about the reliability and validity of standard measures and average ratings as proxies for complex constructs like achievement and admissibility. The way that numbers seem to quickly cut through the ambiguities involved in comparing students who are different on many dimensions has made them a vital decision-making tool, particularly as applicant pools have grown. Faculty in the programs I worked with quantified their judgments in several ways. They interpreted small increments in test scores as significant differences, for example, and condensed holistic evaluations of applicant files into numerical ratings that guided subsequent decision making.

Test score increments. Early in the review process, many faculty fixated on small increments in test scores or grade point averages, treating them as the equivalent of significant variance in intelligence, preparation, or general admissibility.[19] Describing the motivation for this practice to me, a sociologist explained, "If you've got a stack from here to the ceiling, you've got to try in a small amount of time to get them down to a small list. The grades, the GREs, the letters do a big work *[pause]* in trying to decide who is on the short list." A biologist made a similar point on the clarity that GRE scores provide. Individually composed aspects of the application like the writing sample or personal statement are not only more time consuming to review, he argued, but ultimately are incommensurable.[20]

> It's just too easy given quantitative data like that, it's just too easy to just rank, you know, to use that to differentiate . . . Not only is it obviously a time savings but . . . trying to judge and tease apart these factors and distinguish applications—sometimes it's not too bad but a lot of times it is, and so to be

able to just say, "Okay, oh, this person clearly had a better GRE set of scores than this person. We should rank them in." . . . It's something that common. You know all applicants took the same test, presumably under the same conditions, *[Laughs]* you know, they were watched over. But anyway it's one thing that we can standardize in the sea of variability in these applications.

As the applicant pool increases, so does the burden of holistic review, and with it, the difficulty of sorting out who should have a place on the short list. The GRE's standardization thus becomes central to justifications about its utility and appropriateness.

Applicant ratings. A second form of quantification involves rating individual applicants. Faculty in nine of the ten programs translated their holistic evaluations of individuals on the short list into overall ratings, usually on a 1–3 or 1–5 scale.[21] As one participant described it, ratings offer "the most efficient way to focus in on the people that really need to be thought about"—that is, the applicants whose admissibility was debatable. Two recurrent debates in the committee meetings I observed involved who should receive the hallowed "1" rating on the one hand, and what that rating actually meant, on the other. One of the philosophy committees waxed eloquent on these matters, as I discuss in Chapter 3, leading off the conversation with one member ruminating, "What *is* a 1?"

In the end, the meaning of a 1 rating was perhaps best revealed by the qualities of applicants for whom faculty reserved it—those whom readers were most enthusiastic about, impressed by, or otherwise eager to admit. Faculty recognized that, no matter how many seemed worthy of admission, giving more applicants a rating of 1 only delayed the inevitable task of rejecting most in their pool. Allocating the 1's grew even more difficult in later rounds of evaluation as the share of promising prospects increased. An economist explained,

> It's really hard. Once you get down to the final forty, you could conceivably admit all of these people . . . They probably would come here and do quite well. It's just you can't admit everyone who is actually above a certain bar. You've got to keep raising the bar just to accommodate the numbers that you want.

Above a general threshold of admissibility, faculty were forced to make difficult choices.

A number whom I spoke with justified their preference for making those hard choices sooner rather than later by asserting that awarding too many 1's in the first round of evaluation created more work for one's colleagues. After observing that a junior member of the astrophysics committee received some teasing from his colleagues for being a "softie," I asked another member of committee in a follow-up interview to explain the teasing:

> If you put forward thirty out of the sixty that you want everybody else to read—you're not doing your job to whittle it down to the best of the best. You're just making more work for the four other people on the committee who have to read your thirty—instead of them all having to read your twenty. I think that's really the only reason why being harsh would be valued. You're trying to pick out the best people. You want to cut the fat away.

Another member of this committee affirmed this:

> The list needs to be cut down. We have 180 applications and we had to cut it down to eighteen admissions or something like that. We had to make cuts. You know so—you actually need to distinguish them between the merely good and the very good, and being a harsh critic is helpful for making that distinction. In some sense, the committee can't function if we're all softies. There needs to be some who are more harsh and demanding. Otherwise it's impossible to cut it down.

The perceived need for some reviewers to be "harsh and demanding" was not limited to the hard sciences. In one of the philosophy departments, for example, the admissions chair apologized profusely for the number of 1's she had awarded, sparking a longer conversation about what constitutes the "boundary between a 1 and 2" and how each of them had approached the ratings. The chair exclaimed, "Sorry about all of my 1's! My 1 might be another person's 2 . . . We are all intelligent, competent people trying to do our best." A senior colleague replied, "1's are the crème de la crème. I was very disciplined. I made a list of all the 1's, and then I was ruthless to get to ten 1's."

Still, rejecting a large majority of applicants can be a tough pill for new reviewers to swallow. Many of those who are ultimately rejected could probably succeed in these programs, and achievements of even rejected applicants may surpass reviewers' own accomplishments at a similar stage of their career. Everyone recognized the difficulty of cutting ostensibly qualified students, and seasoned veterans of admissions review often adopted a tough attitude to match the toughness of the task. Being "harsh," "demanding," "disciplined," or even "ruthless" with one's ratings was thought to ultimately serve the committee's best interests by moving the process along more efficiently than a "soft," "generous," or "lenient" approach. A sociologist clearly explained the importance of individual ratings, which many faculty slipped into calling "rankings," and their influence on admissions outcomes:

> There was very much a sense that we all went off in our little corners and read and submitted our rankings. That's where the decision really got made.

Individual ratings were key ingredients of collective decisions, both in determining an individual's place in the rank-ordered list of applicants, and as a starting point for conversation about his or her particular strengths and weaknesses.

Rank-ordering applicants. The quantification of judgment continued into the next phase of the review, as committees averaged individual reviewers' ratings to develop a rank-ordered list of applicants that would guide subsequent discussion and decisions. Here, committees associated each applicant with two numbers: the average rating of the application (for instance, 2 out a possible 5) and their rank on the overall list (such as a rank of 11 out of 20 total applicants on a short list). The list, aptly regarded by one philosopher as the "collective assessment" of the committee, thus linked individual judgment with collective selection.

Several participants described the simple computation of the rank-ordered list as an efficient substitute for the hard work of comparatively evaluating the applicants.[22] With just a few keystrokes using spreadsheet software, individual judgments of hundreds of unique applicants could be transformed without discussion into an apparently clean distribution of their admissibility. Several marveled to me about this substantial feat, with one humanities professor describing the computer's work with a flourish of his arm that resembled waving a magic wand.

Letting the computer generate the committee's collective assessment of each applicant was functionally important in that it saved time over consensus-oriented discussions, but its social importance lay in the *reason* it saved time: it clarified where agreement already existed and inhibited debate over disagreements. "Consensus at the top tells you that the process is working," one social sciences professor summarized. To save time, committees felt they did not need to discuss areas of agreement, which the spreadsheet of individual and average rankings allowed them to assess at a glance. A senior sociology professor elaborated:

> Years ago they didn't score these things. It's become more bureaucratic. I think they want to move things along, so once you put a score on it, you just tabulate and rank-order . . . When I was at Cornell, we didn't use this kind of system. We spent the whole morning deciding the admit list, and in this one it took us less than an hour after we had already rank-ordered. So we had done our homework before the meeting.
>
> Once we see the list, then we could discuss, so it becomes very clear. There's not much debate . . . I think it's a good one, because otherwise you can debate

for a long time. They know how to debate and they know how to engage all these rhetorics . . . If we can keep debating about who is a better student all morning, we still can't convince each other . . .

In the end, it's personal taste. Everyone has good scores on different aspects. You know, "I like this person's experience, that person's background, this person has better quantitative skills."

Similarly, one philosopher who reflected on the process noted, "There was always a consensus that way or another . . . but we didn't have to agree on why." In essence, less time was required for discussion because less negotiation was required. Given the small scale on which ratings were assigned, average ratings disguised disagreements about individuals' relative ratings as minor differences of opinion about appropriate standards, criteria, and applicant strengths and weaknesses.[23]

Some committees relied on the list more than did others. Some used it as a jumping-off point for identifying and discussing borderline cases. In astrophysics, one member explained,

The first two-thirds of the list went immediately. There were some people it was clear we were going to make offers to and some people it was clear we weren't going to make offers to, and I think two-thirds of the people fell into that category. Those two-thirds took ten minutes and the rest of the time was, "Let's worry about the boundary cases."

Other committees used the list to determine sets of applicants who should be interviewed or whose files the committee should review more closely. Still others simply admitted as many from the top of the list as their projected enrollments and yield allowed. A sociologist explained to me that, with the exception of one case,

there wasn't a whole lot of discussion at the meetings about moving people around . . . We kind of went with the rankings. We felt like we *could* discuss all these people and certain cases but, you know, we had confidence that everyone had read everything pretty carefully. And we had thoughtful rankings. I thought it went really well.

In all cases, allowing each member to have different individual ratings of applicants and using the average of those individual ratings meant that faculty could continue to disagree about student quality while still getting the job done. However, this practice had significant consequences for the transparency of admissions decisions. In highly competitive programs like these, a single reader's classification of an application as a 1 versus 2, or as a 2 versus 3, could spell the difference between admission and rejection, yet with only "the numbers" before them, not even those who assigned the ratings would necessarily be able to pin down the factors that produced this outcome.[24]

Faculty committees conducted admissions as a "numbers game" in other ways. A few readers, for example, took individual rating a step further by imposing numerical identities onto applicants based on the ratings ("She's definitely a 1"). And all programs gambled on their yield rate in determining how many admissions offers to make. Nevertheless, the three most common ways faculty quantified judgment were by interpreting small increments in test scores as substantive differences in admissibility, applying numerical ratings to applicants, and constructing rank-ordered lists of applicants using the averages of reader ratings.

"We Definitely Try to Make People Happy"

Admissions may officially be a matter of choosing students, but the selection process itself is an institutionalized compromise that balances and reflects multiple, sometimes competing, faculty values.[25] And to many professors, the easier it is to find this compromise, the better. Therefore, amid awareness of the tendency toward bureaucratization, the faculty I observed made concerted efforts to build two professional norms, deliberation and collegiality, into the admissions process. Perhaps the clearest evidence of this was in widespread effort to downplay fundamental disagreements about what the appropriate evaluation criteria should be. About the tacit agreement to disagree on this matter, a sociologist remarked:

> Invariably, we wind up having conversations about norms and priorities, but there's no effort to put people on the same page. I would resist that as an individual faculty member . . . People weigh pieces of the application packet differently and I respect that. I would never try to create that kind of consensus.

Another sociology professor related these differences of opinion to the diverse viewpoints that he believed were central to research and faculty culture:

> I absolutely believe that the best work I've ever done is a pathetic, groping approximation to some very complicated truth out there. And the more methods, the more angles of vision I can bring to bear on that complicated truth, I feel, the better, the closer I get to it, without ever getting there.
>
> I think we're in the same business when we're doing admissions. The complicated truth is this person's ultimate ability as a sociologist. And I've got different metrics. I've got different items of information that are supposed to be giving me a handle on that. And when I've got a faculty member that says, "Oh, GREs will predict that" . . . I think, "You've got to be kidding, right? We know there's almost no predictive power there." But it is a piece of information. I agree.

So, I'd rather have members of the committee not saying, "It's GREs." If everybody went, "It's GREs," we'd have an easy process . . . and a deeply flawed process. To me it would be very, very far away from that complicated truth. So I want people coming to it, hopefully, from different angles.

Whether it was to avoid conflict over their colleagues' divergent approaches to evaluating applicants, or out of respect for their "different angles," the importance of collegiality to perceptions of a legitimate selection process is clear.

Faculty also displayed a commitment to collegiality in several other ways through the review process. For example, rather than discuss the thorny details of many cases, committees redirected most of their deliberations to less controversial issues, such as the rules of the process, what the numerical ratings mean, and where to "draw the line" for admitted students on the rank-ordered list. They debated the merits of delegation and quantification, philosophically and in practice, reminding one another of the value of deliberation and making appeals to shared values such as fairness and peer review. Discussing this level of detail and philosophy about procedure permitted the appearance of a deliberative process without broaching disagreements that stemmed from differences of priorities.

Moreover, it was natural to discuss procedure because so many faculty were ambivalent about the admissions process. In both interviews and committee meetings, participants freely acknowledged imperfections in the system, such as the false precision introduced when quantifying student quality through a rank-ordered list. A political scientist compared the challenge of admissions to that of selecting faculty for awards:

Partly for reasons of expediency, we need some kind of scoring system. It's easy. I've been on lots of committees on campus this semester deciding award winners. When the pool is twenty-five and you have time to think about your top fifteen who should get this teaching award, the numbers and the myth of precision [are] readily acknowledged because you have time to talk about all of this. But if you have a hundred good people, then . . . [we] say that the confidence interval around these numbers [is] thirty spots plus or minus, but we still have to go by them.

Members of one philosophy program spoke at length about this problem as part of a longer conversation about their discomfort with quantifying judgment and the implications of the subjective nature of the ratings themselves.[26]

Along with false precision, another frequently debated set of procedural questions was whether, how, and where to impose numerical thresholds for GRE percentiles, TOEFL scores, and average applicant ratings. These

debates provided clear examples of admissions decision making as improvisation, with faculty constructing the process as they went along. A linguist summarized the process and his committee's discussion:

> They were ranked, and some of the candidates were already on top of the rank-
> ings, so that simplified a lot of the conversations. More disagreement was on
> the edges. We cannot admit everybody. You need to put a line somewhere, and
> it's where do you put the line? And then, the people close to the line? That's
> where it starts. And so that's where the disagreement emerges.

The hard truth for decision makers in programs such as these was that the
admissions process requires many more rejections than admissions. Drawing
a line to separate the two groups, even with a wait-listed set to buffer them,
felt uncomfortable both because it made the scope of the rejections so
plain to see and because it provoked the sort of disagreements that faculty
try to avoid.

Compromise: When Collegiality Trumps Taste

Substituting discussion of uncontroversial procedural matters for questions
of who and what should be valued worked for another reason: Not only did
faculty feel ambivalent about how work was delegated and numbers were
used, but they felt that most admissions decisions were not worthy of argument, especially when compared to faculty-related decisions about
hiring, tenure, and promotion. In most cases they saw their collegiality as
a bigger priority than their individual preferences. A natural scientist
explained, "I think everyone on the committee wants to have an opinion.
That's the nature of scientists: they always want to make an opinion. But
I don't know if a lot of people feel very strongly." A first-time admissions
committee member in the physics department expressed surprise at the relative ease with which decisions were made:

> I think on the whole there were relatively few, quote, disagreements. Nobody
> was—that I could see—no one was particularly adamant that this person must
> be admitted. I didn't see any of that. I was expecting a little bit of that where
> students might have contacted directly a professor to say, "I would very much
> like to work in your group and your group exclusively" . . . But I didn't see
> any of that. I didn't see anybody pushing internal candidates. I thought it was
> all very congenial and, "Let's talk this over. What did I miss?"

Indeed, across the six committees I observed, committee members limited
hard advocacy to one or two cases per committee member.

Deferring to a colleague's judgment, not challenging it, was the norm. Faculty rationed their confrontations, treating agreement as more important than the marginal differences in the quality among those on the short list. Instead, and somewhat ironically, although admissions committees agonized about the integrity of the process, it was only through deliberation about its imperfections that they were able to move forward together.

Costs of Deliberative Bureaucracy

The goal of deliberative bureaucracy was to make the process of arriving at a collective judgment more efficient while preserving core norms such as deliberation and collegiality. The process clearly accomplishes these aims, but it also comes with unintended consequences.

Compromising recruitment networks. Bureaucratic practices made it more difficult for these programs to develop and sustain institutional pipelines and admit students with nontraditional backgrounds. Comparing current practice to that of thirty years ago, an emeritus physics professor argued that pipelines "could be implemented today if they really wanted to. But everybody is sort of backing off and they want to look at everything and *{Pause}* go through the more formalized process." With decision making both decentralized and formalized, it becomes harder to maintain relationships with feeder programs outside the network of high-prestige universities that everyone recognizes. Bureaucratic processes can also undermine outreach and recruitment programs used to identify talented applicants with nontraditional academic profiles. Kimberly Griffin and Marcela Muñiz came to a similar conclusion; these researchers found that the loose coupling between the administrators responsible for recruitment and the faculty tasked with admissions decision making was a major barrier to the professional efficacy of graduate diversity officers.[27]

Decontextualizing applicant characteristics. The approach to review that I observed during the initial screening, which emphasized the value of standardized categories and classifications over contextualized interpretations and individual uniqueness, fostered what Carol Heimer calls a case-based approach to evaluation.[28] This type of review was more efficient, but it also made it more difficult to identify and admit students with unconventional profiles. One humanities professor articulated: "Students are first sort of presented to us and to other search committees—to our competitors—in a spreadsheet kind of format. There are some that light up. Basically, these things are scores or numerical numbers like GPA, undergraduate institutions, test scores. There are some that will stand out as being *[Pause]* that look promising even without really looking at the application."

Identifying applicants at the earliest stages of the process by standardized categories such as test scores, institutional affiliations, or diversity contributions, rather than a review of their life stories or unique characteristics, had two important consequences. First, it made the few criteria they did consider more determinative of ratings and, ultimately, of students' opportunities. It also compelled an even greater need for committees to repersonalize applicants if reviewers submitted widely disparate ratings. They resolved those differences in most cases not by debating the criteria used to award a rating, but rather by developing narratives about the person behind the numbers, achievements, and standard categories. Here the process resembled what Heimer called biographical analysis, and what Mitchell Stevens called "evaluative storytelling" in his analysis of undergraduate admissions.[29]

Obscuring the basis for ratings and decisions. In addition to making pipelines difficult to sustain and decontextualizing information about applicants, perhaps the most fundamental cost of deliberative bureaucracy was that it obscured the basis for ratings and, by extension, decisions. What really mattered to faculty when they rated, admitted, and rejected applicants faded into the background, and core questions of what counts as a "quality" applicant and which applicants met that definition received only marginal attention. This tendency is closely related to a common critique of quantification, that in the course of facilitating decision making, it "simply evades the deep and important issues."[30]

By the standards of deliberative bureaucracy, utilizing numbers as proxies for complex, debatable judgments had real advantages. Numbers concealed underlying disagreements that faculty would rather not broach and buffered them from charges of unfairness. I was struck to observe that in only two of the ten programs were faculty even asked to compose notes that explained their applicant ratings. Moreover, the very nature of deliberation about borderline cases was so complex and holistic—rich with detail, impressions, and simultaneous weighing of pros and cons—that it was rarely possible to determine why, exactly, a given student was admitted, rejected, or wait-listed. As the chair of the political science department aptly put it, "Everything matters, and nothing matters the most." Vague criteria, unjustified ratings, and ad hoc policy all added to the veil of secrecy that protects these controversial decisions.[31]

Yet by the standards of deliberative democracy, transparency and reason giving are central to a decision's legitimacy. The lack of transparency inherent in holistic review has compromised public perceptions of admissions' fairness. Of particular concern to many are the specific ways that race and other diversity considerations are factored into decisions. Some assume that decisions made in secret must be largely a product of committee members' personal tastes or subconscious biases. Others assume that race plays a pivotal role in outcomes, instead of serving as a "factor of a factor of a factor of a factor," as Justice Ginsburg noted in her 2013 dissenting opinion on *Fisher v. University of Texas,* in which the U.S. Supreme Court evaluated the constitutionality of the admissions policy at the University of Texas.[32] Openness about the basis for ratings and decisions may open the door for disagreements, but it also forces accountability for evaluation criteria in use and enables committee members to learn from each other.

Friendly Debate and Drawing Group Boundaries

That reason giving and disagreement need not compromise collegiality—and indeed can be harnessed to improve admissions work—was exemplified in three committees: linguistics, political science, and astrophysics. In these programs, deliberations were characterized by vigorous, friendly debate in which faculty corrected each other's misperceptions and proposed alternative interpretations. They made explicit their tacit assumptions and, in select cases, challenged one another on those assumptions. An example from a meeting of the linguistics admissions committee exemplifies how faculty draw out the assumptions driving their colleagues' judgments, especially in the presence of implicit bias.

Near the end of an almost three-hour meeting, left with only a handful of borderline cases they had previously tabled, the linguistics committee was losing what little formality had characterized their interactions. Starting the discussion about Maria, a woman who had attended a small religious college, a committee member admitted, "I didn't know anything about the college. I had to look it up." Those with some familiarity spent a little time sharing their impressions and knowledge with the rest of the group.

"Right-wing religious fundamentalists," one said. "You know, they refused all federal monies so that they can resist the socialists."

"Supported by the Koch brothers," another added after a long laugh from the rest of the committee.

"In all seriousness, it's actually supposed to be pretty good in the humanities," one quipped. They started to discuss other specifics of Maria's case, noting among other details that she had been homeschooled and that she had scored at the 99th percentile for the Verbal section of the GRE and the 82nd percentile for the Quantitative section. Although the committee was near the end of the short list that they were slated to discuss, her case was the first in which they discussed GRE scores in more than passing detail. Her educational background clearly had induced skepticism, and they subjected her file to a more stringent review. Those seated on one side of the table wanted to move her application forward into the next round of evaluation, while those on the other side were unconvinced.

"I feel like a jackass for saying this," a male committee member said, breaking a long pause, "but she doesn't seem interested in research to me." Others marshaled evidence from her file to the contrary, and the committee chair smiled and confessed, "I would like to beat that college out of her."

"I think it already has been," a senior member of the faculty suggested, reading an excerpt from Maria's personal statement that signaled independence and critical thinking.

"You don't think she's a nutcase?" the department chair asked, to laughter from most members of the committee. With the three most powerful people around the table having joked about this case, no one tried to top them. They agreed to move her forward to the next round but a few weeks later, when making their final decisions, chose not to extend her an admissions offer.

Driving home that evening after the meeting, I thought about how the committee had discussed this case. I wondered what their meetings must usually be like if this was how they spoke to each other with a researcher in the room? It was a question I asked myself more than a few times during the course of my fieldwork, in response to seemingly unfiltered discussions of candidates with uncommon profiles. It had been an amusing conversation, but whether Maria had received a fair hearing was debatable, and the tenor of their discussion was consistent with results of an experimental study that found disclosing a religious background in one's application to psychology doctoral programs reduced the chances of admission.[33] On the one hand, it was frustrating to hear faculty describe any applicant as a possible "nutcase." On the other hand, rude comments like this affirmed for me that I really was seeing behind the curtain. Further, their exchange had perfectly exemplified how individual and collective judgments could be refined when a committee takes time to work through the details of a case, especially an unconventional one that might otherwise fall through the cracks of implicit, collective stereotypes.

On another level, this episode in linguistics showed that interactions of committees characterized by vigorous but friendly debate were often less formal and used their deliberations to draw group boundaries. That is, they used admissions deliberation not only to choose students, but also to send messages to one another about who they were as a community and who they were not. It was hardly the only time I observed committees ease negotiations over sensitive cases by introducing the entertainment and shock value of humorous or rude comments. Such comments compromised norms of professionalism, but served an important social function of cutting through tension, encouraging camaraderie, and clarifying shared values. Sometimes one committee member would tease another, but more often jabs were outwardly focused—joking at the applicant's or another discipline's expense.

The astrophysics committee was another whose meetings were characterized by friendly debate and humor. In one case, they had reached a point of deadlock over an applicant, and a junior professor noted that one of the letters of recommendation in his file seemed "weird and brief." Another shot back, "That's what happens when engineers write," to cathartic laughter all around. Whether it was astrophysicists distinguishing themselves from engineers or members of a large research university distinguishing themselves from those in religious colleges, faculty used evaluative deliberations to affirm their identities and organizational boundaries by admitting those who were believed to fit and rejecting those who did not.

As my fieldwork progressed, I couldn't help but note how unique the interactions were in linguistics and astrophysics—how comfortable they seemed to be with the each other and with the work of ruling out qualified students. To understand this from a department member's perspective, I asked each committee's admissions chair to reflect upon it in follow-up interviews. The linguistics chair affirmed the value of their deliberation-rich process,

> I think the experience of doing this together is good for us even if we weren't admitting anybody. I mean just to read these applications and talk about them, you find out, you know, about how your colleagues think or find out more about how they think about the graduate students . . . Their perspective is often useful and sometimes they know things about such-and-such an institution that the rest of us wouldn't know about.

The linguistics and astrophysics committees not only framed critique and disagreement as natural to social and academic life, they also *valued* disagreement as an opportunity to build knowledge and understanding. And although the political science committee did not seem unanimous about their comfort with the presence of dissent around the table, its chair encouraged the members to remember that "disagreement is not a sign that something is awry." This perspective stands in contrast to those committees who perceived disagreement as a precursor to conflict and conflict as a problem to be avoided. Better, those participants might say, to conceal disagreements behind numbers and celebrate the average as a compromise achieved without controversy.

Finally, subtle details hinted at the sort of relationships present in committees that are characterized by friendly debate. Astrophysics, linguistics, and political science were the only three committees to serve food during their meetings, for example. The political science committee had pizza delivered to what they called their "marathon meeting." There were custom deli sandwiches ordered for one of the linguistics committee's meetings, and the administrative assistant serving on the committee in astrophysics circulated a tin of homemade cookies in one of their meetings. I noted also in two of these three programs that small talk preceding the meeting included recounting time spent together outside usual work hours and settings. In astrophysics, two male professors laughed about the play date they had arranged for their children, and in linguistics, half of the committee bantered about the mountains they had seen from the air while traveling together back from a major conference. Obviously, the formation of trusting relationships is a complicated process involving much more than a sandwich or some informal time together. Yet it's also possible that when a group of professionals will be engaging in potentially contentious work, taking time for food or fellowship may encourage social conditions, not to mention blood sugar and energy levels, in which differences of opinion are less likely to be interpreted as hostility or disrespect.

Conclusion

In some doctoral programs, the sheer volume of applications can make democratic deliberation about every applicant a near impossibility, especially if there are profound disagreements about how scarce spaces should be allocated. The model of decision making I observed, deliberative bureaucracy, is an organizational adaptation to these challenges whereby faculty reduce the potential for divisiveness and increase the potential of getting the job done with a reasonable time commitment. Three behaviors—delegating work, quantifying judgment, and shifting the focus of discussion to process matters—serve the interests of bureaucratic efficiency and safeguard professional norms like collegiality and deliberation.

Deliberative bureaucracy also helps explain why faculty overrely upon GRE scores. Committees looked to quantitative metrics for efficiency's sake, often decontextualizing test scores from their students' backgrounds. Yet failing in many cases to discuss the basis for applicant ratings or to read scores in context allowed narrow framing and misperceptions of what test scores mean to continue unchecked. Deliberative bureaucracy may serve faculty interests, but it is a costly model for applicants whose GRE scores are noisy signals of potential.

Most research on elite preferences in educational settings emphasizes how common selection *criteria* can reinforce existing patterns of privilege, and this is a major theme that runs through subsequent chapters of this book. However, deliberative bureaucracy demonstrates that the preference for efficient, collegial decision making also plays an important role in maintaining inequality by helping explain unexamined use of those criteria in reference to most applicants.

One of the keys to understanding organizations is understanding how they coordinate their values and beliefs with their practices and personnel.[34] Faculty valued consensus achieved through deliberation, but felt daunted by the prospect of finding consensus amid the range of disagreements they held—about acceptable criteria and how applications should be interpreted, to name just two. Finding consensus required a level of conflict that most programs preferred to avoid. Moreover, they recognized that *any* process they adopted would be seemingly unfair because it would deny enrollment opportunities to scores or even hundreds of qualified candidates. Absent the feasibility of consensus or fairness as grounds for legitimate admissions, they built a case for the legitimacy of their practice on other organizational priorities—namely, efficiency and collegiality—while permitting a modicum of disagreement on less controversial matters of process.

Discussing the roots of democratic decision making, Pericles wrote, "Instead of looking on discussion as a stumbling-block in the way of action, we think it an indispensable preliminary to any wise action at all."[35] Using numbers as proxies for collective judgment and refocusing discussion away from controversial matters may get the job done, but deliberative bureaucracy is ultimately a missed opportunity for organizational learning. The discussions that lead to selecting students are about more than selection; they are an annual opportunity for leaders to reassess their department and discipline's mission, values, and what they have been and are becoming.[36] Through gatekeeping deliberations, faculty can come to understand and appreciate others' perspectives and more thoughtfully align their organizational identities and goals as scholars with the people they are initiating to help fulfill them.

CHAPTER TWO

Meanings of Merit and Diversity

V IVEK, the admissions chair, started the conversation about Denpa. "He grew up in a yurt in the Himalayas. He was raised by his mom and grandma after his father died at an early age, and the next neighbors were two mountains over. He then found his way to a major U.S. research university and has since started the only organization for the discipline in the Himalayan region."

On the other side of the table, William, a recently tenured professor who seemed to play the role of resident skeptic, asked, "But do we think he can succeed?" There was a long, loaded silence. None of the five around the table dared to register a prediction. In an earlier meeting, the committee had decided *not* to move Denpa forward in the admission process because his GRE scores came in after the deadline and because when they did, the Subject score was at the 10th percentile. They were having this conversation only because a senior professor in the department, Harold, had petitioned the committee to reconsider his application. Harold had received a personal email from a longtime friend who was serving as one of Denpa's references, discussing how impressed he was with the student's research experience and motivation. Harold asked Vivek via email to reconsider their decision and to offer him admission, conditional on "passing certain remedial courses." Vivek deferred to the committee in making this call, and after receiving some pressure from others in the department, they invited Harold to their meeting to discuss the case.

Breaking the silence, Vivek acknowledged, "He's the most amazing case we've ever seen."

Finally Harold, himself, spoke up. "He would bring some personality to the department. I commit to look after him and fund him through the prelims. He presents himself as quite intelligent."

"Excellent idea to give him a chance," the graduate student member of the committee affirmed, and with that, Denpa's case was closed. He was ultimately admitted. He enrolled. He passed the "remedial" coursework, the core courses, and his qualifying exam. And at the time this book went to press, Denpa had submitted a paper for publication, was working on his thesis, and was active in scientific outreach in both the United States and his home country. Harold remained his advisor, and he collaborated with William.

Debatable assumptions underlie judgments of quality, which underlie assessments of merit and admissibility. I argued in Chapter 1 that running admissions as a deliberative bureaucracy effectively prevents difficult conversations about those assumptions from dominating or extending the review process. Yet regardless of whether the politics of quality remain tacit—due to consensus or avoidance—or are made explicit because individual judgments of applicants do not align, they are always present in admissions. They are at the heart of committee and broader debates about how opportunities should be distributed. Through cases like Denpa's—in which faculty debate judgments of unconventional, borderline applicants— the politics of evaluating student quality and the multiple meanings of merit are revealed.

I found that the standard used to assess merit during the initial screening of applications varied substantially from the standard of merit used to judge candidates who made the short list. The distinct notions of what made a desirable applicant at each stage of review had distinct implications for the equity and diversity of who might eventually enroll. Given the distributions of GRE scores by race, ethnicity, and gender, for example, the extremely high bar of conventional achievement with which faculty in these programs initially assessed the pool adversely affected opportunities for Latino, black, Native American, and female applicants.[1] I found that meanings of merit included diversity only when faculty worked to distinguish among those on a short list of well-qualified applicants, at which point the ideal of merit was rooted in envisioning the future of the discipline. Even then, however, faculty conceived of diversity very broadly. Black, Latino, Native American, or Southeast Asian applicants might stand out on the short list because they rarely appeared there, but race/ethnicity was just one of many dimensions of diversity they weighed in making judgments about quality. And as Denpa's case demonstrates, regardless of how faculty assessed individual student quality, *department* politics also contributed to the politics of quality and the operational meanings of merit.

Thus, if a cost of the secrecy and lack of transparency in admissions is uncertainty about how decision makers are incorporating student identities into their assessments, an important point in these programs' admissions story is this: Even in closed-door conversations, race, gender, and other student identities came up very rarely. When considered at all, race was a "factor of a factor of a factor of a factor," as Justice Ginsburg concluded.[2] Indeed, it was not opponents of affirmative action but rather its proponents who would be likely to take issue with the standards of merit by which graduate decisions were made.

How gatekeepers in elite organizations relate merit and diversity is a question of deep importance. The Association of American Colleges and Universities proposes that joining principles of merit and diversity in an integrated notion of inclusive excellence is "critical to the wellbeing of democratic culture."[3] Lani Guinier's advocacy of democratic merit is consistent with this view, emphasizing that a tendency to narrowly judge excellence on the basis of individual achievement or aptitude flies in the face of higher education's responsibility to cultivate leaders with democratic capacities such as collaboration, problem solving, and creativity.[4] At the institutional level, higher education researchers have argued that inclusive excellence in admissions enables postsecondary institutions to "leverage diversity for student learning and institutional excellence."[5]

Theories of Organizational Excellence

Sociologist Michèle Lamont found that faculty on interdisciplinary review panels define excellence and rationalize their judgments through evaluative scripts. The idea traces to Erving Goffman's dramaturgical theory, which compares social life to the theater and public behavior to the performance of familiar roles and scripts. Following prevailing social scripts ensures that others will find our behavior (the performance) realistic and acceptable, which led Goffman to conclude that social behavior consists of managing others' impressions as much as it consists of managing our own principles or commitments.[6]

Applying this idea to the context of evaluation, Lamont found that faculty use scripts to link formal evaluative criteria with the meanings those criteria hold. Usually these meanings are rooted in reviewers' shared identities and work, and they therefore serve as decision pathways or stories that reviewers tell to justify their judgments.[7] Following these pathways is a bit like peeling back the layers of an onion. A surface-level criterion has meaning, but there are reasons—often implicit—that the meaning is itself important (that is, the meaning carries its own meaning). For example, a common evaluative script I observed was that some faculty perceive grades to be a function of academic ability or effort, perceive ability and effort to be signals of future success, and perceive likelihood of future success to be a justification for the investment that admission represents. Evaluative scripts thus allow even controversial outcomes to be regarded as legitimate, because criteria are understood as proxies for shared, self-evident values. Definitions of excellence thus come to constitute boundaries that define groups of scholars and become the terms by which they define others.

Shared goals may also factor into the ideals of excellence that guide decision making, and this is particularly the case in elite organizations because they attract many applicants who meet basic qualifications. Organizational theorist Robert Birnbaum concluded that a key factor in elite academic selection is the degree to which a particular applicant "represents the optimization of one or another institutional goal."[8] Knowing the goals of highly ranked graduate programs can therefore offer insight into the desired qualities of applicants and what will likely count as merit. For example, graduate education and academia have a basic goal of advancing knowledge, and the importance to an academic program of pushing knowledge in particular directions may help explain the importance in admissions of perceived "fit" and "match" with departmental intellectual foci or disciplinary norms, often over and above conventional academic achievements.[9] In broad-based departments or interdisciplinary fields, where fresh perspective is desirable, committees may be more inclined to select students with diverse knowledge and perspectives. By contrast, niche programs or disciplines with a strong orthodoxy may seek conformity over novelty.[10]

Status is another important organizational goal in doctoral programs like the ones I studied, and in higher education more generally. To justify and maintain their high ranking, leaders order program activities and priorities for maximum consistency with the norms in their field.[11] In admissions, that work of alignment includes adopting selection criteria that carry academic cachet, such as high GRE scores and degrees from elite colleges and universities.[12] Whether they name status as a consideration or simply reveal it as such through their behavior, faculty are attuned to organizational status competition in defining what counts as merit.

Within this broad framework of priorities, however, research about decision making and the selection of social and academic elites portrays it as highly negotiated processes that depends on a variety of structural and cultural conditions, as well as the characteristics of the applicant pool and quirks of reviewers themselves. As such, we can predict that some outcomes of selection processes in departments like these will seem far from predictable. We need to keep these factors in mind in examining how faculty define and relate merit and diversity in selecting doctoral students.

The First Cut: Merit as Conventional Achievement

In almost every program, review began with assessments of applicants' academic achievements, especially GRE scores and prior grades. As we saw in Chapter 1, faculty saw these measures as useful metrics for the first cut in part because they could be used to quickly compare applicants. The general rule was the higher the grades, the better, but the meaning of a particular GPA could be further calibrated by considering the reputation of the institution where those grades were earned. Similarly, most insisted upon interpreting GRE scores in the context of national origin, although they were reticent to do so on the basis of race, gender, or socioeconomic status.

Programs varied by discipline in the specific grades and test scores they weighted most heavily at this point in the review process. Physicists and astrophysicists reported that they looked first and foremost to scores on the Physics Subject test of the GRE. In response to my usual first interview question, "What are you looking for in prospective students?," an astrophysicist admitted, "I would say—and you will see it in our discussions— it's very unlikely that we would consider anyone who has a low Subject GRE." One of his colleagues concurred, "If you don't score high, you're probably not going to make the cut." Those in the humanities emphasized the GRE's analytical writing score in their initial screens, and in economics, high quantitative GRE scores were crucial. The admissions chair in the economics program disclosed his approach to making the first cut of their 800 applications: "Personal statements have almost no role. I don't read them. I look at the transcript and glance at the GRE. If the quantitative score is not perfect, don't bother applying."[13] Broadly, these findings about the vital role of quantitative metrics support Robert Klitgaard's assessment of admissions in Harvard University's Graduate School thirty years ago, that test scores and grades form the "backbone of the evaluative process," with test scores especially attractive due to their "magic simplicity."[14]

Yet faculty felt that the rise over time in GRE scores and, in particular, GPAs had decreased their usefulness in culling the pool. Facing a ceiling effect, in which distinguishing among candidates was impossible because so many applicants' scores and grades were concentrated at the top of the scales, reviewers felt they needed additional information to compare applicants. As an astrophysicist put it, "Grade point, most people said it doesn't really affect them very much because basically everybody in the pool—everybody in the final pool—has such high GPAs that it's not meaningful." In response, many reviewers considered grades in light of the reputation of the institution in which the grades were earned and the rigor of the student's curriculum. A sociologist, for example, compared his department's admissions process to its process for faculty hiring. I quote him at length:

> *Robert:* What's great about hiring professors is we have direct evidence of exactly what they did . . . It's not easy, but it is information rich. Whereas I would say graduate admissions is information poor. So then one tends, or we tend, a lot to rely on signals that are low quality, like, one of the frequently used ones is the quality or prestige of the undergraduate school. Lousy signal, I think.
>
> *JP: Why is it valued so much do you think?*
>
> *Robert:* Because you have so little else to go on. You have grades, which I think are a good signal. But the people we admit are always going to be right around 4.0. Then you have the ones at the margins coming with a 3.9 or 4.1. So grades are increasingly a lousy signal, especially at these elite places that just hand out the A's. So you don't even have that anymore. I think only if you *don't* get a straight A average or close to it that it's something you attend to.
>
> Then you have test scores, which are lousy for all the reasons we know . . . But what else do you *have?* So you have the tests, and yeah, we definitely sort of have an expectation of high scores on the test even though no one *likes* to use them. But increasingly, you have plenty of people who are really high on the test scores and really high on grades. Tons of those people. So *now* what do you use?
>
> *I: It sounds like you're looking for variance.*
>
> *R:* Right, right. So you use the prestige of the school.

Reviewers could never be sure how much grade inflation had distorted a given student's GPA, and they doubted whether prestige of an undergraduate institution actually predicted student success. Still, they continued to read grades in light of college prestige because it effectively broadened the range of grades and test scores. On one end would be a low GPA from an unknown college or one whose training in the field was regarded as weak.[15] On the other end of the spectrum was a high GPA from an Ivy League or other institution with a reputation for strong undergraduate preparation in the discipline. A "good" grade from a "good" college "carried more weight" or could be awarded "higher marks."

Rankings were only one way faculty gauged institutional quality, however. Seeing one's alma mater on the application would stir participants on an emotional level, as could peer institutions of one's alma mater. This first- and secondhand knowledge was no more reliable than rankings as a measure of current institutional quality or applicant promise, but it powerfully influenced their willingness to trust. Unsurprisingly, the Ivy League constituted a meaningful institutional trust network, but so did flagship public universities in the natural sciences and elite liberal arts colleges like Reed, Williams, and Wesleyan in the humanities. These variations by discipline and individual experience are consistent with organizational research that finds that "legitimacy ultimately exists in the eye of the beholder."[16]

I probed faculty in the interviews about why they continued using this initial filter, knowing that it disproportionately excluded students who were already underrepresented and knowing there was more to the numbers than meets the eye. By triangulating their answers with observations from the meetings, I began to piece together important evaluative scripts in use—the meanings behind the metrics.

Risk aversion and predicting student success. One evaluative script emphasized risk aversion. Faculty believed that they had an institutional imperative to avoid risky candidates. And because slots in their program were so coveted, they had the luxury to reject those candidates whose test scores and grades failed to reach a very high standard.

Worried about the possible financial and status consequences of student attrition from their programs, faculty read applicant qualifications with their own formal course requirements in mind. They sought students whom they thought would work hard, but who would not struggle too much with the curriculum. Often, this curriculum demanded prerequisite skills not communicated to students and for which they offered few to no opportunities to learn once on campus. Reflecting on their program's tendency to prefer students whom they felt "pretty confident can get through," a classicist explained,

> Graduate admissions is one of the things I think you have to be very humble about. And there's always a tension here because we're always under pressure to have good numbers for completing a program, completing it in a reasonable amount of time, and so on. The effect of that is to make you risk averse because it's not that hard just to go for the students you're pretty confident can get through.

Others discussed risk aversion in terms of the investments of time and energy that students require of faculty. During an interview with a physicist, I commented, "You've mentioned a couple of times: 'Can they be successful?'"

and 'Do I think they'll be successful?' It sounds like that's a really key question you're asking." He responded,

> Yes, because it's a big investment for the faculty member who takes on a student. And so if you work with the student so closely and then he walks away or doesn't make it, then it's a waste of his time. And in a way, I mean, it's our mission to teach, but I'd rather spend my time teaching somebody who actually can continue my mission and then teach other students than somebody who realizes, "It's just too difficult. I can't do it."

The tendency to avoid risk was ubiquitous, but it was especially potent in programs with small cohorts and those that offered full financial support to their students. Under these conditions, each student has a relatively large effect on completion statistics and represents a significant financial investment. Perhaps it should come as no surprise that faculty repeatedly compared admissions to "risk taking" and "gambling."[17]

Participants in this study approached admissions as risk taking in a variety of ways, but for most, the risk was entirely uncalculated. The vast majority were unaware of research about what affects graduate student outcomes, and only one program had analyzed their own applicant data. Nevertheless, I heard a common refrain that a weaker record of upper-level coursework on student transcripts could be assumed to represent weak preparation and a good chance that the applicant "may not know what they're getting into." Several participants admitted their tendency to "feel spooked" when an applicant's profile called to mind a past student who had struggled or ultimately not completed. Still others, consistent with research on decision making in elite organizations, preferred to eliminate *perceived* risks rather than estimate or calculate the level of risk.[18]

Another approach to risk was born of the tendency toward credential inflation at the undergraduate level. As more and more students report higher grades and GRE scores, not to mention other skills, research experiences, and honors, some faculty interpreted the *absence* of such distinction as a sign of risk. Finally, four admissions chairs—whose programs were ranked in the top five for their disciplines—voluntarily discussed the "luxury of risk aversion" that their large, highly qualified pools permitted. Some preferred conventional overachievers in the first round of admissions simply because they could.

Intelligence and belonging in elite intellectual communities. An evaluative script of intelligence and belonging also helps explain the enduring influence of GRE scores and student grades early in the review process. Many associated "the numbers" with intelligence, and intelligence with belonging in an academic community near the top of their fields.[19] I asked each participant in individual interviews what they thought GRE scores signaled, and the first response from more than 50 percent of them included comments like "innate ability," "sheer intellectual horsepower," and "native intelligence." These comments were reflected in admissions meetings, where more than half of the comments about intelligence coincided with comments about high grades and/or Graduate Record Exam (GRE) scores. In linguistics, one professor commented, "Those are astronomical scores!" with another responding, "And check out the stellar grades. There's no question she's smart." Following up with the department chair, he reiterated, "Someone who does that well on the GRE is unlikely to be lame-brained. They are likely to be smart."

To the extent that faculty connect GRE scores to intelligence, these supposedly objective, standardized criteria may take on a personal quality, for intelligence is central to academic culture and faculty self-concept.[20] I examine the nuances of how faculty conceive of intelligence in Chapter 5, but for the sake of understanding conventional achievement as a standard of merit early in the review process, the key point is that programs' legitimacy as elite intellectual communities in some ways hinges on the perceived intelligence of those whom they admit and hire. As the linguistics committee chair put it, they used admissions to "reflect the view the department has of itself" because the department's character is "so determined by graduate admissions."

That faculty associated quantitative metrics with intelligence and belonging helps explain why faculty relied upon them so much when making the first cut.[21] Yet, a sense of the applicant's belonging mattered deeply in later phases of review as well. Explaining his committee's decision not to admit a borderline applicant, a biologist commented, "[He was] from a different planet and we were confident that this person was not going to be one of us. He's not going to be a full member of the scientific community." Committees often framed belonging in terms of "fit," which was a seemingly unassailable criterion and, in many cases, a bottom-line consideration.

Convenience. Reading to this point, one might assume simple elitism and outdated views of intelligence explained why faculty relied so much upon GRE scores, grades, and institutional prestige. And, indeed, one sociologist in the sample quipped,

> This is an elite university and a lot of the people at the university are elitists. *{He laughs.}* Simply said. So they make a lot of inferences about the quality of someone's work and their ability based on where they come from.

However, the tendency toward bureaucratic decision making suggests there may be more to the story. Faculty didn't simply rely upon grades, test scores, and institutional prestige because they believed they were the best indicators of achievement. They also relied upon these metrics because they were convenient.

Time demands and incomplete information were the most frequently cited answers to my interview question about what makes admissions evaluations difficult, and quantifying quality and judgment helped faculty cope with these difficulties. Some committees went so far as to sort long spreadsheet lists of applicants by scores and grades. In the physics program, which drew hundreds of applicants, the chair shared with me his instructions to the committee for the first round of review: "In reports to me, just summarize the test scores and GPA because I'm fully capable of reading a spreadsheet, but I prefer not to have to read the entire file." Especially in large programs, some expressed regret that every file did not receive a truly holistic review in the initial review, including this sociologist:

> We receive so many applications, and we are always in a crunch with time—always. And I have impressions that some of my faculty—senior members—were simply looking at the GRE. They have a threshold such as, "If it's not over 700, I won't read anything." And that cuts usually two-thirds of the applicants.

Drawing large numbers of applicants, faculty sacrificed the multidimensional ideal of quality they believed in to process applications quickly and efficiently. Letters of recommendation required reviewers to "read between the lines" and "sift through the superlatives." Many worried that personal statements were "subject to gaming," and not only were writing samples extremely time-consuming to review, but it was impossible to know how much support students had received in preparing them. Given these ambiguities, numbers like the GRE and grade point average seemed to carry an apparent—if illusory—clarity, simplicity, and precision. A sociologist noted that unlike work experience, research experience, or awards, which might not be available for comparing all applicants, "The GRE is something they all have in common. The fact that it is common to everybody is really useful." Valuing scores and grades, then, was not only a matter of perceived belonging and risk aversion, but also of *ambiguity aversion*. In the absence of clarity, and given their shared values of risk aversion and intelligence, faculty settled for the convenience of the entrenched standard when making the first cut.

The cultural meanings of conventional achievement—risk aversion, intelligence, belonging, and convenience—help explain why faculty often maintain a standard of evaluation about which they feel some ambivalence and doubt. In addition to the problem that this standard has only marginal relevance for scholars' long-term outcomes however, rigidly pursuing this vision of academic excellence disproportionately prevents women and domestic students of color from advancing beyond the first cut. As long as systemic disparities in GRE scores and elite college enrollment persist, it will be more difficult for programs to diversify if their initial standards of quality rely heavily on these qualities.

Two pathways toward more equitable enrollments are available to faculty. One involves preserving the current admissions regime, waiting for more equitable patterns in student scores and institutional affiliations, and accepting that until that occurs, admission decisions may reproduce within the academy the racial and gender inequalities present elsewhere in society. Another pathway involves faculty stepping back from screening customs and assumptions about student quality that are entirely taken for granted. They could explicitly treat diversity as a dimension of quality from the beginning of the review process, for example, or reevaluate how they think about and weigh the GRE.[22]

The Short List: Merit as the Future of the Discipline

Faculty revealed their preferences both in the initial criteria they used to narrow the applicant pool and in the hairs they split to make final selections. Through holistic and individualized review, faculty adopted a much broader view of merit in judging the short list. They opened their eyes to the very minutiae in qualitative components of the application that initially they wanted to avoid. Evidence of having mastered course material or a bank of test items was insufficient to impress reviewers at this point, because the list was replete with such conventional achievers. Rather, they looked for applicants who had a different relationship with knowledge. Seeking potential for independent scholarship and innovation born of fresh perspective, faculty combed through details to make a fundamental inference: Who might advance the future of the discipline?

Faculty from disciplines that were far afield intellectually shared the sentiment that such prediction was very difficult work. An astrophysicist explained:

> You're really basing it on their potential to be great scientists. But it is much harder—much harder. What you look at for a particular person varies from person to person.

And an economist elaborated,

> That's so hard because at one level what you're looking for is so easy. You're basically looking for people who are going to be first-rate researchers and leaders in the field . . . who are going to be great economists. But figuring out in a twenty-one-year-old what traits are predictive of becoming great intellectual leaders is incredibly hard. You have to look for proxies at some level. One of the proxies you look for is, is the person sufficiently quantitative and mathematically sophisticated? . . . You want to find someone who is creative and asks great questions. That is so hard to tell. You might look at their thesis or maybe they worked as a research assistant or their recommendations. It's very hard to assess if someone is—{Pause} it takes a certain type of person to be a researcher.

In classics, fluency in ancient languages mattered at this point as much as mathematical training did in economics and research experience did in astrophysics, but in each of these fields, professors struggled to identify talent. An associate professor of classics described it as "guesswork":

> From the department's perspective, we want to have somebody who is going to finish the program and thrive—thrive here and go on and be a successful faculty member somewhere. So we want to be careful about who we pick . . . They're really pretty young, just finishing college and a lot of students really still are quite unformed in a lot of ways, still taking a lot of other classes on top of their classics courses. What will that person be like in one or two years? You know, where will they go? That's where the guesswork comes in. I think the more experienced—the more you teach, the more you know students, the more you choose them and see how they turn out, the better feeling you have for it. But there's something. It's not quantity. A score doesn't tell you, answer that question.

Across the disciplines, what faculty sought were displays of potential to become what the Carnegie Initiative on the Doctorate called a steward of the discipline, one who "considers the applications, uses, and purposes of the field and favors wise and responsible application . . . [and] how to foster renewal and creativity."[23] Reviewers assessed a range of personal characteristics that might affect whether and how their skills and abilities would be realized, including affective dispositions and noncognitive qualities that they associated with exemplary scholarship. A physical scientist explained (emphasis mine): "I look for people who have had research *experience* and show a great deal of *enthusiasm* for it. I look for *creativity*. I look for *energy*. I look for possibilities, potential for *innovation* . . . a *passion* for research." And in a social sciences program, a senior scholar born outside the United States listed similar qualities:

> If the person is intellectually *creative,* I think he or she *will grow to be a really, good scholar.* To me that is the most important trait I look for . . . He or she is *really thinking.* It's not like—I know this language. I have that skill. I have learned these courses, all this typical knowledge. I'm *curious* about all of the new, interesting phenomena in society or this or that. And I *want to explore.* I want to find what's going on . . . That would make a good scholar.

Such qualities connote a relationship with knowledge that cannot be measured quantitatively but may be inferred from elements of the application that many claimed were too onerous and ambiguous to emphasize in the first round.

Professors were especially eager to glean these qualities from evidence of previous research experience. Given the importance of conducting original research to success in doctoral education, their hope was to evaluate research potential as a function of prior accomplishment, as if they were hiring a faculty member. A biologist commented,

> I wanted to see some independent research because I think if you haven't done independent research then you don't really know whether you have a passion for it. And you kind of don't know what you're getting yourself into. This is what it is all about.

Respondents were divided, however, over whether the most reliable testimony of a student's research experience and potential came from letters of recommendation or from students themselves. In four of the programs, reviewers wanted students to personally communicate their experience with research (in the personal statement and/or interview), and in astrophysics a majority of the committee discussed the importance of "sell[ing] your ideas." The admissions chair explained,

> Here, we judge them about how well they can explain things. So the selling component of being an astronomer and selling your ideas is very important. In theory it's actually even more important because we discuss ideas all the time to get new ideas. It's all about the discourse and why are you doing what you're doing. Challenging the fundamental, physical concepts behind it—a student has to be well versed as to how to defend their own ideas and how to express them.

Committees also took seriously the alignment of student research interests with faculty expertise. Some described this alignment in terms of the potential for mentoring, others in terms of the applicant's capacity to support faculty research. In spite of being listed as an author on seven publications, for example, an applicant in the physical sciences was not admitted under a rationale that included worries about the depth of her involvement and weak alignment between her interests and the department's strengths.

The importance of intellectual fit applied across the disciplines. "We don't want clones," one humanities professor laughed. "But on the other hand, we do want people who really do match reasonably well to what we're good at."

Defining diversity. During later rounds of review, faculty invariably preferred students who would add to the program's or discipline's diversity. If an applicant with merit is broadly defined as one who deserves admission, then diversity was not in tension with merit in the later phases of the review process. Instead, diversity was simply one component of merit.

Why is diversity important to graduate admissions committees today? Research suggests a variety of reasons that postsecondary institutions seek diverse student enrollments and strive to be *known* as diverse. For one, the educational benefits of diversity is currently the only constitutionally accepted rationale for affirmative action; therefore, institutions that utilize race-conscious admissions often lean on the diversity rationale. Others have found diversity a politically palatable rationale for efforts toward racial or gender *equity*, because diversity can be defined with a sufficiently long "laundry list" of identities to make anyone feel included.[24]

Diversity also has a clear business case in academe, given its documented relationships with established metrics of scholarly excellence. Political scientist Scott Page found that a randomly selected group of amateurs outperformed a homogeneous group of experts in tasks that involve creativity and problem solving, for example. And through an analysis of the citation patterns of 1.5 million scholarly papers, economist Richard Freeman found that papers with author lists that appear ethnically diverse are cited more frequently. Freeman surmises that ethnically diverse authorship produces greater diversity of ideas. In graduate education, studies also find that diversity contributes to innovation in research and to preparing professionals who will work effectively in increasingly multiracial communities.[25] Both because diversity aids universities in fulfilling their educational and public missions, and because the image of insufficient diversity may compromise an institution's reputation, many universities and their departments strive to *present themselves* as diverse and are explicit about diversity as a goal that they should use admissions and hiring to pursue.[26]

The faculty I interviewed and the committees I observed may not have agreed about exactly which characteristics should "count" as diversity or why it should be an informal criterion in this phase of the review process. They did agree to disagree on the matter, though, and in keeping things vague, made it possible to make the argument that by some standards they were diverse, in spite of deep gender and racial inequities. Still, the default mindset about diversity started with racial, gender, and, for a few people, class stratification. Committees in all three universities adopted the language of "diversity candidates" to refer to those who would be eligible for university fellowships targeting underrepresented groups. Philosophers and physicists expressed the most concern about gender parity. Some tried to explain long-standing inequality by painting philosophy as "a macho profession," evocatively describing current levels of representation as "abysmal," "atrocious," and "awful," and so on.[27] Physicists, however, felt that progress on gender equity has been made in recent decades. One elaborated:

> I think the drive for broadening gender representation has been quite successful, and not without its problems but we have *[Pause]* we have very strong representation of women. You can see that in the profession now. *[Laughs]* You look at university presidents for example. I think the highest paid president in the United States is a woman PhD physicist, Shirley Jackson . . . Anyway, we now see in our research groups a very strong representation of women and they're doing well. So whatever risk we took there, we haven't had to worry there. With African Americans, it's often a different story.

When I asked faculty to describe how their department defined diversity, they most frequently started with race. Only a few mentioned socioeconomic status, and then only in concert with race. A white female graduate student on the political science committee was one such individual. Sighing, she said, "I guess I'm like with *[Pause]* diversity meaning like class, race, and gender. It's a plus. I'm going with like Supreme Court language here because I just talked about this with my students." In sociology, a male faculty member of color expressed that, throughout higher education,

> socioeconomic diversity is something I think we don't talk enough about. It's not mutually exclusive with ethnic and racial diversity, but there have been enough privileged minority kids out there that schools like Harvard and Princeton can feel like they have a fairly diverse student body if all these kids are, like, children of doctors and lawyers and second-generation Harvard students.

In each committee I observed, at least one applicant was counted as a "diversity candidate" on the basis of class, socioeconomic status, or family financial hardship.

Diversity may be thoroughly institutionalized as a value, but some forms of diversity are easier to achieve than others, and this appears to have ramifications for how faculty frame their department's diversity efforts and goals. Faculty in the disciplines with the deepest racial inequities were also the ones to most vigorously defend the value of national origin and disciplinary concentration as meaningful types of diversity. In economics, several participants held up international students as evidence of achieving diversity, in spite of persistent gender and racial stratification.[28] A professor of economics who had been born outside of the United States described his department's international character in relation to racial and ethnic diversity:

> It is incredibly diverse. There are people from every continent . . . we have South American and Asian students, European students and Eastern European students, U.S. students and Canadian students. We get Mexican students every year. We're spanning the globe with our students. We're amazingly diverse in people's backgrounds. Everyone, of course, has had a lot of higher education. But people do have diverse backgrounds and perspectives. And in that sense, there is a lot of diversity. But in other dimensions of diversity, particularly the ones you would traditionally measure in U.S. institutions . . . like how many African Americans do we have? How many Hispanic Americans do we have? How many women do we have? The situation is dismal. They're a distressingly small number at every level.

Similarly, a philosopher defended his department's strong focus on international students for the diversity of viewpoint it introduces. He argued that "new kinds of diversity matter" in an increasingly global graduate education market, with its changing knowledge production system. In Chapter 6, I will discuss an exception to this general rule: Applicants from China occupy a tenuous position due to their strong representation in the pool and the influence of model minority stereotypes, which carry both positive and negative connotations.

Whether any personal quality that may introduce a unique perspective should be considered diversity, or whether diversity efforts should focus on interrupting historical patterns of inequality, are major questions in many academic departments today. The tendency of the last few decades to approach the problem of *inequity* using a strategy and rhetoric of *diversity* may actually help explain why progress has been slow. Research by Liliana Garces found that statewide affirmative action bans have significantly reduced graduate school enrollments among students of color in all fields studied except business, suggesting that, when permissible, race-conscious admissions make a difference, and that a general interest in "diversity" without explicit attention to race may be insufficient to realize equity aims.[29]

Evaluative scripts of diversity. In the presence of divergent ideas about how diversity should optimally be defined, faculty expressed clear patterns in what diversity means to them. Their answers fall into two themes: obligation and opportunity.

OBLIGATION. Many faculty whom I spoke with thought about attending to diversity as a professional obligation of admissions work. They felt a sense of duty, and in a few cases a personal commitment, to improving the representation of women and racial/ethnic minorities in their programs and disciplines. According to professors in both philosophy programs, the attention by disciplinary professional associations to gender inequality in their fields has heightened the sense of obligation to admit more women. And in another sign that insufficient diversity may compromise organizational legitimacy, an awareness among philosophers that other predominantly male fields have made better progress in attracting and retaining women has only sharpened their sense of responsibility. A male philosopher elaborated: "We were sort of going backwards while the fields that you think of as the most paradigmatically male fields were inching towards something."

However, obligations to diversity were conditional on another obligation they perceived: protecting well-established standards of conventional achievement. I started the data collection process expecting to observe some debate about when diversity should be factored into evaluations, and was surprised that it only came up in one of the ten programs. In the others it seemed to be taken for granted that diversity should be weighed only in the late stages of decision making. However, in the one philosophy program where this was not the assumed practice, the question generated the committee's first real disagreement. During a preliminary committee meeting held to set norms for application review, a senior scholar asserted, "We aren't supposed to consider diversity in the first round. We're supposed to select out the top students and seek in the second round to weight the students who meet diversity criteria." Two of the five committee members—one male, one female—questioned him on this. They argued that at least one member of the committee should be responsible for "reading for diversity" from the start, so as to ensure that someone would advocate for unconventional students with exceptional promise. Their minority position was eventually overruled on the basis of a belief that if diversity were defined broadly enough in the second reading, that they could achieve the diversity they sought without using multiple standards of evaluation in the first reading. They, like so many others, eventually decided to consider diversity only if academic achievements were roughly equal. A senior sociologist put it this way:

> That's one of the difficult issues, because I would say this: I try not to pay too much attention. I try to admit students that are the best in my intellect with no regard for gender or race. And so I understand, I perfectly understand, that because the world out there is not equal, this simply reproduces inequalities. I understand that. But at the same time—so I will say this—if there are

two students that are, in my view, equal on intellectual merit, *then* I will prefer a minority. And I think it is the same—at least from what I observed— it probably was the same for my other colleagues on the committee. It's something that everybody pays attention to—the minority race, gender—for good reason.

To "pay attention" to diversity in the committees I observed was not to seek it out in a consistent way from recruitment to admission, but to put it on the table among the many factors in play and perhaps use it to give select candidates a positive nudge. Reviewers felt they could uphold diversity as a legitimate consideration in the review process only by using it to compare applicants who had already surpassed an extremely high threshold of academic accomplishments.

OPPORTUNITY. Other evaluative scripts for diversity reflect a deeply pragmatic turn that centered on diversity's organizational benefits, including financial and intellectual opportunity and the opportunity to maintain a competitive advantage with other elite programs.

One reason reviewers felt obligated to consider diversity only after candidates had sufficient achievement on conventional metrics was because they believed other top programs in the discipline applied the same standard. Attracting accomplished, highly sought-after applicants from underrepresented groups may not be part of the algorithms used by *U.S. News and World Report* or the National Research Council, but it has become a way that programs informally evaluate themselves against one another. Composing student bodies that reflect both traditional notions of academic quality and demographic diversity was an informal aim of these highly ranked programs.

Like other top recruits, high-achieving students of color (and, in some fields, women) were viewed as organizational assets. When a philosophy professor learned that an Ivy League–educated applicant was also from an underrepresented minority group, for example, he commented offhand, "Sounds like he'll get in everywhere. Everyone will love him." Conversations about yield, in which committees worried together about where admitted students would choose to enroll, were especially useful in revealing this mindset about diversity. They shared their goals of enticing underrepresented students away from peer institutions. Asking one other, "Can we get her?" "Who are we going to get? It's a gamble," or "We'll lose him to Princeton and Caltech," they constructed students as human resources in the struggle for status among peer programs.

Inquiring into these comments in follow-up interviews, participants framed African American and Latino student underrepresentation using a

set of popular beliefs about the challenge of faculty diversity—that qualified scholars of color are a small pool and those individuals have many attractive offers. An economist, for example, discussed his program's struggle
to attract black students:

> Gender is an issue in that we get good—we get top-notch women as well top-
> notch men. Black—we get fewer blacks. It's true. But we do try—in the past
> we've tried to attract them. But then they get the same attractive offers from
> Columbia and Yale and Stanford and Berkeley and so forth. So it's a small group
> typically who get a lot of attention.

A sociologist of color expressed an almost identical perspective:

> We all kind of admit the same pool of applicants—the top ten departments.
> Harvard's going to admit them, Princeton's going to admit them, Stanford, Co-
> lumbia, Michigan, Wisconsin, and Chicago. And so we're all fighting for the
> same applicants, and there's a lot to compete with, and you know there are a
> couple programs right now that are just kind of doing phenomenally well in
> terms of placement and training—just dominating sociology.

In a study of faculty hiring, however, higher education scholar Daryl Smith
debunked the claim that enduring inequality is due more to minority
scholars' many professional options than to institutional decision making.
In a 1996 study of faculty diversity that focused on the trajectories of national fellowship winners, data from 298 in-depth interviews revealed that
only 11 percent had been through a hiring experience that was anything
akin to a bidding war, and that especially in the STEM fields, faculty of
color began to consider industry positions only after repeatedly feeling that
their credentials were not taken seriously by the institutions to which they
had applied.[30] Moreover, diversity within the faculty, even at top-ranked
programs, has failed to keep pace with the increasing numbers of underrepresented PhD recipients in several fields, which creates conditions for
isolation and other negative experiences that recent PhDs may be eager to
escape.[31] These studies suggest that the supply-and-demand and bidding-
war arguments used to explain lack of faculty diversity are "more rhetoric
than reality."[32]

At the program level, where gatekeeping decisions are made, the awareness that diversity represents an *intellectual opportunity* was one of the
three most common evaluative scripts for factoring it into evaluations of
those on the short list. Websites for all three universities' graduate schools
proclaimed the importance of diversity for promoting excellence and the
mission of graduate education. When I asked an associate professor of classics how her program conceptualizes diversity, she said:

We welcome it. We want it. It's so much. I think everybody is committed to it on principle, and we know from past experience how much it enhances our classrooms and our life in our department. And the university really supports it, I think . . . Students who come from other backgrounds will have other, will just focus on other, um, moments or ideas in the text. Also, students who have different backgrounds will have studied different things. There's a kind of desire, there's {Pause} more of a drive in some of the students who come from different backgrounds.

Consistent with a desire for fresh perspectives on the discipline, diversity considerations rarely stopped at whether a student identified with a specified racial, gender, or other social category. Instead, faculty sometimes comparatively evaluated applicants within these categories against one another, reading between the lines of the personal statement or letters of recommendation to gauge how students' identities would inform their perspectives as students, and how these perspectives affect their communities. Five of the six committees I observed discussed diversity in this way.

Discussing a female applicant, for example, an astrophysicist asked his colleagues around the table, "Is it enough to be a woman in science?" This group of five men proceeded to catalog the ways that women on their short list had used the personal statement to disclose gender-related experiences in science. They offered informal judgments of what they thought about these narratives, and speculated what it might be like to have these students in the program, noting one applicant's admission of self-doubt and another's desire to mentor young women because she had personally lacked role models. In reference to an applicant who disclosed experiences with "teasing and bigotry" from male teachers and peers, the graduate student member of the committee quipped, "I'm less persuaded by that story," and went on to defend the teacher and suggest she might have an "axe to grind" if she enrolled in their department. Ultimately, that interpretation was overruled when an associate professor of color noticed in her personal statement that she was now "taking action, organizing a lecture series" on women in science.

Their conversation demonstrates the tendency for the identities and experiences of "diversity candidates" to be scrutinized more critically than those of applicants from historically privileged backgrounds. Previous research on the hiring of academic administrators has come to similar conclusions. In "Held to a Higher Standard?," Roberto Haro found that 80 percent of subjects judging a Latino and 75 percent of those judging a white female for positions in higher education administration cited the doctoral institution as very important to their judgments, but only 55 percent of those evaluating a white male cited it as very important. Another study found that African American women applying for administrative positions in universities were subjected to additional "filters" (sets of criteria) that white men and women were not subjected to, including personal values, personality, and whether she would be likely to "rock the boat or embarrass the employing unit or university."[33] My own research here found that university websites and program publications communicated unequivocal support for diverse perspectives as a means of enriching the learning environment, but that at the level of file review, faculty inferred that some applicant perspectives would be more appealing than others.

Faculty in these programs also associated diversity with *financial opportunity* due to fellowships that all three universities made available to select students who contribute to the university's racial, gender, and socioeconomic diversity. These fellowships were especially powerful incentives for faculty when they enabled a program to admit more students than they expected. Some committees even adopted the university's conceptualization of diversity to ensure they would maximize the opportunity to add a few fellows to their programs. When I asked an associate professor of sociology how his program conceptualizes diversity, he admitted:

> I think roughly in whatever way the university will pay for. Our conceptualization is the university's conceptualization, and that's putting it a little harsh. But because the university's commitment is quite good and there are lots of incentives, we don't need to add any interests . . . So we'll just do whatever. We define diversity as the university defines it.

Depending on your perspective, his admission could be read as promising or concerning. On the one hand, it suggested that their program's commitment to diversity is simply a matter of following the money, implying that they had yet to adopt it as one of their own priorities. On the other hand, his comments—and my observations in other programs—imply that institutional financial incentives can change faculty behavior. Whether such incentives can help shift the composition and culture of the professoriate so that, in time, such incentives are no longer needed, is a question that remains open.

To summarize, when faculty evaluated students who made it to the short list, they invariably considered both qualitative and quantitative elements of the application, privileging students who seemed to have the research experience, disposition, and fresh perspective to become leaders and innovators in the field. At this stage, diversity informed broader ideas about merit and was justified through evaluative scripts about obligation and opportunity.

Diversity entered higher education discourse in the 1970s as an alternative basis for affirmative action programs.[34] Presidential executive orders during the previous decade had mandated affirmative action to remedy the effects of discrimination, but in *Regents of the University of California v. Bakke,* the Supreme Court challenged the constitutionality of the remedy rationale. They ruled that the educational benefits of diversity, broadly defined, are a compelling state interest that justifies the consideration of race in narrowly tailored admissions policies. Amicus curiae briefs informing that critical case in 1978 included one written by four of the Ivy League universities, which has special relevance for graduate education:

> A central function of the teacher is to sow the seeds for the next generation of intellectual leaders, and this, indeed, is a main reason why many university instructors find that an ethnically diverse student body helps them fulfill their teaching roles. In short, we hope that by these efforts, the leadership of the next generation—majority and minority members alike—will be the better, the wiser, and the more understanding.[35]

Debate continues today over gender- and race-conscious admissions, the appropriate basis for it, and the meanings of diversity. In 2015, eight states had passed bans on affirmative action, but the U.S. Supreme Court and the 5th Circuit Court of Appeals upheld the University of Texas's affirmative action policy and the educational benefits of diversity rationale.[36]

In this uneven policy environment, the multiple definitions and meanings that professors attach to diversity hardly come as a surprise. Their ideas about diversity were sometimes principled and sometimes pragmatic, and could be mobilized to serve a wide range of faculty interests. Yet even as diversity shaped conversations about individual, borderline cases, delaying its consideration until the review of the short list meant that criteria associated with conventional achievement carried the day in shaping access to these selective doctoral programs.

Disconfirming Evidence: Risk Aversion and Academic Preparation as Final Considerations

I close this chapter with an extended episode that illustrates how faculty negotiated ideals of merit and diversity in practice. It also is one in a handful of cases I observed in which questions of preparation and risk resurfaced in the late stages of decision making. Two such cases occurred in linguistics. Toward the end of their second meeting, Peter, the committee chair, raised the need to discuss two "diversity fellowship students" who had attended a local college from which the department was striving to develop a pipeline. He had previously described this recruitment effort to me in an interview:

> We decided to interpret diversity broadly, not just race and gender and all those things. We have very few students from local colleges so we contacted a local college and told them that if they have good undergraduates to apply here because there's this image that we are snobby so there is no point to apply here. So we had several applications from the local college and two made the short list.

And, indeed, last year they did admit one student from the college. This year, although a majority of the committee had voted them through to the short list in their first meeting, a majority also raised concerns over whether one student's research interests were clear and whether the other posed too much of an academic risk.

After reviewing some basic information about the first of these applicants, whom I'll name Amaya, the department chair, Nancy, commented, "If we're serious about diversity, these are the students we need to take seriously." Interrupting, Lin asked, "Can I please speak up? We want diversity, but we want excellence in diversity. And when I read that statement, it was all over the place." Another member affirmed this view, comparing her to others in the pool. "We need evidence of research skill, which we had with both of the last two applicants we discussed." A third added, "I tried to talk with her when she visited campus and couldn't get a line."

Just as it seemed energy was building against Amaya's case, Denise, an associate professor, raised the diversity-risk relationship. "In most cases, diversity will involve some degree of risk on our part. We have to not be so risk averse that we miss opportunities."

"That's true," added one of the people who had expressed concern just a moment earlier. Then, in the first and only mention of an applicant's race or ethnicity I heard in this program, she continued, "And students from her ethnicity are very unlikely to apply to graduate school." She did not formally advocate for the student on this basis, but rather reminded the group that the opportunity to enroll a student from this group—especially in linguistics—was rare.

They tabled the decision on Amaya, and moved to discuss the other student from the local college, Nikki. Peter began by reading an extended portion of a letter of recommendation, which closed with the words "I hope you get to meet her." He followed this reading with, "And we will. She's coming to campus this Friday for a visit." Like Amaya, it became clear as they dug into Nikki's application that no one felt strongly about moving her forward in the process.

Peter in particular sounded unsure about her, but Nancy highlighted the extreme personal struggles the student had faced, concluding, "She might be a bet, but it could be a good bet." She also reiterated an earlier point. "If we are going to increase diversity, these are the students we need to take seriously." This perspective reflected a view I heard frequently: that some bets are safer than others, and improving diversity requires decision makers to identify applicants who contribute to diversity and have acceptable risk profiles.

Tentatively, Lin asked, "What's the diversity?" Denise and Nancy, who by now were unified in advocating for Nikki, responded with "family financial hardship." The committee agreed at that point to leave her on the list, but discussion about her and about building diversity continued.

Nancy said, "It will be good for the whole faculty to take a look at her file. It seems pretty clear that she's a risk, but if we're going to increase diversity, we have to take risks." Concurring, Denise added, "And she seems like a good bet. Increasing diversity will also require these pipelines."

Two weeks later, after the next faculty meeting, both Nikki and Amaya visited campus for the recruitment weekend. However, in the final selection meeting following their visit, in which the goal was to cut four people, the committee decided not to admit either of them. In Peter's description, the committee came to this decision "in the first five minutes, with very little discussion." He elaborated:

> There was universal agreement . . . No one thought they were up to the bar. So that got us down to ten. We liked them both [but] we thought they didn't have the intellectual capacity to excel in graduate school.

I probed, "What was it during the campus visit that gave you the sense of that?" He responded,

> In the end they just didn't have the right preparation. They were just, there were others from universities with great, active linguistics departments where they probably had taken two years' worth of graduate courses already, things like that. The local students just didn't have that preparation. So they might have been perfectly capable, but in comparison . . . We felt horrible. We really wanted them, but it just wasn't going to happen . . . I'm still wondering what necessarily the right thing to do is. Both of them may have had the intellectual ability, but they didn't have as much background as the other students. So maybe if there were a way to guarantee them a sixth year of funding so that they can take an extra year to catch up, but that's not something we have.[37]

I followed up with another member of the committee as well, and his narrative corroborated Peter's:

> They were applicants that we were hoping to be able to take a chance on, that we invited to campus. Sadly, once they got here we decided it would not be a good gamble. Um, and in fact, I mean we really were disappointed because we did personally *like* the people involved and a lot about them but again you

have to think about what you're doing to their lives as well. *[Pause]* Some of the sort of last stage of discussion was, which of the people . . . are likely to be a good enough risk?

As Peter acknowledged and anyone who has participated in admissions knows, "the right thing to do" is never a straightforward determination in borderline decisions. Tough calls like these emerge only through a rough calculus involving risk assessment, principles, emotions, implicit biases, and experiences. They are, however, almost always made easier by consensus among decision makers, as uncomfortable as they may be with their conclusion.

Bringing a critical eye to this episode raises questions about the assumptions underlying the committee's decision. What *is* "the right preparation"? What would it have looked like for these two applicants to be "up to the bar"? Did those qualities exist in reviewers' minds before they encountered the applicant pool, or did they become salient only by comparing applicants with one another? When gatekeepers conflate something as difficult to judge as the "intellectual capacity to excel" with "the right preparation," what does it do for their reputation for "snobbishness"? A case like this demonstrates that how admissions decision makers conceptualize, assess, and act on "risk" can have significant implications for diversity. Risk aversion pervades assessments of which applicants are worthy of the investments of time, money, and energy that doctoral education requires.

Conclusion

A 6 on the GRE Writing section.
A grade of C– in Organic Chemistry II followed by a change in academic major.
President of the Black Student Union.

When reviewing admission applications, each of these lines is likely to elicit reactions and value judgments rooted in the meanings a person infers from them. Those meanings are fragile however, subject to change if one were to imagine it as a set of qualities from the same application. The perfect writing score might elicit a different reaction if exchanged for a quantitative score, and President of the Black Student Union may mean something different to a reviewer than President of Delta Delta Delta or Phi Beta Kappa. Admissions work involves countless little value judgments made through what behavioral economist Daniel Kahneman calls "fast thinking," the same mode of thought by which we automatically recognize and react to subtle facial cues or hit the brakes to avoid a collision.[38]

I found that in the moments that faculty individually and collectively judged applicant merit, that they instinctively drew upon evaluative scripts. They wove together available information with cultural meanings, rooted in shared values, to construct justifications for their applicant ratings and admission decisions. In response to seeing GRE scores, institutional affiliations, and students' social identities, for example, faculty employed scripts like risk, belonging, and opportunity to justify their evaluations. That scripts of merit play out so quickly in the mind, sometimes without deliberate thought, poses a challenge for decision making. Professors I spoke with recognized that the world is full of complexities that invalidate their instincts and commonly held assumptions. They would be the first to admit that the assumptions and stories embedded in prevailing scripts might be incomplete or even inaccurate, especially as they concern individual applicants; nevertheless, they leaned on those scripts because they help to get potentially divisive work done on the basis of shared cultural meanings and values that are incontrovertible to the community.

In the early rounds of application review, faculty often misconstrued merit and diversity as a trade-off due to the evaluative scripts they used and the timing at which they considered key criteria. The excellent applicant was one with a very high GRE score who had earned very high grades from a well-respected college or university. Such individuals were thought to have a low risk of failure and to "belong" in a department like theirs. Just as importantly, faculty thought of these criteria as convenient means for sifting through the pool. However, evidence of disparities in GRE scores and enrollment in highly ranked colleges, and of grade inflation in that sector, demonstrate that rigidly defining merit as "conventional achievement" when sifting the pool is likely to perpetuate enrollment inequities.[39]

The findings in this chapter have several implications for admissions decision makers that I will introduce here, in addition to discussing in greater detail in the Conclusion chapter. First, the interpretation and use of GRE scores by faculty decision makers requires attention. Female, black, Latino, Native American, and low-income students may have lower mean GRE scores,[40] but those scores are poor predictors of long-term outcomes, and research studies have been mixed about whether scores predict the success of different groups equally well.[41] Therefore, ETS advises that admission decision makers treat GRE scores not as a singular window into a student's future of success or struggle, but rather that they interpret scores (a) in the context of the student's profile of identities, native language, and previous educational opportunities, and (b) as one piece of information in a more holistic review.[42]

Professors would do well to assess for themselves—either individually or as committees—the engrained scripts about merit that shape their judgments, which are crucial to cultures of faculty gatekeeping. Take the risk aversion script, for example. For programs to be self-critical about their use of this script might mean taking stock of the skills required for doctoral students' introductory coursework. They could also gather data to examine which doctoral student characteristics are associated with success (as they choose to define it) in their program or discipline, so as not to operate on assumptions about risk that are invalid for their context.

Like merit, admissions decision makers will give careful thought to defining what they mean by diversity and equity, and recent scholarship suggests that academic organizations will benefit from a critical look at diversity, itself, as an aim. For no matter how "elaborate [the] organizational infrastructure for diversity," sociologist Ellen Berrey notes, it "beautifully symbolizes inclusion but only sometimes, and only partially, undoes racial hierarchies."[43] Higher education scholars Alicia Dowd and Estela Bensimon have also argued that colleges and universities need to enact equity as a goal distinct from diversity, and specifically, to build organizational capacity for talking about race. They note, "The majority of diversity initiatives are directed at improving human relations and tolerance rather than on achieving equity . . . which calls for directing more resources and support toward students who have greater needs due to social inequality."[44] I observed that many faculty felt a strong obligation to remediate underrepresentation of African Americans and Latinos in their disciplines and the professoriate, but that they also felt (a) a strong obligation to uphold the standard of conventional achievement, (b) unsure about what the current legal parameters were for considering or talking about race in admissions, and/or (c) discomfort raising race, because their colleagues would regard it as a controversial issue. In short, my findings corroborate Dowd and Bensimon's conclusion about the need to build organizational capacity in this area.

Committees wanted to construct "balanced" cohorts and entice well-pedigreed students of color, and they believed that this combination is now a status signal among top-ranked programs.[45] Yet several behaviors suggested that racial equity and diversity were not integral to their vision of excellence, but at best, secondary to and separate from it. Under the current review process, many students whose diversity contributions might have been considered assets in later rounds of review had already been filtered from the pool. An important conclusion of this chapter is that *when* a committee factors diversity into recruitment and admissions may matter much for the outcomes they achieve.[46]

In these core disciplines of the academy, and in both phases of review, faculty acknowledged that doctoral students are critical members of their intellectual communities—not only because of what they would accomplish as individuals, but because their presence, perspectives, and effort would affect faculty productivity and the program's stature. Selecting students was therefore not only about *predicting* who would be successful in the future. It was about *creating* their programs' futures by selecting new members who would uphold the core, identity, and status of the group. Sociologists call this organizational boundary work, and as subsequent chapters will examine in greater depth, faculty in these programs did not privilege applicants who would push their elite communities in bold new directions. Instead, they favored students who would "fit" and add a bit of fresh perspective.

An unspoken program identity—that of elite academic community— clearly shaped admission preferences in these ten programs as well, but what makes the politics of quality in graduate admissions so intriguing is that faculty negotiated much more than their program's priorities in choosing among students. As I'll discuss next, they also negotiated disciplinary norms (Chapter 3), their own personal identities (Chapter 4), and ideas about intelligence (Chapter 5), as well as unexamined assumptions about the differences between American and international applicants (Chapter 6).

CHAPTER THREE

Disciplinary Logics

To be a Shakespearean scholar, to absorb oneself in black holes, or to attempt to measure the effect of schooling on academic achievement—is not just to take up a technical task, but to place oneself inside a cultural frame that defines and even determines a very great part of one's life.

—CLIFFORD GEERTZ

D OCTORAL PROGRAMS have long been regarded as "the academy's own means of reproduction."[1] They sustain academic departments and disciplines by developing subject matter expertise, awarding credentials, and socializing rising scholars to norms, identities, and affective dispositions such as a sense of "stewardship" for one's discipline.[2] And although the career paths of PhDs now vary widely, departments like the ones in this study saw themselves as leading producers of knowledge for their respective academic disciplines. For them, doctoral admissions was about identifying rising stars, and doctoral education was about preparing a corps of disciplinary experts. Through the characteristics of those whom they admitted, faculty brought to life imagined academic communities.

As Clifford Geertz noted, to do the work of one's discipline is more than a "technical task." The disciplines play an integral role in all of faculty life and, as I will argue in this chapter, were a critical source of faculty tastes. Cultural sociologists have portrayed academic disciplines as social worlds unto themselves,[3] and education scholars have examined disciplinary variation in such aspects of doctoral education as mentoring, persistence to degree, and research socialization.

In my case, I expected that faculty in different fields might use or weight admissions criteria differently. I was also curious to learn whether committees in fields with relatively unified intellectual paradigms would come to consensus about criteria, ratings, and decisions more easily than committees in fields known for using a greater breadth of theories and methodologies. Within the social sciences, for example, economics has a reputation for being more paradigmatic than political science. In the humanities, philosophy has a more centralized intellectual tradition than linguistics,[4] a once centralized field into which other disciplinary perspectives and quantitative research have made significant inroads in recent decades. To ensure that my sample offered a broad view of core disciplines, I selected three disciplines each within the humanities, social sciences, and natural sciences. Then, to compare whether disagreements on admissions committees varied by the extent of disciplinary consensus, I chose fields within each broad subject area that have more and less consensus about preferred theories and methods for advancing knowledge.[5]

The Latin for discipline, *disciplinare,* means to train or to teach. And, indeed, the patterns of evaluation in programs from centralized, hierarchical fields like economics, philosophy, and physics exemplified how disciplinary socialization can train faculty judgment into specific forms. In these high-consensus fields, admissions preferences and practices exhibited clear trends. I also observed that, in such fields, the raw material of disciplines— the prevailing theories, methods, epistemologies, and practical priorities— produced shared logics by which committee members could legitimize preferences and decisions to one another that outsiders might find debatable. A key finding of this study is that, like deliberative bureaucracy, strong disciplinary logics facilitate decision making while discouraging the selection of students with unconventional profiles. Disciplinary logics bring shared priorities into focus, but those shared priorities tend to privilege applicants who "fit" the disciplinary culture as currently constituted.

In fields with weaker intellectual consensus, such as political science and linguistics, disciplines also trained individual judgment, but underlying debates in the field manifested in committee deliberation. One participant called these incidents "worldview moments." In these moments, the absence of a common disciplinary logic that might have helped facilitate consensus became clear to the committee. Admissions in fields like political science and linguistics therefore involved more disagreement—about applicants, ratings, and what the appropriate process for making decisions should be. With less underlying common ground to stand upon, the process resembled interdisciplinary review and involved some unique features such as deference to seniority and the use of serial impressions to describe candidates.

To illustrate these trends, in this chapter I explore in depth two high-consensus disciplines, economics and philosophy, and then present an extended episode from deliberations in political science, a low-consensus discipline. Through these portraits, we see how admissions evaluations become patterned by disciplinary content and consensus. In Chapter 4 I highlight an additional feature of review in low-consensus disciplines: preferences among individual reviewers for applicants like themselves.

Economics

Stavros Ioannides and Klaus Nielsen argued that economics is "now widely seen as the most advanced of the social sciences with its mathematical formalization, public prestige, and Nobel Prize awards."[6] Justin Wolfers, himself an economist, recently dubbed it "the queen." Across macro and micro levels of analysis, economics possesses a cultural coherence around numerical evidence and algorithmic thinking that is stronger than any other social science discipline. In both the theoretical (mathematical modeling) and empirical (statistical analysis) approaches to economics research, scholars rely as much upon numbers as words to communicate their findings to one another. One priority in economic scholarship, which is reflected in their emphasis on mathematical reasoning, is precision. Economists have made inroads into other disciplines by spotting topically related research whose methodological or theoretical precision could be improved with economic ideas, reasoning, or analytic approaches. Some argue that their doing so has simultaneously weakened the intellectual consensus in target fields and broadened the intellectual jurisdiction of neoclassical and Keynesian economics. However, a sharp rise since the early 1990s in "heterodox economics," such as behavioral economics, and in membership in groups like the International Confederation for Associations for Pluralism in Economics suggests that the field's orthodoxy may be weakening and/or that other disciplines shape economics, just as economics is shaping them.[7]

The viewpoints of economics faculty whom I interviewed epitomized how common theories, methods, and practical priorities could combine to create a common logic by which professors could legitimize admissions evaluations and practices that others might question. Decision-making tactics and priorities reflected foundations in theories of rational choice and human capital, methods that are mainly quantitative, and a shared priority of maintaining prestige in the social sciences. Like other disciplines, how economists represented their values in admissions revealed preferences that were thought of as self-evidently preferable rather than the result of common socialization and professional practice.

Relative risk aversion. In a discipline that prizes its status in the social sciences and a department that prizes its standing in the discipline, the economics program I studied designed its selection process, curriculum, and funding model to minimize threats to their status. This orientation comports with one of the most treasured principles of neoclassical economic theory: relative risk aversion. Their pool was extremely large (about 800) and academically qualified, so members of this committee routinely denied admission to anyone whose long-term success they doubted, perceiving such failure as a financial or reputational risk to the program. As one committee member explained, "Because we run the program to be highly ranked . . . basically we have a good chance of getting people if we accept them. We have the luxury of getting to look at the pool and say, 'Let's just take the people we think have the best prospects as an economist.'" Another faculty member said,

> The people that the top programs admit—we admit basically the same people . . . [Programs in the next tier] don't want to admit the same people that we admit because they're going to lose them . . . I think we have the privilege of taking less risk than other universities of lower ranking.

He went on to acknowledge that his program's prestige-focused, risk-averse orientation had consequences for judgments of applicants with traditional versus nontraditional trajectories:

> If we have a letter from someone who had a difficult background, then I think that would count a little. I wouldn't say that that would be the reason why you get admitted. Based on the experiences we had in the past, these things are even less important now than it used to be, when some deviation from the rule that "We only admit the best" was made and it didn't work out well. So based on that experience, I think the committee will be more cautious.

Successful organizations generally tend toward risk aversion when facing the prospect of loss,[8] but in this program the intersection of prestige as a practical priority with risk aversion as a widely shared tenet of economic theory justified relative risk aversion as a modus operandi of decision making. The other programs in the sample, which were also highly ranked for their fields, also revealed risk-averse approaches to admissions, but none so overtly as in economics.

A foundation of quantification. Perceptions of "the best prospects as an economist" cannot be understood apart from the quantitative foundation of the field, for as one participant put it, "Mathematics is the language in which to explain your argument or your story." On my asking what intelligence in economics looks like, an associate professor responded, "Many people who become successful . . . first of all, they all have some basic level of mathematical sophistication." Interestingly, economists not only looked for quantitative expertise; they relied primarily on quantitative measures to gauge it.

The trend toward quantification seems only to be strengthening with methodological developments in economics. As one associate professor explained, "At some point in the middle of the last century, the nature of discourse among economics became based around models and using mathematics for precision and to precisely state hypotheses." What counts as high-quality economic research must be cutting-edge, he continued, which demands cutting-edge statistics. A junior faculty member also volunteered this position, "Over the decades the field ages, and there's more and more work you have to know in getting to the frontier. The frontier is more technical and deeper." As the statistics have advanced, so have mathematical prerequisites for admissions. Today that preparation consists of "ideally a double major in math and econ," as one professor summarized.

Thus, this economics program was not unlike the top 25 in the field for requiring a perfect or near-perfect quantitative GRE score and for giving careful attention to the score's percentile, due to the concentration of scores on the right tail of the distribution.[9] They interpreted the score as signal of competence with skills, and competence as a signal of how the student would fare in coursework. A junior professor, new to admissions, laid it out for me:

> They do look at whether the student is going to struggle. Technical expertise is a fact. The trouble is, if a student doesn't have enough mathematics, they don't see the economics the first year. They just see it as mathematics, and it's a real problem. What you want is somebody who has enough to distinguish the math from the economics. I do believe the admission committee does try to determine whether a student is going to struggle and is prepared. A master's program is not necessary but it helps.

Economists' priorities of near-perfect GRE scores and advanced academic preparation in mathematics manifested foundations of their field in rational choice and quantitative evidence. These criteria also supported the discipline's interest in maintaining its prestige in the social sciences. Together, these practical, theoretical, and methodological priorities guided admissions practice and converged in a logic to which they collectively deferred in justifying their judgments—to me, to one another, and to themselves.

Philosophy

In contrast to economics, "good philosophy," according to an associate professor of philosophy, consists of "charitable conversation with controversy."

The heart of philosophical scholarship is analytically dissecting ideas about fundamental questions, and reconstructing them in strong arguments. Having survived thousands of years, philosophy is among the oldest of disciplines. Over its history, the topics philosophers have taken up reflect the diversity of interests of their societies and cultures. Today, there are six primary strands of work within the field: ethics, epistemology, metaphysics, philosophy of language and mind, philosophy of science, and aesthetics. Yet across time, culture, and content, the core of the field has been defined and preserved as an ongoing conversation about the nature of knowledge and reality.[10]

Biglan's original disciplinary classification system named philosophy as a soft discipline relative to all other fields,[11] but it is among the most paradigmatic in the humanities. The most well-known series of teachers and students in early Western philosophy—Socrates, Plato, and Aristotle—initiated modes of discourse that continue to guide Western philosophers' communication with one another, and most aspects of disciplinary socialization in philosophy departments in American universities reflect these scholars' influence. The Socratic method, in which hypotheses are eliminated discursively by identifying ideas that produce contradictions, remains central to philosophical discourse. Aristotelian logic and its syllogisms are another enduring branch and method, and training in the use of syllogisms to argue one's point is fundamental to the preparation of philosophers.[12] It may not come as a surprise that philosophers' top priority in evaluating applicant files was the writing sample or that they engaged in more prolonged and intense deliberations than did the committees I observed in other disciplines. Those deliberations covered their evaluations of applicants, the rationales for those evaluations, as well as self-critical analysis of their own ability to judge and select students fairly.

Interpreting the writing sample. Philosophers felt that the writing sample evinced the substance, skill, and style of what an individual would bring to the conversation of philosophy. They revealed the crucial role of the writing sample in several ways. In our interviews, all members of the philosophy committees I observed at both institutions volunteered to me that it was "very important" or "the most important" component of the application. In meetings, they referred to applicants not by name, but by the topic they had chosen to explore in the writing sample. Philosophers also devoted more time to discussing writing samples than any other component of the application, and it became quickly clear to me that applicants needed to receive a positive assessment of the writing sample to have a chance at an admission offer. A senior professor explained his approach to evaluating the writing sample:

> When you have eighty of these things to read and you come in in the evening, you want to get home and watch TV and go to bed. So, you're looking for a reason to stop reading. And so I tell [students] what they have to do in their writing sample especially—they have to try to counteract that tendency. They have to give me something to make me keep reading.

What holds a philosopher's interest may vary, of course, and participants from both philosophy programs were conscious of stylistic differences among traditions that shaped their interpretations of writing samples. An associate professor regarded one student's writing as "murky" and "complexified," only to learn from a senior committee member that these qualities "come with the territory" in the latest expressivist writing. Admitting her distaste, because it was not like "her own sort of philosophy," she deferred to the judgment and expertise of another committee member. To guard against uncharitable assessments of writing samples based on style, one committee structured the review process to ensure that each applicant's writing sample was read by individuals with expertise in that subject area, bringing in readers from outside the committee as needed.

Sensitivity to subjectivity. Philosophers revealed in other ways their culture of self-scrutiny and their emphasis on interpretation as a way of knowing. They exhibited high levels of introspection about the evaluative process, for one, and displayed sensitivity to the implications of a process laden with subjectivity. They tested the defensibility of their judgments, challenging each other when the grounds for an outlying rating seemed weak. Yet they almost always crafted these challenges in an exceedingly respectful manner— as a matter of inquiry, not attack. An associate professor explained the difference between persuasion born of rhetoric and the philosophical argumentation they practiced as a committee:

> Rhetoric is not a craft. It's an empirical knack that enables you to please people. But philosophy is [a craft], right? And I think Plato is right. There is such a thing as learning to give good arguments for what you think. And it's different from the skill—such as it is—of just persuading people.

As in their scholarship, philosophy committees approached admissions as "charitable conversation with controversy." They were the only committees to grapple with certain aspects of subjectivity that nearly all other programs also experienced but seemed to take for granted: the role of emotional responses and quantification of their judgment.

Enthusiasm and other emotions. Enthusiasm for applicants affected individual ratings and committee deliberations across the disciplines, but philosophers were the only ones to explicitly acknowledge it. Even one committee member's enthusiasm could determine an applicant's chances by shaping whether she advocated for the applicant, and this trend became especially apparent in discussions of borderline applicants. When I asked one philosophy professor what helped the committee decide among relatively qualified applicants, he admitted:

> Well it's very hard. Let me try to answer your question in a way that may make the whole process seem a little less credible—but that's the way it is. What happens is that one or more members of an admissions committee will catch some enthusiasm for some applicants but not others. If you go back over, if you are forced—practically, they'd have to grab you by the scruff of the neck and force you to look again at a recommendation that you have consigned to oblivion. There probably are some of them where if you were to say, "Why weren't you enthusiastic about the person?," I'm not sure I could answer. And I'm sure every year there are . . . people who could easily have been among the top ones but nobody picked up on them. They just didn't light a fire under anyone.

Certainly, graduate admissions is not the only type of elite selection in which decisions can come down to feelings and gut responses. In an observational analysis of hiring for investment firms, sociologist Lauren Rivera used Randall Collins's theory of emotional energy to explain how "evaluators used their own emotional responses to candidates as both metrics of merit and mechanisms of candidate selection." So influential is emotional "buzz" generated on behalf of a candidate that it can trump traditional metrics such as achievement, performance, or ability.

Resigned to quantification. Although every program in this study played "the numbers game"—collecting ratings of applicants and aggregating them to simplify selection—the two in philosophy were the only ones to debate whether it was justified and how it should be executed. Unlike most other committees, for example, they were explicit about what their rating scales meant. One committee used the following scale: 1 = admit; 2 = maybe; 3 = wait list; and 4 = a bit of a risk. The other committee used a five-point scale, and distinguished 1's from 2's by the enthusiasm of their own responses.[13] As in other fields, philosophers relied upon quantification to transform an applicant pool that was diverse along countless dimensions into a single distribution of admissibility, yet they were deeply uncomfortable with the false precision these ranked lists implied.

Philosophers actively discussed subtleties of evaluation that remained unspoken in most other disciplines, such as the link between enthusiasm and evaluations and the imperfections of numerical metrics of applicant excellence. Whereas economists' comfort with quantitative metrics allowed them to perceive applicant quality in black and white, it seemed fitting that during one philosophy committee meeting, every member of the group wore gray.

Comparing the Cases

Pairing economics and philosophy clarifies how the prevalence of positivist or interpretive epistemology within a discipline is not isolated to scholarly research, but can affect how professors carry out administrative, evaluative work. Philosophers vary in their analytic foci, arguments, and conclusions, but are distinguished as a group by their method. Similarly, economists share a strong belief in the value of quantitative analysis and are committed to making social science as scientific as possible. Though of course there is some epistemological diversity within both fields, the predominant orientations were clearly recognizable in their approaches to admissions. This conclusion fits well with the findings of previous social research on the power of epistemology in shaping disciplinary cultures.[14]

In addition to epistemology, however, other disciplinary cultural qualities were evident in the patterns of faculty evaluation I observed, including common theories, vocabularies of practice, and practical priorities.[15] Table 4 points out these qualities in economics and philosophy, as well as in physics—the other high-consensus discipline I studied. Given the important role that admissions and other forms of faculty gatekeeping play in determining the next generation of the academy, I contend that we should not interpret evidence of the disciplines in admissions work as a spillover effect from the intellectual domain to the administrative, but rather as support for the view that, for professors, administrative and evaluative work is inherently intellectual. This view is consistent with the perspective on disciplinary cultures expressed in the quotation by Geertz at the start of this chapter—that disciplines establish "cultural frame[s]" that shape all sorts of activity in the lives of scholars.

Particularly in more paradigmatic fields, to work from the vantage point of a particular discipline leads one to see the world in a particular way. Committees representing disciplines with stronger intellectual consensus— such as economics, physics, and philosophy—understandably displayed more agreement about what counts as a legitimate admissions preference and less disagreement in their judgments of individual applicants. In the social sciences, economists tended to draw upon a shared logic more than

Table 4 Indicators of Disciplinary Logics in High-Consensus Fields

Discipline	Theory		Epistemology & Methodology		Practical Priorities	
	Indicator of Disciplinary Logic	Related Preferences	Indicator of Disciplinary Logic	Related Preferences	Indicator of Disciplinary Logic	Related Preferences
Economics	Rational choice & human capital theories	Risk aversion; applicants with strongest GRE & academic preparation	Positivism; deep methodological frontier	"Mathematical sophistication"; applicants with math degrees & near-perfect Quantitative GRE scores	Concern for prestige in social sciences	Use of admissions criteria with widespread legitimacy (e.g., college prestige & high GRE scores)
Philosophy	Valuing prudence	Risk aversion; deliberation about as many applicants as possible	Interpretivism	Emphasis on letters, personal statement & writing sample	Desire for "distinguished" philosophers	Applicants with pre-professional writing samples & pedigrees from elite institutions
Physics	Goal of discovery	Efforts to identify "spark" and "diamonds in the rough"; interviews that go beyond credentials	Highly technical work	Applicants with significant, relevant research experience	International collaborations in English	International applicants with strong English skills

political scientists, and in the humanities, a common disciplinary logic was more apparent in philosophy than in linguistics.

Yet some disciplinary qualities are admittedly difficult to disentangle from scholars' individual identities and program prestige. There was, for example, the way in which status concerns were engrained in the economics department, and the seriousness and pride with which philosophers discussed the distinctiveness of their own training and work. It is no coincidence that economists admitted they must resist the temptation to be "dazzled" by applicants with elite pedigrees, or that philosophers frequently used the word "prudent" to describe their ideal standard of judgment and "distinguished" to describe their ideal applicants. Such default tendencies reflected underlying disciplinary values, which may not be fully independent from personal or program values. Regardless of their origin, revealed preferences were for both specific qualities of desirable applicants and specific practices for identifying those applicants.

Struggling for Consensus

In contrast to the high-consensus disciplines, which were natural sites to observe faculty using a common disciplinary logic to build consensus, lower-consensus disciplines were ideal for seeing how divergent disciplinary logics could lead faculty to very different interpretations about the same applicant's admissibility or criterion's appropriateness. In previous research on academic disciplines, some scholars have found that disciplines with competing schools of thought struggle to achieve collective intellectual progress. For example, scholars in lower-consensus disciplines have a harder time building upon each other's findings, are more likely to have turnover among department chairs, and are less likely to obtain significant research grants.[16] In this study, committees in lower-consensus fields revealed how individual tastes can shape collective decisions, and were key sites to observe three other mechanisms of evaluation: serial impressions, worldview moments, and homophily. I'll examine the first two ideas in the remainder of this chapter before devoting Chapter 4 to the third.[17]

Serial impressions. In fields with weaker disciplinary logics, faculty explained their ratings of applicants to other committee members using what I call serial impressions. Drawing on a seemingly bottomless arsenal of adjectives, some faculty sketched their judgments and rationales using long lists of casual judgments that provided a glimpse into the personality of the reviewer as much as the qualities of the applicant. It might sound mundane, even self-evident, that faculty would use adjectives to describe applicants. But the adjectives faculty chose were revealing: scholars used clusters of words that reflected their particular tastes and temperaments. Furthermore, though they stated their impressions as individual responses to individual applicants, these impressions were often given as much weight in deliberations as universal criteria such as grade point average, work experience, or positive references.

In political science, for example, the committee maintained an online, password-protected spreadsheet for tracking their responses and ratings for each applicant. There was a row for each applicant with corresponding columns that indicated one's subfield, scores, and comments from each reader, readers' average ratings and standard deviations, and the final decisions on each person. Throughout the file review period, this spreadsheet was available online for committee members to enter their ratings and comments. Then, at the meeting, they projected it on a screen for common reference, and I was struck to see the comment fields. The notes from two readers about two of the applicants contained: "mature, sophisticated, honest, stunning, stellar," and "worry about fit, lukewarm, passionate, committed, thoughtful, moving, and able." A few rows down, notes about an applicant who was ultimately admitted included, "Killer backstory" and "quirky, which I like."

In his introductory comments to the group, the political science committee's chair noted that one function of their discussion would be to "help calibrate one another's comments." This calibration proved critical as it became clear that some committee members were more effusive than others in their written praise, and harsher in their judgments, and that at least one did not provide any notes at all. Moreover, some committee members were more likely than others to accept their colleagues' serial impressions—devoid as they were of reference to the evidence that prompted them—as valid or trustworthy depictions of the applicants.

In other low-consensus disciplines, a similar use of serial impressions took place through discussion, though not always with a shared record of everyone's notes. In classics and linguistics, most discussions of applicants took a predictable structure. Faculty would open the discussion of a new individual with one or two expressing their overall impressions (such as "He wasn't the most exciting"). The impressions would be followed by an attempt to jog others' memory about who the person was through an institutional affiliation or research interest, and another round of adjectives to summarize the profile ("naive," "creepy suck-up," "amazing," and so on). Then they would then move into a discussion of the writing sample, letters of recommendation, and/or personal statements, which were summarized by invoking several more vague judgments (such as "not entirely lucid," "brilliant," "misguided," "pretentious"). Discussion would continue, often comparing the applicant to others in the pool, until at some point the admissions chair would gauge the energy and emotion around the table to discern what action to take ("There doesn't seem to be much enthusiasm around the table"; "So we're not very enthusiastic"; "Let's wait and see if anyone more interesting comes along"). By reiterating individuals' impressions of the applicant and the file details that inspired those impressions, committee members resolved their differences of opinion and developed working conclusions that guided their decisions. Building and attempting to justify their serial impressions was a process for translating individual judgment into collective consensus.

Worldview moments. In programs representing lower-consensus disciplines, intellectual differences did not prevent committee members from getting along well on a day-to-day basis or even from becoming friends. A quantitative linguist brought coffee for a qualitative colleague on the committee for their three-hour admissions meeting. An experimental astrophysicist and a theoretical astrophysicist spent time together on the weekends with their families. Within departments, what separated scholars from different intellectual traditions was not so much a "gulf of mutual incomprehension"[18] as a difference in intellectual worldviews, despite residence in the same organizational space.[19] Yet, because disciplinary and evaluative cultures are not independent from one another,[20] collective evaluation, especially defending one's ratings and advocating for particular individuals, may prime scholars in low-consensus disciplines to recognize and engage worldview differences that most of the time remain comfortably latent.

I observed that weaker underlying intellectual consensus manifested in what a political science participant astutely called "worldview moments," when scholars realized that the differences in how they evaluated an applicant stemmed from different assumptions about intellectual, theoretical, and metaphysical matters. They recognized that the absence of consensus delayed their progress on decisions. They also understood that agreeing to disagree would not move them closer to a resolution. In these cases, the basis for deliberations often shifted to power relations within the committee and program. For example, if a reviewer's advocacy was grounded in disciplinary assumptions that were different from those held by senior members of the committee or by the committee's majority, it was unlikely that the advocacy would bear fruit. Worldview moments provoked some of the strongest disagreements I observed and, in some cases, led committees to settle for decision by majority vote in lieu of consensus. I offer an extended illustration of one such episode in political science.

Worldview Moments in Political Science

Political science can be considered a low-consensus field, with subfield concentrations that range from political philosophy to mathematical modeling. The program I studied, however, has been known for its strength in statistics, with one participant remarking to me with pride, "We are a hard-line quantitative program." Indeed, all doctoral students except those admitted to study political theory were strongly encouraged to take a se-quenced curriculum of statistics courses in their first year, and admissions committees typically looked to quantitative GRE scores to predict students' likelihood of success in that statistics sequence.

On that year's committee of eight, a full professor whom I'll call David explained how scores were typically interpreted. "Lots of eyebrows are raised if both [sections' scores] are around the 50th percentile. But if you're above 60 and one [section's score] is high, I think you're totally solid and no one is going to bat an eye." However, if it had been up to that year's admissions chair, Thomas, the department would not even collect appli-cants' GRE scores. A political theorist, Thomas took seriously the messages conveyed in the university's workshop for faculty involved with graduate admissions about downplaying the GRE and utilizing holistic, individual-ized evaluation.

The committee's disagreement about how GRE scores should be inter-preted and weighed in the context of real applicants revealed the difficulty that competing disciplinary norms can pose for collective evaluation. In the group's initial meeting, Thomas presented his plan for the admissions pro-cess and suggested how committee members might weigh various criteria. He discouraged them from using the GRE, noting findings from "a study at Yale University" that the only thing they could predict was first-year grades. He also remarked that the graduate college was collecting the scores only because some programs still wanted to use them.

At this comment, Roger, a full professor on the committee who conducted quantitative research, interrupted. "I want to respectfully disagree. Evidence from the research on the GRE can't give advice to committees like ours be-cause those studies use censored samples consisting only of those students who were admitted." It was the first time someone other than the chair had spoken since the official beginning of the meeting. David, who was also a statistician, affirmed this interpretation of the research, adding, "I myself am going to use the GREs."

An uncomfortable silence followed, with tension hanging in the air. Linda, an associate professor, inquired, "What about people who are in, say, the 40th percentile?" Thomas noted that traditionally there "had been sort of an informal 50th percentile threshold," but an assistant professor, Emily, chimed in that she agreed with the two senior statisticians. Recognizing her expertise, Thomas affirmed, "And you're the methodologist here. However, I do strongly discourage you from using it as the first or only threshold, as some sort of a litmus test." After another period of silence, he moved on to another topic, the question unresolved.

This discussion exemplified how a worldview moment could induce a more overtly political mode of decision making than was the norm. When Roger, a senior scholar with authority in the methodological approach favored by the majority of the department, interpreted research about the GRE in a way that (1) called into question the *findings'* reliability and validity for their committee and (2) appeared to reinforce the reliability and validity of a *criterion* in which several already believed, it empowered other quantitatively minded people to speak up too. Interestingly, the committee discussed few details of the research in question (a study from 1997 by Robert Sternberg and Wendy Williams) and did not note that its authors anticipated the very critique Roger raised—that the censored range of observed GRE scores would attenuate the odds of finding significant relationships.[21]

In a follow-up interview, one of the two senior members of the committee described his impressions of Thomas and this debate over how research should inform their work:

> He's a brilliant guy. Also, his heart is in the right place, so when he hears evidence from Yale, he believes it. This is just what he's waiting to hear, and so he believes it and he doesn't approach it in a critical way. Roger, on the other hand, has done this stuff. This is his bread and butter. He knows instantly that this is a flawed study. Why did it even get published? Is it just because a lot of people want to believe it?

His comments suggested skepticism not only about the research study discussed in the meeting, but also about the motives of those who marshal its findings to downplay the importance of GRE scores. For his part, Thomas recognized that others' decades of experience with quantitative research surely informed how they approached admissions and GRE scores. He acknowledged to me privately that they had "a perfectly reasonable argument" about the Sternberg and Williams study, but that more discussion should have taken place about the study's nuances than had actually occurred. Finally, Thomas felt that this was a moment in which worldview and power dynamics in the group both became salient as some committee members started taking their cues from Roger and David. Despite his position as chair, Thomas was the only faculty member on the committee firmly committed to deemphasizing GRE scores, and he felt that his minority viewpoint had been essentially overruled. He was not the only person to see it this way. In the course of reviewing this exchange with other members of the committee, I learned that they too thought this was a situation in which a minority viewpoint had been overruled through a combination of seniority and methodological majoritarianism.

The limits of agreeing to disagree. The issue of GRE score interpretation did not resurface for the political science committee until the end of a very long meeting in which their task was to create the final lists of admitted and wait-listed applicants. Committee members frequently cited GRE scores in their rationales for high and low ratings, to little challenge. None of the outcomes seemed to rest directly on the strength of a student's scores, so it seemed they could agree to disagree about how those scores should be used. None, that is, until they reached the very last candidate to be discussed.

Like the other two universities in which my case study departments were located, this university set an early deadline for nominating admitted students for diversity fellowships. With an eye on the urgency of this upcoming deadline, the committee wanted to make a decision on Christian, an applicant with an unconventional academic profile. They did not explicitly discuss what made him suitable for the fellowship, except to acknowledge that he attended a local college that rarely enrolls students in their program. Christian had the earnest endorsement of two noncommittee faculty in the department who had met with him; however, his quantitative GRE scores were under the 20th percentile. "How to think about his scores" was, as Thomas later reflected, "the closest we came to conflict" in the course of working together.

Their worldview differences and views on the GRE's appropriate use unresolved, the committee struggled for more than 20 minutes with whether or not to admit Christian. Emily was participating in the meeting via video conference and initiated the conversation, arguing with some passion that there was no basis for admitting a student with such low GRE scores. She reminded the group that all students except those in the theory concentration would be essentially required to take a statistics sequence, and that the student's expressed research interests did not clearly situate him as a theorist. "When I see him in the intro stats class," she worried, "I see him failing."

Picking up on this implicit risk-aversion narrative, Thomas countered, "All students are gambles in lots of ways. The point is to get local knowledge. Yes, he is problematic on conventional measures, but those are unreliable in this circumstance."

David proposed as a compromise that "putting him on the wait list would be a gesture." Linda interrupted him, but David piped up, "Let me finish. Some indicators are unreliable, but less than 20th percentile is scary. Less than the 20th percentile is not good."

After a long silence, Thomas offered, "I would read it slightly differently. He is less prepared than the rest of the cohort, which is his biggest risk." He also mentioned Claude Steele's research on stereotype threat, which found through experimental research that subconscious anxieties about the possibility of conforming to negative group stereotypes can depress the performance of women and students of color on standardized tests.[22] Thomas noted that mentoring would be very important if they chose to admit Christian. At this, David also registered his concern about the student's prospects in the statistics sequence, to which Thomas emphatically responded, "But remember he doesn't *need* to do the quant sequence if he goes the theory route." Still, Thomas conceded that the student's scores suggested underpreparation and that he didn't like the idea of "throwing him into a deep pond" with students whose average preparation seemed to be much greater. One of the three graduate students on the committee then spoke up, affirming the possibility that mentoring could help address the applicant's level of preparation, but also questioning whether there was an individual who might clearly serve as his mentor. Thomas noted that a faculty member with interests similar to Christian's had already volunteered to serve in this capacity, which produced another long silence. The ball was in their court.

Understandably, the committee was tired and a little edgy at this point. They had been working intently together for almost three hours after the end of the workday. The sun had gone down, and the only light in the room for nearly an hour had been the unnatural glare produced by their laptop screens and the image of their applicant rating spreadsheet projected on a whiteboard. Empty pizza boxes, paper plates, and red Solo cups littered their large table. Perhaps fitting for these political scientists, the space had come to feel more like a war room than a conference room. Clearly it was time to start wrapping up the meeting.

It was several seconds more before anyone spoke. "So, what do we think?" asked Emily, who had started the conversation. Thomas proposed a vote by roll call and, to the group's surprise, the seven persons present admitted Christian by a margin of one vote. Further emblematic of the group's ambivalence, the meeting ended with one individual muttering, "I'm really worried about what happens if he sinks."

The conversation had been laced with several disagreements: about whether to admit the student, of course, but also what the appropriate grounds for admitting a student with low GRE scores would or should be, and about what it would mean for a student to "sink." There were points of relative consensus as well. All but one expressed concern over admitting a student with an outlying test score. To me this suggested that an unstated aim of their selection process was to construct a class that would perform at a similarly high level from the outset.

Another point of agreement concerned the importance of faculty mentoring to this student's prospects. Reflecting on the committee discussion about the mentoring this student would require, David explained:

> I think it is a moral obligation to tell him not to take the quantitative sequence . . . I think that if his advisor spends night and day tutoring him, he might overcome this . . . Anything could happen, but I'd say it's highly improbable . . . The summer bridge program offsetting twenty years is kind of unlikely, but it undoubtedly will help . . . It might raise you to the 50th percentile conceivably. From the 19th to the 50th percentile is a huge increase, but the students in this program are in the 98th percentile. It's going to be a very tough competition.

Linda explained that she would not have voted for him if one of her colleagues had not committed to serve as his mentor:

> I think in the end I felt okay with it . . . If over five were in favor, I was at like a 4.5 or slightly under. And I decided not to make sort of any problem with it just because I was very respectful of the committee and I felt {Pause} the fact that there was this professor here already who was willing to sort of work with this student. I mean, if there hadn't been that, it would have been like, absolutely not. Because this person is likely to get lost and then somebody is going to be, in some sense, stuck, on top of everything else we're doing. Then it takes our time away from our research, our other students, and all this kind of stuff. But given that there was somebody who was really saying, "You know I'm going to work with this person," in the end I felt okay with the decision.

David and Linda both identified a role for mentoring students whose formal credentials seem like outliers. Yet whereas David worried that mentoring would be insufficient to offset Christian's competitive disadvantage among his peers and might recreate within their department the same inequalities observed in society, Linda worried about how that mentoring would burden faculty. Her comments suggest a posture of ambivalence—one that I heard

widely expressed—toward working with students who have less preparation than their peers.

With so many well-prepared students, faculty in these programs seemed
to prefer students whose success would be less dependent upon their efforts. After all, these students were not only being admitted to learn; they
would also be the very individuals appointed to teach undergraduates and
support faculty members' own research.

Reflecting on this episode, a graduate student on the political science
committee described support of diversity to me as "a platitude, a noncon-
troversial stance." Like any institutionalized value, diversity seems natural
to support in principle, and especially so when no competing interests are
perceived or personal investment is required. In the real world of negotiation, however, this is rarely the case, and many faculty struggle to balance
the desire for diversity, the difficulty of excluding any applicant who makes
it to the final round of the review, and their untested assumptions about
risk. Depending upon a scholar's own commitments and experiences, advocating for unconventional students may seem natural or it may seem
controversial. David spoke with me about this struggle in a follow-up interview as well.

In what could be read as a sign of a political disciplinary logic at work,
David compared his colleagues' support for Barack Obama's presidential
bid in 2008 to their support for applicants of color with unconventional
academic backgrounds:

> We all voted for Obama. I doubt if there's anyone in the department that did
> not vote for Obama. And we want to believe sort of, "You can pick them at
> random and they'll all do well," and it just isn't true.

David likened the candidacy and election of an inspirational black presidential candidate, who had less experience as a political officeholder than
his white opponent, to the candidacy and admission of compelling applicants
of color with weaker academic credentials than many of the white students they enroll. I sat with his comments for the rest of the day, aware
that they could be interpreted in several ways. A critical perspective might
conclude that "We all voted for Obama" was a disclaimer for me—a political scientist's way of saying they were not racist, despite how they grap-
pled with merit and diversity. One could also interpret his comments as an
effort to convey his colleagues' willingness to select students with profiles
that were statistically improbable for their program. President Obama himself has spoken about his "improbable journey" to the White House, albeit
in language that names his achievements as the product of collective struggle,
not noblesse oblige.[23] Under either of these interpretations, we know that

national political candidates are highly symbolic figures who represent a platform of ideas, policies, and possibilities. And in America today, we know there is strong evidence that race and racism continue to affect opportunities and outcomes in education and politics, regardless of who holds the office of President.

The political science committee's discussion teaches us several things about merit, diversity, and faculty gatekeeping. It offers a concrete example of informed disagreement about the proper place of GRE scores in admissions and of deference to curriculum in constraining who is judged to be qualified. It also demonstrates the controlling influence of seniority and intellectual politics on faculty deliberations in the absence of a shared intellectual worldview, and how, in the end, the outcomes of deliberation may yet surprise everyone at the table. Together, the story from political science suggests that whatever change or stagnancy may be perceived with respect to organizational diversity or equity, that the scale on which changes occur is small—one reviewer, one applicant, and one evaluation at a time.

Conclusion

A comparison of admissions practices and priorities in distinct disciplines like economics, philosophy, and political science brings into focus the implications of disciplinary values for the work of evaluation. Comparing two high-consensus fields, I learned that disciplinary methods, theories, and practical priorities were evident both in scholars' individual judgments and in their collective decision making. Vivid differences in disciplinary cultures of evaluation became clear, as did similarities between the philosophy committees in two universities. I observed that ideas about merit are enshrined and understood within disciplinary assumptions that flow from prevailing theories, methods, epistemologies, and practical priorities. These commonly held assumptions converged as disciplinary logics that committee members used to defend controversial judgments and practices that disciplinary outsiders might question. For instance, the legitimacy of economists' own work often rests on the validity of statistical inferences, and I observed that shared trust in those inferences made it easier for economists to trust inferences from quantitative metrics like college grades, GRE scores, and college rankings than it was for scholars in the humanities and other social science disciplines.

In low-consensus disciplines, scholars are socialized in a variety of ways, which produces a greater variety of theories, methods, and priorities that inform faculty work. When the committees in such fields sat down to deliberate, they exhibited divergent disciplinary logics, which yielded lessons of their own about how disciplines shape evaluation. I was intrigued to find an especially strong role for individual tastes in these fields, and to see those tastes displayed in the use of serial impressions to describe applicants. The episode in political science also illustrated the broader tendency for committees to defer to majority-minority and seniority politics when worldview moments erupt, reminding the committee of how difficult it can be to achieve consensus. A third trend in lower-consensus disciplines—the strong tendency of faculty to advocate for students like themselves—is the topic I turn to next.

CHAPTER FOUR

Mirror, Mirror

Mirror, mirror here I stand. Who is the fairest in the land?

—Wilhelm Grimm, Grimm's Fairy Tales

That people connect through their similarities more than their differences is a fact of social life.[1] We know this tendency affects undergraduate admissions and professional hiring, for example, with decision makers tending to prefer applicants who remind them of themselves or who fit with the organization's status quo. Sociologists call it homophily, and have explained it in terms of simple attraction, reliance on segregated social networks, and self-serving ideas about merit.[2] Preferences for people like oneself and for qualities like one's own have significant implications for equal opportunity, which is especially troubling because such preferences can be difficult to avoid. Often they occur subconsciously. When those with privilege look at others with privilege and instinctively see them as "the fairest in the land," it becomes difficult for those from more modest personal backgrounds to break into the upper echelons of organizations. Sociologists therefore usually discuss homophily as one in a handful of interpersonal processes that reproduce broader patterns of inequality.

I did not set out to study the preference for self-similarity, but it was impossible to ignore in my data. Nothing short of pervasive, it brought to life the tendency for organizational selection to operate as cultural matching.[3] In some cases, reviewers' personal identities and experiences shaped how they emotionally responded to specific applicants' life stories. More generally, self-similarity shaped reviewer responses to applicants by providing a familiar frame of reference. Like previous research on elite selection, I found widespread homophily based on elite academic pedigree. College reputation was central to pedigree, but the details varied somewhat by discipline. Each academic discipline has its own awards, rituals, and experiences that carry cachet, in spite of meaning little, if anything, to those outside the discipline.

As important as pedigree was, other experiences and identities also shaped faculty tastes, especially in the lower-consensus disciplines. I mentioned earlier that when an applicant's expressed research interests or approach to scholarship aligned with a reviewer's, it could earn the application a closer—and usually more favorable—reading.[4] Another type of cultural matching I observed involved reviewers who tried to present themselves as cool, or hip, and who preferred applicants with similar qualities. International faculty often made a special effort to see that all international students' files received serious consideration. They pushed, in some cases successfully, for national origin to be weighted like race in diversity conversations.

Other reviewers felt compelled to pay forward the opportunities for upward mobility that they felt scholars had once given them. Drawing on their own life experiences, faculty who had experienced social mobility also introduced what I call counterscripts—alternative interpretations of admissions criteria or student profiles—into their committees' deliberations. Unlike differences of interpretation rooted in intellectual worldviews, which were unlikely to be quickly settled in the middle of a meeting, faculty more readily opened their minds to counterscripts, perhaps because they came directly from a colleague's personal experience. In cases where socially mobile faculty had a critical mass on committees, counterscripts were more likely to upset the conventional wisdom. And in a few cases, introducing counterscripts even resulted in decisions to admit applicants with nontraditional profiles. Depending upon an admissions committee's composition and how they deliberate, then, I argue that homophily has the potential to either reinforce or challenge conventional wisdom.[5]

Academic pedigree was valued in all programs, but only in lower-consensus fields did I see clear evidence of homophily on international, cool, and socially mobility dimensions (see Table 5).[6] Across settings, identity-based preferences affected evaluation in four ways. Sometimes they provided grounds for a reviewer's claims about an applicant's "fit" with the discipline's focus or department's expertise. Often self-similarity generated enthusiasm or sympathy for applicants, and these feelings translated into higher ratings or advocacy in committee. In some cases, personal identities gave reviewers the sense that they had a unique ability to judge an applicant's potential. And finally, homophily could stimulate discussion about

Table 5   Evidence of Homophily across Disciplines

	Pedigree	Cool	Social Mobility
Astrophysics	x	x	x
Biology	x		x
Classics	x	x	
Linguistics	x	x	
Political Science	x	x	x
Sociology	x		x
Economics	x		
Physics	x		
Philosophy	x		

which characteristics of applicants committee members should weigh and which ones they should try their best to ignore.

It bears noting that the demographic and intellectual composition of the committees I studied necessarily biases my findings about which types of homophily occurred most frequently. For instance, if I had studied graduate programs in applied disciplines rather than ones traditionally designated as pure, I might have found a more pervasive role for professional experience or interpersonal savvy. The sample I have, composed mostly of white and male faculty in pure disciplines in highly ranked programs at selective universities, may help explain the prevalence of pedigree, and may explain why I did not observe consistent or strong preferences for women or for students of color from the United States. I explore this possibility in more detail in the conclusion to this chapter.

This chapter has four sections. First I present evidence that participants are cognizant that personal similarities shape professional judgment. Then I offer profiles of the four types of homophily I most frequently observed. I next describe efforts by socially mobile faculty to rewrite prevailing scripts of merit; here, I illustrate how counterscripts can challenge well-established assumptions. Finally, I present disconfirming evidence that points to instances in which faculty valued cultural differences rather than similarities, either as noblesse oblige or in solidarity.

Awareness of Preferences for Self-Similarity

Homophily often occurs in the moments when we form impressions of others. Nevertheless, faculty in political science, astrophysics, classics, and linguistics expressed that they were quite conscious of this subconscious tendency, especially among their colleagues. One astrophysicist recounted,

"That's how people subconsciously would be attracted to someone—if they see similar interests, or if they see similar sets of skills or similar emphasis or a similar way of thinking." Later he raised the topic again, and spoke at length about the disagreement it sparked on the committee:

> Another interesting thing was the divergence. Different people had very different ways of assessing someone's worth. In particular, the people whose background was in theoretical physics or theoretical astrophysics were more likely to rate a theoretical astrophysicist higher than an observational, experimental astrophysicist. Whereas I thought they had similar overall qualifications.

> There was someone whose background sounded very impressive, and he listed the projects that he had done. But ultimately, it came down to the fact that he was capable of integrating on a computer—differential equations—and that, ultimately, was the basis of all his projects. As an undergraduate that's a great thing to be able to do. It's a skill you could have, and you could do a lot of very interesting things with it. But ultimately, that's what his ability was. And this was a person who theorists on the committee thought was the greatest person ever.

> We also had this guy who was working on building some instrumentation for telescopes—who I thought in the terms of the skills he had—the skills he had were certainly equivalent to the skills this other guy had . . . Some of the theorists in the committee looked down upon this person who was an instrumentalist. They were subconsciously thinking that people who worked in their particular subfield were somehow more talented than this other person.

More often than disclosing their *own* preferences for students with qualities like theirs, participants would volunteer how their *colleagues* responded to self-similarities, although they could also point to specific applicants with whom they personally felt a connection.

Philosophers not only were aware of and discussed with one another how experiences, identities, and self-interest formed a basis for preferences; they accepted this tendency as natural and joked about it. One reflected:

> There are people who write original papers and they show that they're . . . interested in a topic you're interested in. That has something to do with what makes people catch fire about an applicant. If they write a good paper about a topic I know something about and I'm interested in, I can then appreciate the virtues of this paper. This person is on to a subject. They obviously show they're smart because they're interested in the same thing that I am *{He trails off, laughing}*.

Recognizing how difficult it would be for them *not* to be inclined toward work like their own, philosophers downplayed homophily as a threat to legitimate evaluation. Instead, they emphasized how individual expertise gave them special capacity to judge work in similar areas, and they structured the review process to ensure that each applicant's writing sample would be read by at least one person with expertise in the subject area. This practice also addressed their concern that an applicant's writing sample might be discounted because a reviewer could not bracket their personal biases or stylistic preferences.

Participants in other programs discussed the importance of constructing committees that were diverse along several dimensions, including intellectual focus, social identity, rank, and previous experience with admissions. Ryan, an astrophysicist, elaborated, "It's valuable for our committee to have a diversity of backgrounds . . . I think that helps. People tend to view things through their own experience." This approach worked, in part, because admissions committees tended to be relatively small, so adding just one or two individuals from a particular background could easily broaden a group's common sense. On a committee of five, for example, a rating that might have looked like an outlier from one individual would seem plausible from two, and would become the majority viewpoint from three individuals. One person might struggle to build enthusiasm for a borderline applicant, but two or three who shared a particular perspective could shift the entire tenor or direction of a discussion.

Homophily of the Pedigreed

Perhaps unsurprisingly, graduate admissions committees in these top-ranked programs preferred students with credentials that connoted academic prestige. And although participants respected a broader institutional set than the "super-elite (e.g., top four)" universities that Lauren Rivera found professional service firms to privilege in their hiring decisions,[7] college or university reputation was the most frequently mentioned marker of pedigree. Participants also spoke to the value of recommendation letters from superstars in the field and to the honor of Phi Beta Kappa membership.

Faculty members with well-pedigreed backgrounds of their own downplayed how socioeconomic status is related to the attainment of elite academic credentials, offering several rationales for reframing prestige as merit. Some projected their own professional success onto the potential of such applicants, believing that their own early honors set them on a path to later accomplishments. Others made cultural associations between prestigious undergraduate institutions and the doctoral programs in which they taught, believing that applicants from top-tier colleges and universities had, as one humanities professor put it, "been preadapted to a program like ours." A third group recalled the difficulty they had in gaining admission into elite undergraduate institutions (and the intelligence they had perceived among their peers there) as evidence that today's graduates from such institutions must truly be "better." Brian is an astrophysicist who expressed this perspective:

> I was the best at math and physics in my high school, probably the best in five or ten years. That may be a big fish in a very small pond. Then you get into a bigger pond. I got to college and was an undergraduate at MIT. The guy sitting next to me in my intro physics class had been on the American Physics Olympiad Team and was clearly better than I was. I'm good but there's always someone better . . . A letter that says, "This is the best person graduating from Stanford or Princeton" means a lot more than, "This is the best person graduating from Ohio State or University of Texas . . ." We certainly know the caliber of people in there. There was one guy who we admitted that a professor from Princeton said—"this is the best undergrad I've ever worked with." That means a whole lot more coming from MIT than coming from a lesser school. MIT and Harvard are the places where, frankly, the real genius-type people wind up.

Finally, a relatively small group offered the human capital argument for pedigree as merit—that applicants who earned their college degrees from peer institutions must be superior because they had received high-quality training. Brian also mentioned, "Coming from the places that are our competition, we know what kind of background they'll be getting." Across these rationales, the common thread was an underlying preference for applicants whose profiles resembled committee members' own academically distinguished biographies.

Pedigree and Privilege in Classics

Pedigree goes deeper than institutional affiliation, however, and every discipline has its own set of experiences and qualifications that are regarded as distinctive. To illustrate how it played out in one field, I discuss pedigree in classics—a small, tight-knit discipline marked by extended socialization and study of the languages, literature, and art of ancient civilizations. Before asking questions about admissions, I began each of my interviews by asking participants to describe how they had come to be professors in the field, and in classics the responses had clear patterns. All came up through the American or British academic establishment, all but one received an early start learning ancient languages, and several felt that travel and study in Athens, Rome, or England had an important socializing effect on them. Sure enough, in their judgments of applicants, these very traits emerged as salient. Not only did they weigh the undergraduate institutions that students attended (very important), the honors or awards they earned (nice to see), and the eminence of reference providers (expected in this small discipline). They also considered years of Greek or Latin training as a yardstick of preparation, looked for whether students had traveled to and studied in the ancient world, and prized applicants who had connections to the British universities that have been at the forefront of classics scholarship for centuries. Given the discipline's history and its geographic and educational loci (including the relatively small set of elite preparatory schools and postsecondary institutions that provide early training in Greek and Latin), these priorities combined to encourage a system that disproportionately serves the interests of wealthy students.[8]

The committee used the language of risk aversion to maintain that students needed deep, formal training in both ancient and modern languages to be successful at the graduate level. An associate professor of classics explained:

> We definitely want to know how many years have they studied the ancient languages and how many modern languages do they have, because if they don't have that, they're not going to be starting out at a certain level here. They won't be able to read any of the scholarship, the foreign language scholarship. They'll struggle in their classes.

As with committees in other disciplines (such as political science, economics, sociology, physics, astrophysics, and linguistics), they felt that students without formal training would not start out on equal footing with their peers, which was necessary to ensure a common foundation for independent scholarship.[9] Their preference was to admit cohorts of students who would have minimal variation in entering skills, which they thought would ensure similarly shaped learning curves at the doctoral level.

As in other disciplines, faculty in classics liked to see evidence of student effort, but they worried at possible signs of struggle. Rather than selecting students with underdeveloped potential whom they could envision fashioning into disciplinary experts, they preferred to enroll students who already embodied ease with disciplinary discourse and norms. This ease, Bourdieu argued (and other sociologists have agreed), is a hallmark of cultural capital.[10] The disciplinary familiarity that these students already possessed enabled them to easily transition into the role of classics scholar and to immediately support faculty members' research. What is more, a financial aid structure in which students are paid to support faculty research further encouraged selecting on pedigree rather than potential.

Yet the tension between pedigree and potential was not lost on classicists. Paula, an associate professor of classics who grew up with professors in the family and whose institutional affiliations include the Sorbonne, Ivy League schools, and public research universities, admitted that her department was "torn" in how to think about students from less selective colleges. She said, "I mean you can see how torn we are because, um, we want those people. We want them encouraged. We would like to support them. *{Pause}* On the other hand, they're nearly always less of a sure thing." Differentiating herself from such applicants through language like "those people," Paula later made a point to deny "bias" in the department. Yet she also admitted the benefits she personally experienced from her family and well-resourced undergraduate institution. Paula expounded:

> We don't have any kind of bias. We're not, you know, "We only take people . . ." *{Interviewee trails off}*. We don't say that, and we would never say that we only take people from Ivy League schools or from universities as compared to colleges. Because that's not, you just never know who the exciting student is going to be, and it's in no way a guarantee of where they went to college. The only thing that can help, that can be an issue, is students who've gone to really good . . . who have had certain advantages . . . either support from family or support out of a department, have a kind of a confidence that I just myself felt was needed to get through graduate school.

There may not have been an explicit bias *against* less renowned colleges and universities, but there was a clear and consistent preference *for* the sophistication of students who graduated from selective undergraduate institutions.

Students self-taught in ancient languages and those who had attended less prestigious institutions—including public flagship universities—often need a postbaccalaureate or master's degree to be competitive for doctoral classics programs. The postbaccalaureate was started to help students from fields like art history and archaeology who wanted to pursue a doctorate in classics but lacked the language training. Over time, however, students with bachelor's degrees in classics have also begun pursuing these degrees to gain a competitive advantage over other applicants vis-à-vis language skills. Such programs have become a means for current classics students to preserve their competitive edge in admissions. Notably, these programs come with high tuition, fees, and expenses for study abroad, which may work against their original role of broadening access to the discipline.

In short, it is rare in these programs to break into classics at the PhD level without an undergraduate degree in the field from an elite institution. Amy, a female junior faculty member, described the situation to me:

[There is] a structure of privilege which is morally uncomfortable. I was doing an external review at an Ivy League university and we had a meeting with some of their graduate students, not all. And I was really struck that of the eight or so people who actually talked, probably half were Brits. And it came up in the conversation that three or four of the others were from one Ivy as undergraduates. Now, I did ask them and they had told me they had admitted somebody from a rural flagship university a couple of years before. You know if you get classics department students who have been trained in the British system and students from elite Ivy League schools, you can probably have very successful completion numbers. But it doesn't feel right.

In this year's pool, two individuals with self-taught Greek and Latin language skills made it to the short list, but their lack of formal training remained a major concern for the committee, and the committee opted not to send either through to the interview stage. A senior scholar also noted it has been "very rare not to have a senior thesis" among those recently admitted.

The implicit preference of elites for elites reproduces social hierarchies, and in few places is that pattern more apparent than the upper echelons of academia. In the case of classics, participants emphasized criteria in which the lines between human and cultural capital were no doubt blurry. Extended travel to the ancient world and formal training in prestigious institutions had been personally formative for committee members, and hold symbolic value in the field. From their personal and disciplinary frames of reference, reliance on these criteria was understandable.

Yet when opportunities that are available to only a few pass as prerequisites, it creates, as Amy described it, a "structure of privilege that is morally uncomfortable." Unlike fields such as biology or sociology, which have multiple access points and in which nontraditional trajectories are acceptable or even valued, this classics program was more like a typical mathematics program, requiring an early start and years of experience in well-respected programs to be perceived as a qualified applicant. Of course, the term "qualified" is loaded. As recent controversies over hiring faculty and administrators of color at the University of Pennsylvania have highlighted, to be judged "qualified" is not only a judgment of skill and talent. It can also be a function of whether an employer or decision maker feels comfortable with the applicant due to common intellectual interests, social circles, or institutional affiliations.[11]

Inside and outside of classics, participants were mindful of discipline-specific prestige hierarchies, in addition to their awareness of a general prestige hierarchy of colleges and universities. In philosophy, astrophysics, and biology, for example, professors mentioned specific "underrated" universities whose reputations for strong training in the field surpassed their college or university's relatively weak overall ranking. Discipline-specific honors and rites of passage also counted toward one's pedigree. Whether it was travel to Athens or Rome in classics, a journey to one of the major telescopes in astronomy, a summer spent working in a prominent lab in physics, or an award for best undergraduate poster at a national linguistics meeting, accomplishments and experiences unique to one's discipline could distinguish an applicant's pedigree and mark him or her as "one of us."

Homophily of the Cool

In addition to the old-school culture of the academy that is reproduced through homophily among the well-pedigreed, another form of cultural matching that I observed in four programs encouraged characteristics recognized as cool or hip. I certainly did not go looking for this theme. I began to notice it, however, in hearing certain applicants and research interests described as "cool," rather than the more common descriptors, such as "good," "strong," "solid" or "exciting." Taking note of which reviewers used this language, and about whom, clued me into the presence of a cultural archetype. Through further analysis, I came to see it as related to reviewers' and applicants' self-presentation, technology use, manners of speech, and the novelty of their research and personal profiles.

Faculty who presented as cool exhibited carefully managed images, including specific fashion styles that set them apart from the mode. One such style I came to think of as the "ascetic sleek." One male professor seemed to emulate Steve Jobs's look: shaved head, black turtleneck, earring. A female member of that same committee attended a committee meeting with a fresh pixie haircut, cherry red lipstick, white scoop-neck T-shirt, black vest, and leather pants. (By contrast, most of the other committee members wore jeans.) A second type of cool presentation that I observed in several committees was the "rumpled preppy." One young scholar's apparel for both the meeting and our interview could have come straight off of a mannequin in J. Crew, including trendy tortoise shell glasses and a perfectly rumpled and untucked Oxford shirt under a camel wool sweater—all bearing the logos of expensive brands. The vast majority of the committee members counted as cool wore eyeglass frames in trendy styles.[12]

Self-presentation was thus central to coolness, but it came out not only in how these faculty dressed, but also in how they spoke and related to one another. Cool scholars were savvy, with sophisticated social skills. Describing people and things they liked as "cool," rather than good, great, and so on, signaled that they felt positively about an applicant but would not come across as too earnest or passionate (which, by definition, would not be cool). A certain detachment from the matters that others emotionally engaged with characterized the cool scholars on these committees.

Cool scholars also used technology in a performative way, such as through the conspicuous display of devices (especially Apple products) and discussion of popular blogs or their own blogging. In one humanities committee of five people, the gadgets on the table included Mac laptops, an iPad, and an iPod, and several iPhones. The strong presence of technology in the admissions process was not lost on the political science committee, which had the largest proportion of cool members among the committees I observed. In one of their meetings, a senior professor commented, "Technology marches on. Everyone in here has a laptop, some iPads, and some with laptops *and* iPads." During their meeting, they projected a spreadsheet on a screen and committee members searched the Internet during the meeting for more information about applicants and letter writers. At one point, three people on the committee had a side conversation about the blogs they maintained or to which they contributed.

Although I initially passed off this self-conscious technology talk as an insight into the ubiquity of technology and its use to display status and cultural affinity, I began to notice engagement with technology emerge in deliberations about borderline applicants. Against the initial vote of the committee's majority, a humanities program admitted a nontraditional student with "crummy grades" from Princeton, largely due to a cool member of the committee praising the writing skill the applicant had demonstrated through a popular blog for the discipline. And in another case in the social sciences, a preppy cool committee member discussed his rating of a borderline applicant, explaining: "I would be willing to go up. I read this app right after another app in this concentration and wanted to be stingy with my 1's. Plus, she writes articles for Slate. Really cool." An ascetic cool professor added, "She seems like an interesting person."

As these comments indicate, novelty was central to coolness, and in no domain was novelty or originality judged more frequently than an applicant's expressed research interests and experiences. In linguistics, two reviewers described an applicant's intention to study emoticons (symbols, such as smiling faces, inserted in text to add meaning) as "cool" and "really cool." That committee was similarly taken by an applicant interested in conducting experimental research on twins' language use. Political scientists deemed applicants with field research or extended study in unusual places as cool. In astrophysics, an associate professor noted that new instruments generate money, energy, and fertile ground for intellectual breakthroughs that "impose a fashion" for subsequent scholars:

> Astrophysics has become such a large field that you have to be broad in order
> to understand what's interesting—what areas you may move your research to
> [in order to] follow or even impose a fashion . . . For example, if a new instru-
> ment is going to be built—you know exactly that it's going to revolutionize a
> certain number of fields. What are the reasons for that? These projects are so
> large. It's not like someone can say, "I'm going to understand this question in
> the lab. I'm going to set up my own lab to do this." This is a billion-dollar
> project that usually the whole U.S. or international community will use. Students
> tend to understand where the landscape is—where they have to go—where
> are the sexy questions are that people want answered.

Indeed, perhaps the only praise of research interests that trumped "cool"
was "sexy"—a word that participants reserved for research that was timely,
cutting-edge, and somewhat provocative.

By contrast, a committee member in classics audibly groaned as he read
from an applicant's personal statement, then commented, "He's really interested in something that others have done and done and done." A preppy
cool committee member defended his low rating of a student who had generated considerable discussion. "He was strong in a conventional way," he
said. "He was everything you look for, and nothing you weren't expecting,"
to which an ascetic cool professor added, with a chuckle, "Like a Ford."
Neither applicant made their admit lists. To cool faculty, the novelty and
originality of one's research interests and overall profile could make an individual more likable by enabling that student to stand out from the scores
or hundreds of strong, solid applicants.

Interestingly, not a single mention of a research interest being cool or sexy
came from participants in the higher-consensus disciplines of physics, philosophy, and economics. This finding may relate to a trend in Lamont's
study of peer review: that centralized, hierarchical disciplines are more inclined to believe that academic excellence inheres in the individuals who are
being evaluated rather than in the eye of the beholder.[13] It may be that faculty in higher-consensus disciplines are more inclined to judge scholarship
on the basis of shared, well-established standards than on individual impressions. Centralized disciplines possess more of an intellectual orthodoxy in
which novelty—one of the central meanings of coolness—may be of less
value than qualities like precision and methodological sophistication.

Social Mobility Homophily

Eight of the ten committees included at least one member who advocated
for applicants from modest personal backgrounds. Some of these individ-

uals had been first-generation college students, and all had attended moderately selective or public universities as undergraduates. In interviews with me, they expressed mindfulness about how far they had come and how they felt compelled by applicants whose paths reminded them of their own. Having experienced social mobility, they saw admissions work as an opportunity to reach back and promote opportunity for others. Some from this group also felt that their experience uniquely enabled them to interpret applications from individuals from less privileged backgrounds, and they offered alternative ways of thinking about institutional prestige and academic preparation. Contrary to the risk aversion and prestige orientation of these programs, those from less pedigreed backgrounds encouraged their colleagues to take a chance on students who seemed to have potential, apart from their achievements to date.

Narratives from Linda and Louis in the social sciences and from James and Ryan in the natural sciences[14] highlight the unique perspective shared by faculty who did not attend elite undergraduate institutions. Louis, a sociologist, went to a commuter-focused, moderately selective university near his home before earning his PhD at an Ivy League university. The transition for him to graduate school had not been entirely smooth, but after finding his footing, he had a positive experience. Discussing his current program's approach to thinking about college prestige, Louis remarked,

> It's not like we're plucking people from only Princeton, Harvard, Yale, Columbia. But I think prestige is probably a little more important to my colleagues, and maybe they've internalized it more than I have . . . Some of my colleagues, in fact people I know are on the committee, really care a lot more about prestige and think of this university as a much more special place than other institutions—probably more than I do.

Though he said the university was populated with many "elitists," its intellectual enterprise had earned his respect. Moreover, although he felt the degree of coordination between the graduate school's administration and program faculty could be improved, the graduate college was "really putting their money where their mouth is on diversity."

Linda was a social scientist with an international reputation who had grown up in an impoverished community and was one of the only people in her high school class to go to college. She spoke to me at length about her process for choosing a college as a teenager. To save money and stay geographically close to her family, Linda had enrolled in a college that was less selective than what she was academically qualified to attend. Higher education researchers call this undermatching. I asked her whether she felt her own experiences had affected how she read applications, and she responded, "Most definitely."

I will look at somebody who is first-generation *{Pause}*—I think I understand the learning curve that they sort of had to go through a little bit more. So I don't think I *{Pause} favor* them. I mean I've certainly had people I ranked a number 1, the highest score, that had gone to the very best schools all along. But if there's somebody like—I believe there was somebody we admitted who got maybe a 4.0 from Washington State—and had I not had my experience and realized that if you're coming from a first-generation family, nobody is telling you how to apply to college, that you should try to go to the best one. You may be thinking that, if I go here I can help out my family. I won't have huge loans or whatever . . .

I think I'm just much more open to looking a lot at: "They got a 4.0. They did everything they could there . . . The letters of recommendation are really terrific." Whereas somebody who just went to Princeton, you might think, "Even if they have a little bit lower GPA, they might have a better education."

Linda felt she interpreted grades and institutional prestige more broadly than the typical script of associating them with intelligence, likelihood of success, and quality of training received. Her interpretation, she believed, represented a more "generous" and "gracious" approach than that of her colleagues.

Linda also considered "distance traveled," a noncognitive criterion that many in undergraduate admissions are beginning to weigh. Based on her firm belief in the role that effort plays in success as a doctoral student, she assessed not only how accomplished a person seemed, but how far they had come and how hard they had worked. When I asked her to share an example of this, she spoke of her own experience as a first-generation college student, and how that informed her reading of a rural student's application:

So that one applicant, I don't think it's somebody we admitted, but he said from his high school something like 50 percent wind up incarcerated . . . some remote town in Montana. He had to Google how to apply to college. And so somebody like that, I'm going to sort of look at the file and try to understand if you started here and already got there *{Using hands to show relative distance}* versus somebody who started here and just got a little bit higher than you. I'm very likely to look at, sort of, where did you start and where have you been as a very good indicator of where you'll be.

She also relayed the story of a second-generation immigrant:

One person said that his parents were immigrants and some [other family] had been killed in the first war in Iraq. And he came here and he was working in a restaurant washing dishes to get through high school, and in college he had a job and stuff like that. It was a sort of story of *{Pause}* tremendous disadvantages and struggle and desire to make it in, I guess, handicaps. Of course, that's impressive. It implies the person has strong motivation. And also there's a kind of sympathy factor. The spoiled brats who've always been rich and their parents gave them everything, well, they can get in anywhere. We don't need to admit them.

Linda thus set her expectations of applicants not only in an absolute sense and by comparing applicants with others in the pool, but relative to the student's own previous opportunities and what the person had made of the chances they had been given.

James and Ryan, two junior scholars in a natural sciences department, both of whom had attended midwestern land-grant universities, adopted a similar approach when evaluating institutional affiliations. In their committee's initial meeting to develop a short list, they discussed Wilson, a student with a near-perfect GPA in the discipline and considerable undergraduate research experience.

"He went to the University of Nebraska," James commented. "He's a lot like me."

"Defend your alma mater!" Matthew exuberantly responded, with a swoop of his arm.

After a moment's pause that appeared to me to be a pointed nonverbal response, James calmly continued. "I trust Janine, his letter writer. If *she* says he's one of the best in forty years . . ." He trailed off, and there was another pause in the conversation.

"I like him," offered Ryan. "I think he'd be a good fit."

"Let's move him up and then do death match against the others," Matthew urged.

For context, Matthew earned his PhD from Columbia University, and "death match" was a term he used multiple times to refer to comparing a small group of applicants with one another in order to identify weaknesses.[15] In a follow-up interview, James spoke at length with me about how he felt Wilson and his alma mater had been evaluated.

There was the student from Nebraska who ended up getting in our top thirty. There was an interview, and I couldn't make the interview. Apparently the interview didn't go very well, and so he didn't make the top twenty-two. But that guy, personally, had a research record that looked very much like mine. He had a very high GPA. If you want to stand out going to a big, state school, you have to have a really high GPA. Someone from Columbia doesn't have to have a 3.9 but if you're from Nebraska you do. So anyway, we're advocating for other people. I try to generally take a second look at people from big, state universities. I know there are a lot of fantastic students there who for very good reasons decided not to spend $50,000 a year on their undergraduate education.

James continued, discussing how both his own judgment and that of his colleagues were situated in personal experience:

> The people on the committee who have an Ivy League background thought about things a little differently. That's why my colleague was trying to criticize someone who went to Nebraska for going to Nebraska . . . I think people understand what their [own] experience was, and maybe don't think the others on the committee may value the experience that they personally went through.

Recognizing that some of the distinctions that their colleagues valued were also functions of class or wealth, socially mobile faculty made a special effort to disentangle potential from achievements. Looking back on their own paths, some expressed skepticism about how well an elite pedigree would predict long-term scholarly success. They rated unconventional applicants more highly than their colleagues did, and advocated for unconventional students in ways that both improved such students' admissions chances and, in a few cases, helped their colleagues think more broadly.

Counterscripts and Critical Mass

Rosabeth Moss-Kanter's breakthrough research on group dynamics coined the idea of critical mass, "that groups with varying proportions of people of different social types differ qualitatively in dynamics and process."[16] And, indeed, in contrast to typical committees in which expectations of elite academic pedigrees were normative, deliberations in more diverse committees—those with a critical mass of people with a different identity than the norm—engaged in more debate about the conventional wisdom around merit. Linda, James, and Ryan's committees did so, as well as one of the two in philosophy. In these conversations, members corrected misperceptions and pushed one another on their rationales for particular applicant ratings. Members of these committees also went beyond correcting and challenging each other, proposing altogether different interpretations of common criteria. For how these interpretations deviated from standard evaluative scripts of merit, I call these perspectives counterscripts.

A common script associated elite pedigrees with belonging in elite communities like theirs. Maintaining this preference helped uphold their organizational identity, and was thought to protect them against financial and reputational risks of admitting students with lower odds of success. Linda, Louis, James, and Ryan each pointed out that their current programs and universities were resource-rich and therefore had the most to give—not just the most to lose. Contrary to those who saw their programs' status as bestowing "the luxury of risk aversion," these professors associated status with an obligation and opportunity to invest in underdeveloped potential. They advocated for students whose credentials may have seemed less impressive but who seemed to possess "spark" or potential to be "a diamond in the rough." In committee, they named the faculty who once took a chance on them and in one case expressed aloud that they wanted to pay it forward, as the phrase goes. Breaking with the usual script, they argued for opportunities to be expanded rather than for their own status to be protected. Their higher ratings, advocacy in deliberation, and challenges to their colleagues' rationales shifted deliberations of borderline applicants and, in a few cases, the outcomes of deliberation as well.

One person introducing a different interpretation would rarely be sufficient to shift the group's common sense. Usually it took a coalition of sorts, a combination of advocacy from someone who shared an aspect of the student's profile and support or advocacy from committee members with more privileged backgrounds. Often that support from more privileged members was no more than a token gesture toward a few applicants rather than a reorientation toward the pool or of the value of elite credentials. A senior professor of philosophy illustrated:

> As things go on, the privileged get more privileges. One thing I like to do when I can is to include in any class a kind of long shot. That is, a person from a smaller college or something—someone who has written a writing sample that really grabs you. Even though you don't know the recommenders, so therefore you don't really trust the recommendations. You don't know what it means that they got a high GPA at this school because it's not much of a school. But you know—it looks like this is the sort of person that needs to be plucked out of mediocrity and given a chance. And I like to do that.

Such noblesse oblige seemed to give those faculty the sense that they had fulfilled their responsibility to encourage opportunity and mobility in a system fraught with obstacles. Yet it shifted opportunities for only a very small minority of applicants, and is unlikely to shift the overall profile of doctoral students away from the power of pedigree and wealth.

In a few cases a critical mass emerged through ally behavior—individuals working across different social identities toward a common interest. In philosophy, for example, there was the case of Gerald, who supported Liana's and Olivia's argument that they should not prioritize high quantitative GRE scores because it would systematically undermine women's access. In contrast to noblesse oblige, allies joined with individuals from historically marginalized groups in questioning the usual review process or rethinking common criteria with an eye to opening opportunities for categories of students, not individual cases. Whereas noblesse oblige would selectively extend support and opportunity in spite of perceived risks, allies poked holes in the common narratives about "risk." From an organizational learning perspective, ally behavior carries the potential to stimulate longer term cultural change by encouraging critical thinking about aspects of admissions that often are taken for granted. And although examples of advocating across different identities were rare enough to be considered disconfirming evidence, they suggest a culture of evaluation that is more complex than simple theories of homophily suggest.

Conclusion

Especially in lower-consensus disciplines, reviewer tastes were inextricable from their own identities and experiences, especially their educational, social, and national origins. James promoted students from flagship public universities because he had attended one himself, for instance, and had come to believe they provided undergraduates a training that his colleagues underrated. In classics, Paula liked to see evidence of extensive travel and study in Greece, Rome, and British universities because those experiences had been formative to her socialization. Jimmy encouraged his colleagues in biology to closely consider every East Asian applicant because he had immigrated to the United States to attend graduate school and has since become a citizen. The examples are numerous.

Yet what appeared on the surface as a single trend toward homophily consisted of specific interactions that collectively offer a richer picture of cultural matching than "birds of a feather sticking together."[17] Sometimes similarity with applicants provided grounds for claims of fit, which was a critical consideration in late stages of admissions review. Connecting personally with an applicant's experience or trajectory could also generate an emotional response that affected ratings and spurred reviewers to speak up in committee deliberations. I also observed scholars treating their identities and life experiences as knowledge that positioned them to better interpret the stories and possible trajectories of applicants with similar experiences—better, that is, than their colleagues who lack such perspective. Similarity with applicants was thus not only a source of attraction. It framed participants' subjective ability to judge and their desire to speak up.

Process-level patterns like these generally align with the organizational, affective, and cognitive mechanisms that Lauren Rivera identified in her study of hiring in professional investment firms.[18] However, I draw out dynamics unique to more diverse selection committees and examine an evaluation context in which pedigree is not rooted in a single institutional prestige hierarchy. Whereas Rivera's research found that elite firms privileged degrees from a small handful of universities, I found that faculty doctoral programs were also mindful of discipline-specific status hierarchies.[19] The Ivy League retains a cultural mystique, but faculty in these doctoral programs were less compelled by an Ivy League institutional affiliation if the department from which they graduated was different than their own field or did not have a strong reputation of its own. Likewise, they might be impressed by affiliations with a land grant, state flagship, or other moderately selective university when it was home to a respected program in the discipline. To identify future stewards of the disciplines, the pedigree that counted most was pedigree in the discipline.

Interestingly, gender, race, and ethnicity may have been the primary types of inequality about which faculty expressed concern to me in interviews, but the committees I observed rarely raised race, ethnicity, or gender in an explicit way. It could be that distinguishing racial or gender-based homophily from the review process itself was almost impossible because straight white men were so well represented on these committees. Indeed, because white males established most U.S. universities, preferences for cultural qualities associated with whiteness and traditional masculinity are subtly interwoven into the fabric of values, rules, rewards, and selection processes in elite higher education. It can thus be hard to see gender and racial homophily, and social reproduction can occur along these dimensions without explicit preference or advocacy.

Sociologist Shelley Correll's research provides excellent evidence of how judgments of professionally relevant qualities associated with traditional masculinity reinforce gender inequity. She found with collaborators Stephen Benard and In Paik that employers judged working fathers as more "competent" and "professionally committed" than working mothers. In another experiment on the "motherhood penalty," they controlled for an employee's competency and commitment to see whether this removed the preference for males. Interestingly, they found that male and female research participants alike rated fathers more highly, because they were judged more "likable" than professionally successful mothers.[20]

There are similar dynamics in graduate admissions. Having developed a suite of professionally relevant rationales for the value of elite college attendance (such as human capital, cultivation of academic ease and confidence), faculty can uncontroversially make explicit their preference for elite college attendance, in spite of its tendency to rule out many who might succeed. The focus on personal qualities, which reviewers may subconsciously associate with social identities, allows more forms of homophily to persist than those that a committee explicitly discusses. Without a lively debate among diverse reviewers, particularly one in which individuals debate the rationales for their rating, committees may not even realize how much their own identities are shaping the selection process.

Each of the last several chapters has emphasized a social context in which faculty judgment is situated—one's program or department, discipline, committee, and individual identity. Depending upon the situation and group, different identities can become salient, for identity is multidimensional and dynamic, not uniform or static.[21] In admissions, faculty members' identities may be triggered through the committee's composition, through engagement with applications, and through discussions of those applications with colleagues (whose own identities have also likely been triggered through evaluation). The mix of experiences, identities, and preferences that results reflects a fragmented organizational culture—one composed of multiple priorities and of fluid perspectives and values. Organizational theorist Joanne Martin articulated this viewpoint:

> Organizations, environments, and group boundaries are constantly changing. Individuals have fragmented, fluctuating self-concepts. One moment a person thinks of himself or herself as belonging to one subculture, and a minute later another subcultural membership becomes salient. People fluctuate in this way because they are faced with inescapable contradictions, as well as things they do not understand.

Increasing diversity in the upper reaches of America's labor market, Martin also argues, is only likely to increase the complexity of individual identities and, by extension, how fragmented our organizational cultures are.[22]

It is hard to predict what the effects of such complexity might be for faculty evaluation. On the one hand, it could weaken the influence of specific identity-based preferences. On the other hand, complexity could effectively increase preference for students like oneself by creating ambiguous conditions under which decision makers look for something familiar. Fragmented organizational culture might open space for counterscripts that pose a challenge to conventional wisdom, but these alternative interpretations could just as easily be folded into the tendency to extend noblesse oblige without rethinking the system. My data do not suggest any clear answers, but there are hints to suggest that the cultural profile of the ideal student is no longer singular, but rather is diversifying. I observed two types of coolness—the rumpled preppy *and* the ascetic sleek—as well as the influence of both traditional and disciplinary-based prestige hierarchies. There is also a growing value placed on a student's "distance traveled" and some disdain for applicants whose applications imply that they have led a charmed life.

One thing is clear. The more that *departments* hold up a mirror and notice in the reflection not only their collective fairness and beauty, but also the flaws that stem from who is absent from the image that the mirror presents, the closer they may come, in time, to embodying the image of diversity they aspire to project.

CHAPTER FIVE

The Search for Intelligent Life

Definitions and understandings of intelligence, like all meanings,
are sensitive to the contexts in which they are developed.
—JEANNIE OAKES ET AL.

WILLIAM JAMES once hypothesized that self-worth is fragile when grounded in qualities that are sensitive to others' judgments. Social psychologist Jennifer Crocker and her colleagues have amassed an impressive body of evidence for this idea through research on prospective graduate students. They found that graduate school applicants' self-esteem—which in most cases is a stable quality—fluctuates dramatically between the days when they receive acceptance letters and days when they receive rejection letters. For participants who rate academic competence as central to their self-worth, the boost to self-esteem that accompanies admission offers is greater, and the loss of self-esteem from news of rejection is stronger.[1] Findings like these, as with the research on human tendencies toward homophily, support a central tenet of social psychology, that people define themselves in relation to others.

Interestingly, the areas in which we may feel judged by others, such as our gender, class, appearance, or intelligence, tend to be the same ones in which we judge ourselves and others. Our inward judgments create a foundation for identity and self-esteem (self-respect or self-worth). Applied outwardly, we use social judgments to discern others' worthiness to receive social goods—anything from an admissions offer, to a vote in an election, to a compliment. Often we subconsciously reserve the harshest judgments about qualities that are most important to our own self-concept.

In academia, an enterprise oriented around knowledge production, intelligence is an important domain of judgment and an informal grounds for distributing opportunities and rewards. Central to academic culture and the self-concepts of academics, faculty expect intelligence of themselves and of one another, and they look for it in those whom they train and hire.[2] It may come as no surprise that a senior professor would sum up all of graduate admissions as "finding smart people to replenish the gene pool."

What "smart" means, however, is of course deeply contested. The status and opportunities that accompany judgments of intelligence raise the stakes associated with our definitions, as do historic tendencies to emphasize measures of intelligence with racial, socioeconomic, and other inequalities. Disputes also emerge from the wide gap between psychometricians' formal measures and the implicit ideas (lay theories) that people use to judge one another on an everyday basis.[3] A related source of disagreement involves the degree to which intelligence can be separated from cultural context. As with all meanings, the everyday meaning of intelligence varies widely, depending upon where you are and whom you ask. In a fascinating study of American kindergarten classrooms, for example, Beth Hatt found that teachers regarded as "smart" those children who started the school year with the knowledge that kindergarten aims to teach. This knowledge included reading skills, of course, but also the skills of sitting quietly and interacting with docility. A study in Taiwan found that the flexibility to apply the right ability at the right time was central to judgments of intelligence, whereas Japanese college students and their mothers rated quick thinking, decisive judgment, and a strong memory as important.[4]

Few researchers have systematically examined the lay theories of intelligence within specific disciplines or disciplinary cultures. The insights that have emerged from previous studies are intriguing, however. Lamont's study of interdisciplinary peer review found that literary scholars were especially prone to lapse into weakly substantiated claims of smartness as they evaluated others. Data presented in Becher and Trowler's famous exploration of the disciplines, *Academic Tribes and Territories,* suggests that hard scientists compare scientists' relative intelligence on the basis of subject matter complexity. One chemist cited a "hierarchy of arrogance" in the sciences rooted in intellectual activity and qualities of mind: "Physics represents the hardest, most abstract reasoning—people know they're smart. Chemists feel defensive in relation to physicists, but superior in relation to biologists."[5]

I did not intend, when I started this research, to examine how faculty conceive of intelligence across the disciplines or how faculty ideas about intelligence shape admissions. Yet when four of the first five people I interviewed cited intelligence or brilliance among the characteristics they were looking for in prospective students, it became clear that this was something important to them. To understand how they thought about admissions, I needed to attend to intelligence as well. Disciplinary foundations to ideas about intelligence and brilliance became quickly apparent as well, because I conducted early interviews with admissions chairs from a variety of fields.

I learned as the fieldwork continued that intelligence is one of the most fundamental values driving faculty efforts to create the futures of their respective disciplines. In admissions meetings, I observed that like assessments of a student's "fit," assessments of this nebulous quality almost always went unchallenged. When an applicant was understood to be "brilliant," a host of other flaws could be forgiven or ignored. When an applicant was believed to lack intelligence, either in degree or in qualities that serve the discipline, admission offers were unlikely at best. At issue in my analysis is not whether judgments of intelligence *should* matter for admission Rather, I focus on other questions: How do professors conceive of and attempt to assess intelligence in doctoral admissions? How do their ideas about intelligence vary by discipline?

I discussed in Chapter 2 the differences between the criteria that faculty used in early and later phases of review and how, in each phase, they sought to infer applicants' intelligence. Here, I distinguish between two common ways that faculty understood and assessed intelligence: as a general impression and as a disciplinary cultural practice. Committee members frequently expressed summary judgments about how smart they believed an applicant to be, linking those perceptions to predictions of a student's likelihood for success. These overall impressions treated intelligence as a fixed attribute that some people were assumed to have more of than others. Yet when prodded in interviews to elaborate on what intelligence means for scholars in their discipline, faculty transitioned away from impressions and broad judgments into a view of intelligence as a disciplinary cultural practice. By assessing applicants' writing samples, personal statements, or interview responses, faculty tried to glean qualities of thought and mind, especially as evinced in research experience and other forms of engagement with the discipline. Assessments of intelligence thus rested upon a combination of general impressions and locally defined behaviors—something that an individual *is* and something that an individual *does*.

General Impressions of Intelligence

In offhand comments, reviewers often described applicant intelligence as a noun or adjective, implying that it is something that one has or is. I mentioned in Chapter 2 that at least half of those in the sample instinctively associated GRE scores with intelligence, although they frequently equivocated on this. I asked each participant, "What, if anything, does the

GRE signal?" and some caught themselves, mid-answer, overcoming their instincts with more thoughtful responses. In sociology, for example, an associate professor responded to my question with the following:

> I suppose it signals a certain kind of *{Pause}* I was about to say native intelligence, but I know that's not true, because people can dramatically improve their scores by taking classes—these Kaplan, Princeton Review classes. So *{Pause}* I have a hard time knowing what it signals.[6]

Another sociologist proposed,

> GREs tell me something, probably, about—I don't know—crude about native intelligence or general intellectual horsepower or something like that. I think that's a relevant piece but it doesn't tell me about the person's creativity or sociological imagination or something like that. I tend to look for things in letters, personal statements, much more than past achievement. And even that obviously is a real thin predictor.

In committee meetings, discussions of each applicant began and ended with faculty enunciating their overall impressions of students, and often, that included at least one comment that I came to think of as an example of "smart talk." Such talk involved language like "intellectually capable" and "plenty of intellectual horsepower" when judgments were positive, and comments such as "lame-brained" and "I question she has what it takes" when negative. Broadly, committees in the humanities disciplines displayed more lenient interpretations of lower scores and grades, but high numbers still often impressed them. Low scores might be the result of "a bad day" or "few opportunities for test preparation," they claimed, but they also said, "You don't earn perfect GRE scores by accident."

Is it appropriate to infer intelligence from scores on the GRE or other college entrance exams? This question is deeply fraught territory because of the origins of college entrance and intelligence tests in the eugenics movement and continuing gaps in scores that fall along lines of social identity.[7] And like the broader question about what intelligence is, answers about what can be inferred from GRE scores depend whom you ask. Even the Educational Testing Service sends somewhat mixed messages. On page 4 of their document "GRE Guide to the Use of Scores," the ETS insists that the test measures skills—specifically "verbal reasoning, quantitative reasoning, critical thinking and analytical writing skills."[8] They emphasize this point by placing it inside a large, gray text box within the running text. On the cover of that same document, however, in fine, italicized print in the upper right-hand corner, are the words "Assess Ability."

Rebecca Zwick, author of *Fair Game: The Use of Standardized Tests in Higher Education,* acknowledges that if the SAT is the "grandchild" of intelligence tests, then the GRE and other graduate admissions exams are "certainly cousins." Designed to assess skills that are useful apart from disciplinary content, Zwick argues that the GRE General Test, along with the SAT, LSAT, and GMAT, tends toward measuring *aptitude,* whereas the ACT and MCAT assess specific *subject matter learning*.[9] However, ACT and SAT scores are highly correlated, and both are promoted as predictors of college grades. The "IQ test versus achievement test debate is a tempest in a teapot," she writes, a minor distinction that has been blown out of proportion. Zwick quotes sociologist Christopher Jencks:

> Many people—including federal judges—think that both intelligence and aptitude are innate traits . . . Yet almost all psychologists now agree that while an individual's scores on an intelligence or aptitude test depend partly on his or her genetic makeup, it also reflects a multitude of environmental influences.

Zwick concludes that neither intelligence *nor* standardized admissions tests measure "native intelligence" or ability.[10]

Notably, across the committees I observed, only in the case of one applicant to one department was a general impression of intelligence—along with its perceived indicators—enough to generate consensus about admission. This individual had perfect scores on all three sections of the GRE and a 4.0 GPA from Harvard University. Unbeknownst to him, he became an inside joke for the committee when a senior—and typically dour—professor declared him a "freaking genius." For the remainder of their meeting, he became the standard against which many others were jokingly compared.

Qualities of Thought and Mind

Offhand comments like labeling an applicant a "freaking genius" can speak volumes about engrained assumptions, and they highlight the tendency to reduce complicated profiles to stereotypes. During interviews, I therefore probed respondents to describe more fully what intelligence means for scholars in their discipline and how they recognize it when they see it. In these comments, participants indicated that intelligence is not only something that students have, but something that students *do*—something that one embodies and practices. Judging these dimensions of intelligence was thought to be best accomplished by evaluating students' experience with research. As summarized in Table 6, they spoke about intellectual dispositions as well as qualities of thought such as novelty, rigor, and insight. A common theme in the humanities was to value qualities of mind that

Table 6   Qualities of Thought and Mind Cited in Relation to Intelligence

Novelty	Rigor	Insight	Intellectual Dispositions	Intellectual Virtues
Creative	Analytic	Deep	Spark	Humility
Curious	Systematic	Reflective	Passion	Honesty
Imaginative	Theoretical	Perceptive	Intensity	Courage
Original	Independent	Intuitive	Grit	
Open-minded	Abstract	"Big picture perspective"		
	Critical	"Can see questions"		
	Precise			
	Useful			

were fundamentally moral in nature, which I characterize as intellectual virtues.

Intellectual dispositions. Notable among the qualities of mind faculty that care about are intellectual dispositions, in which reviewers attributed personal characteristics to the ways in which applicants think, research, or otherwise approach their subject matter. Paradoxically, such dispositions capture what some would call noncognitive qualities of students' cognitive engagement. For example, when speaking of applicants whose approach to learning or research displayed "spark," faculty used words like "lively," "energetic," "enthusiastic," and "excited." I observed that perceptions of spark could be especially important as a counterbalance to skepticism about atypical academic trajectories or subpar test scores or grades. In one philosophy committee, which held high standards for prior disciplinary socialization, the committee chair successfully advocated for an applicant who had attended a small college in the Deep South and lacked formal training in philosophy. Self-taught, this applicant nonetheless demonstrated exceptional insight and energy in her writing statement, the chair argued, and was potentially a "diamond in the rough" who could inject fresh perspective into a corner of the discipline that sorely needed it. In the biology program, which was slightly less selective than most others in the study, faculty worked hard to recruit students on the basis of spark. The chair emphasized their interest in students whom other programs might ignore but who would still likely be successful.

Spark was closely related to affective intellectual dispositions such as "intellectual intensity" and "passion," which were frequently mentioned in answers to my question about what intelligence means in one's discipline.

Other respondents made direct links with love, such as "You're supposed to love truth" and that one should be "in love with research."

The analogy with love is instructive in that it draws out the distinctly personal, relational elements of intellectual life that scholars experience but rarely discuss. In her book *Professing to Learn,* higher education scholar Anna Neumann used vivid faculty narratives to illustrate affective and aesthetic aspects of scholarship that contribute to ongoing scholarly learning. She concludes that the "construction of subject matter knowledge is hardly free of emotion and is intimately connected with themselves."[11] Neumann's participants relayed stories of rare, but powerful, "experiences of passionate thought" wherein the beauties inherent in their work eclipsed the usual struggles that accompanied research, their understanding intensified, and they felt a sense of exhilaration or intimacy with the subject matter. As fleeting as these experiences may be, their inspiration fuels everyday academic life, she argues, and they matter deeply to what it means to be a scholar.[12] It may be that faculty were seeking in prospective students glimmers of the same passionate spirit that animates their own work and careers.

In the unique relationship that scholars have with their work, however, participants shared with me that intelligent scholars are not only "*gripped by* whatever they're working on." They also *stick with* the research process when the going gets tough. Respondents associated "intellectual grit" and "tenacity" with intelligence, especially when considering the long haul of the PhD and today's competitive research climate. Determination and resolve were difficult qualities to infer from the records of these mostly young students. For those applicants with more experience, however, "persistence in a research area" could signal persistence through the dissertation. For others, comments in letters of recommendation that an applicant was "driven," "hardworking," "steady," or "reliable" in research offered hints that a student might have the intellectual determination that academic life demands. To extrapolate from such evidence and become persuaded that such hints were more signal than noise, reviewers might also look to patterns of grades and courses within a student's transcript.

Intellectual virtues. In the humanities, participants actively sought intellectual virtue in applicants. Moral qualities such as "intellectual honesty," "intellectual courage," and "intellectual humility" came up regularly in relation to how applicants seemed to manage their subjectivity and approach the work of interpretation. Faculty believed intellectual courage could be inferred from applicants' willingness and ability to undertake contentious, complicated, or otherwise difficult projects. They also commented on the value of intellectual honesty and humility. Students could display these qualities in writing samples through their respect for opposing viewpoints and disconfirming evidence, and in sensitivity to how their own background potentially biased their interpretations. For the clearest description of these qualities, I quote at length Jack, a senior professor of classics:

> *Jack:* One thing you're very much looking for is a kind of intellectual honesty that's a real feature of quality-of-mind.
> *JP: What does that mean?*
> *Jack:* Above all, that means looking at reasons not to agree with what you're saying and treating them fairly. That means making nuanced arguments instead of overstated ones . . . *[Pause]* It also involves a certain humility about—you know, if you are arguing about what a certain expression simply means at a semantic level. You know if important scholars have taken views with which you disagree, you are looking for people who have the courage to disagree but also are aware that . . . there are people with whom one does not disagree, likely.
> *JP: That's very helpful. I also heard intellectual courage mentioned a couple of times.*
> *Jack:* Right. They go—they're not at all the same. But, do they typically go together? Yeah, I think so. A lack of profound intellectual honesty is often a form of cowardice because the kind of intellectual honesty I'm thinking about requires accepting that you can be wrong—that others' views are often entitled to quite a lot of respect. And to be able to be aware of that and still say what you think is at least one important form of intellectual courage.

In many cases, faculty folded specific qualities of thought and mind into broader judgments of intelligence. In a handful of cases in the humanities, however, they became bottom-line considerations in wrestling with borderline candidates. For example, in the classics program, the committee debated two applicants from the same, moderately selective public university in New England, and ultimately made their decision on the basis of an applicant's failure to embody intellectual humility. Jack introduced the first candidate to the committee by reminding them, "He got his degree in 2010 and has been a legal assistant since then. Has also been a volunteer editor for a classics website."

Bill noted, "His letters praise 'diligence,' and that he is 'on the way to originality.' "

"He's bright and lively," Linda, the department chair, followed. "Has been to Athens. There are errors in his Greek, but he seems to have intellectual courage. He's curious and is an original character. He has studied with my old student."

Jack reminded them that the applicant grew up in rural New England, and commented, "The place is ideal in some ways for pursuit of classics. Very pastoral."

Moving on to the next applicant, Linda expressed amazement that the student had checked the "some high school or less" box to describe his parents' education level. Jack said, "He seems bright enough. A little naive. Paper seemed misguided but intelligent. It's a good treatment of a new problem."

Another noted that he "qualified as a diversity candidate," and Sandy admitted, "I've rated him lower than you all have. The letters stressed drive and energy more than talent."

"On general principle, it would be nice to have someone from that part of New England, from a modest state university," Linda added. "It's impressive that they can produce two reasonable applicants."

Yet with an entering cohort of only four students, the committee agreed that they should not admit both—that they needed to choose just one. As they dug into the details of the applications, a committee member discovered a line in one of the letters, describing the second applicant as insensitive to what fellow students thought of his "academic zeal." Worried that this alleged lack of intellectual humility might encourage competitiveness in their small graduate student community, they opted to admit the first applicant. Qualities of mind, which in the humanities included intellectual virtues, could thus build up or break down a committee's enthusiasm and trust in an applicant.

Research Experience and Disciplinary Engagement

Implicit judgments of intelligence often emerged through inferences made from GRE scores, but it was through letters of recommendation and applicants' records of research engagement that participants gleaned discipline-specific evidence of intelligence. Consider the comments from Vincent, a biologist:

> JP: *What do you think intelligence means here in biology?*
> Vincent: With how fast science is moving, you have to be able to keep
>   thinking about the next thing. And so students who can read primary
>   literature and kind of take several papers and distill them and put together
>   an idea for what the next experiment should be is really important . . . I'm
>   looking for students that can critically think about the scientific literature
>   and students who also have good hands in the lab who can carry out
>   those experiments they think of.

Intelligence may be fundamental, but it is only valuable to the extent that it can be demonstrated and thus recognized. In the following narrative from William, an economist, I highlight qualities of thought in italic, disciplinary engagement in bold, and overall impressions in bold italic.

> *JP: What does intelligence mean in economics?*
> *William:* That's a hard question. There are obviously a lot of dimensions of intelligence . . . First of all, they all have some basic level of **mathematical sophistication,** but that can vary a lot. There are people successful in economics who were **mathematically brilliant.** They were **International Math Olympians or they were Putnam exam winners** and particularly in economic theory . . . Some of them probably could have been successful mathematicians. I'm certainly not in that category *{Laughing}* even though I was a math major. But then other people are intelligent in the sense that they *think really creatively.* And other people are intelligent in the sense that they're **really good with statistical patterns and data.** You're thinking about **how to use data to get at a particular question** . . . You're looking for the combination of **skills that will serve you well to do research in the field** and it's some sort of combination. In every field you want people who **think super clearly** . . . who are just incredibly *clear, logical, precise thinkers.* Although to be honest, there are people who are successful researchers who think clearly, but they have a hard time articulating clearly, but *they're so brilliant.*

In the same way that successful economists bring a unique blend of tools, knowledge, and perspective to their scholarly work, the intelligent applicant was understood to be one whose combination of preparation, achievements, skills, and qualities of thought signaled capability for producing exceptional research. For those students who demonstrated substantive research experience in their application materials, the committee could more easily recognize those qualities and, thus, associate them with intelligence.

As William noted, "in every field you want people who think super clearly." It was only in humanities, however, that applicants submitted research that faculty could use to personally judge lucidity of thought.[13] Faculty in the humanities scrutinized writing samples with a fine-toothed comb for evidence of this quality and for evidence of fresh perspective on an issue of importance to the field. Some social scientists I spoke with lamented the lack of a writing sample from their applicants, while also acknowledging that its absence came with positive trade-offs such as reducing the time required for each file's review, eliminating ambiguity about how independent the writing process had been, and obviating the need to debate whether co-authored work merited the same consideration as a single-authored paper. Moreover, in the social and natural sciences, an applicant could often demonstrate clear thinking through facility with quantitative reasoning as well as the written word.

The importance of research experience. Patricia Gumport, vice provost for graduate education at Stanford University, wrote that organized research is the foundation of American graduate education, and selectivity "the key ingredient reinforcing the pivotal role of the graduate school as a site for professional socialization and disciplinary reproduction."[14] Especially in doctoral programs that strive to develop and produce future "stewards of the discipline," it is therefore only logical that evidence of research experience would serve as a foundation for admissions selections.[15] And indeed, I found that when judging among students on the short list, experience with and potential to advance the discipline were among the most important considerations that committee members brought to bear on their decisions. A professor of biology explained:

> Probably the most important criteria or variable that I look at is whether the student has been engaged in research. Because that's really what we're trying to figure out: whether the student can successfully finish a dissertation research project . . . It's not to say that I would automatically rule out a student who had no research experience. But I think my point of view is probably fairly common amongst most of the faculty.

The physics admissions chair used even stronger language. "If the person hasn't taken advantage of [research] opportunities, it's effectively the kiss of death, at least from my point of view. I think that probably speaks for most of the people I've talked with about this process."

With widening opportunities for undergraduate research, faculty increasingly expect that at the point of admission students will already have had some research experience, but they are not always sure how to accurately draw meaning from the experience that students report. There were two common refrains I heard on this topic, and both related to the broader challenge of incomplete information that plagues admissions decision making.

One interpretive challenge with respect to student research experience is the question of how well a student's past experience signals current skills or future performance. A number of professors expressed to me that they would ideally like to replicate in admissions their process for hiring faculty or postdoctoral fellows, in which reviewers judge the quality of completed manuscripts as a signal of future contributions. Unfortunately, forecasting a student's contributions from the admission application and prior research experience was much more difficult. Substantial learning has yet to take place, for one, and the nature of skills and dispositions a student may have gained through undergraduate research experience are difficult to discern with any accuracy. Faculty in the humanities may have some direct evidence in the writing sample, but elsewhere, reviewers were forced to make inferences from applicants' curricula vitae, interviews, and the testimonies offered in letters of recommendation and statement of purpose.

Another common challenge of interpreting student research experience concerned uncertainty about the relative quality of experiences themselves. As knowledge spreads among college students that research experience is desirable for graduate school admission, more students are pursuing these opportunities and highlighting them in their applications. In some fields, especially those in STEM, undergraduate research experience is well-institutionalized in the structure of access to advanced education and becoming a scholar. In response, faculty feel compelled to "sort out the quality of undergraduate research experiences." The gold standard, which several reviewers offhandedly called "real research," was understood to consist of following a study from conception to either publication or presentation at a national association. Exhibiting some degree of independence was also critical to "real research." By contrast, some students' research experience was assumed to involve little more than "pressing a button" to analyze a faculty advisor's data.

An effect of trying to sort out the relative quality of student research experiences has been to raise faculty standards about what is necessary to qualify a student for the research training that doctoral education offers. The depth and breadth of research experiences available today do indeed vary widely, with opportunities of course more widely available for students who attend research universities. Reviewers from several of the programs admitted their concerns about the rising expectations for research experience. One, who asked that I not name her discipline, argued that desiring a degree of independence is understandable, but that admitting increasingly pre-professional researchers threatens to undermine the developmental, educational mission of doctoral education.

Among these ten programs, rising expectations of research experience were especially salient in philosophy and the natural sciences. About one-third of the philosophers in each of the two programs I studied worried that doctoral education was becoming overly professionalized. Whereas successful applicants might once have been able to submit a slightly revised term paper, today's admissions committees expected something much more sophisticated, original, and polished. Writing samples should demonstrate the author's courage and capacity to—in philosophers' jargon for how the discipline advances—make a "move" that shifts discourse in the field. However, several acknowledged that this expectation presumes a level of socialization that privileged applicants who had received considerable training and editorial support. In the natural science programs I studied, a strong base of research experience was valuable because they did not have structures in place for graduate students to learn the basics; most students engage as a full collaborator on faculty-supervised research projects from their first day onward.

A concrete example of a committee discussing a specific applicant's research record may be useful here as an illustration. Lara had applied to astrophysics, and her curriculum vitae listed multiple research publications accumulated in a full-time research job at a major public university after completing her bachelor's degree. This record sounded impressive to me at first, but the committee was strangely unimpressed. So quiet were they about this unusually productive student, I wondered if there was something they were leaving unspoken in my presence. Then they began discussing the very technical, task-oriented nature of involvement in research, according to the letters of recommendation. At this, the reason for their ambivalence became clear. After scrutinizing her background, an associate professor asked, "Is it our goal to bring in someone who is very productive and can be productive for me? Or to select those who can be leaders in the field? The application provides evidence of coding skill, not science."

This shifted their discussion to the similarities and differences between admitting graduate students and hiring postdoctoral fellows, and how these activities seemed to be increasingly similar in their aims. The committee chair eventually brought their conversation back around to Lara, asserting, "What is missing is evidence of scientific intuition, scientific leadership."

Another associate professor added, "I find no evidence of creativity or any synonyms for it in the letters." Ironically, how the committee read her wealth of technical research experience became her Achilles' heel. Because she had years of experience, the committee felt that her potential for scientific leadership, intuition, or creativity should be plain to see. The committee did not offer her an interview.

Conclusion

Scholars have argued that the informal mental models about intelligence that each of us hold are at least as important as formal measures of intelligence in how social goods and opportunities are distributed. By their very nature implicit, these informal views often go unexamined. I found that there were two dimensions to the implicit model common to many faculty members in this study. They described intelligence both as something that a person has or is in a general sense ("they're so brilliant"), and as something that one embodies and does (dispositions and "skills that will serve you well to do research in the field").

It is possible that a lack of clarity about disciplinary boundaries or quality standards may compel scholars in low-consensus disciplines, generally, to cloak the unknown thing they are looking for in vague words whose value to the whole community is incontrovertible.[16] But comparing across fields, professors expressed specific ideas about intelligence that reflected their varying disciplinary cultures. In the humanities, faculty assessed how students seemed to manage subjectivity, inferring from this such virtues as intellectual honesty and intellectual courage. In one case, doubts about a student's intellectual humility—which they inferred through a single line in a letter of recommendation—even became the deciding factor in that student's rejection. By contrast, it was a strongly quantitative political science program that admitted a student dubbed a "freaking genius" on the basis of his perfect test scores and perfect grades from a famous university. A study recently published in *Science* demonstrated that disciplines vary in gender and racial inequality based on whether scholars in that field believe innate brilliance is necessary for success. Embedded beliefs about intelligence within the disciplines are thus an important part of the academic opportunity structure, and arguably a topic worthy of further research.[17]

When describing to me what intelligence means within their disciplines, many participants used active, detailed language to describe specific research-related skills and qualities of thinking that facilitate scholarly work. To divine this aspect of intelligence, the applicant's record of disciplinary engagement was key. Committees might get excited about what they perceived as "raw intellectual horsepower," but they also wanted to see intellectual dispositions conducive to creative, insightful, rigorous research. Their ideal applicant would have a clear record of engagement in the discipline with which to assess these intangible qualities. Their goal was to admit students who were not only capable of passing their courses, but whom they could envision becoming respected scholars. As one economist put it, ideal doctoral students are "the smartest, most creative people you can find."

In envisioning applicants' possible futures as scholars, I was struck by my participants' almost single-minded concern with potential for research. Only in the natural sciences did they even mention an applicant's potential for teaching, and no one speculated on applicants' potential for service or advising. This emphasis on research may simply have been a matter of the social context. In elite doctoral programs located in research universities, teaching is fundamental, but research and writing are sacred. Regardless of how many people read or cite them, one's publications create a physical, indelible legacy of scholarship. More pragmatically, research is the activity rewarded in research universities' systems of evaluation for hiring, tenure, and promotion. It follows that research would also play a formative role in evaluations for graduate admissions. Over and above their possible futures as instructors, faculty sought applicants with potential to make independent, creative contributions to their collective intellectual record.

Although faculty could speak eloquently about intelligence as a disciplinary cultural practice, it was the other dimension of intelligence— something innate, decontextualized, and perceived through general impressions and GRE scores—that dominated the "smart talk" that I observed in committee deliberations. Ideas like "native intelligence" and "raw intellectual horsepower" were also the most frequent type of answer to my interview question about what GRE scores signal. Such thinking is reminiscent of Harvard law professor Lani Guinier's critique of admission test scores' misuse:

> It is as if this test functions as a thermometer. And you give each person the test as if you were taking their smartness temperature. And that, unfortunately, is not how the test functions. Even the test makers do not claim it is a thermometer of smartness. All they claim is that it correlates with first year college grades.[18]

ETS has taken steps to revise the GRE away from the format of an IQ test. Its most recent overhaul, which they have promoted as a more "friendly . . . flexible test-taking experience," reduced the amount of rote vocabulary required for high scores on the Verbal Reasoning section of the exam, among other changes.[19] Their revisions have the potential to reduce group disparities and better distinguish among test takers on the upper end of the score range, but improvements to the instrument will not change how faculty interpret the scores.

From professors' hedging about what GRE scores mean, and from the nuanced views of discipline-specific intelligence that they articulated, it is clear that many of them possess a more sophisticated mental model than the one implied in their discussions with one another. Most know that GRE scores are only modestly correlated with measures of intelligence, and that admission tests are not designed to measure it at all. Yet in contrast to some thoughtful and measured discussions I observed about other topics, smart talk in committee meetings was off the cuff, to the point of appearing performative. Why? I have spent some time trying to make sense of this, because faculty falling back, in practice, on a more simplistic view of intelligence than the one they actually hold could be seen as a significant flaw for the integrity and legitimacy of admissions evaluations.

Reflecting on my own assumptions as a researcher in light of Goffman's dramaturgical theory was instructive.[20] Compared to faculty perspectives obtained through recorded interviews, which might be tainted by participants' desire to express socially desirable views, I viewed the admissions meetings as an opportunity to see behind the curtain and engage with "backstage" faculty behavior. But committee members themselves may have conceived of their group meetings differently. For them, the meetings were in some ways the *front* stage of admissions work. The meetings were a place to perform evaluation using roles and scripts that they thought their colleagues would interpret as socially appropriate. Awarding ratings to individual files was a more private, backstage type of work. Further, it is impossible for me to know what email communication transpired in the nine programs in which I was not on the committee email list, or what additional deliberations about students may have occurred in hallway conversations or private office meetings. To the extent committee members thought of their meetings as a site for front stage behavior, their glib associations of GRE scores with intelligence (as described here and in Chapter 2) can be understood as performance of an evaluative script and scholarly role that they expected their colleagues would find appropriate.

And indeed, whether it was due to either mutual agreement about its appropriateness or faculty conflict aversion, I observed that it was rare for people to speak up and correct their colleagues for uncritically using GRE scores as proxy for either the intellect that graduate school requires or a student's likelihood of success. Current research indicates higher scores are positively associated with first-year grades, but the relationship is more complicated when analyzed in terms of real grades earned. A compendium of research published in 2014 by ETS reported that less than half (43 percent) of the students who earned combined GRE scores in the top quartile also earned first-year grades in the top quartile. GRE scores explain only about 10 percent of variance in first-year grades, and they have only modest relationships with formal measures of intelligence and longer-term outcomes.[21]

A more sophisticated treatment among decision makers is therefore critical, both to improve the integrity of admissions review and because misconstrual of the GRE as a "thermometer of smartness" may feed racial and gender stereotypes that can contribute to test score disparities. A large body of research has found that women and non-Asian students of color may underperform on standardized tests due to underlying fears of earning scores that will conform to negative stereotypes about their identity group's intellectual abilities. For students subject to this risk, which is known as stereotype threat, the test score is a noisier signal of their skills. And in a painfully ironic twist, the threat of underperformance is especially strong among students who feel most closely identified with academic success. The prompts included in test instructions appear to shape susceptibility to stereotype threat. One of the first experiments on this phenomenon, which was published by Claude Steele and Joshua Aronson, administered a test to students that included items from the GRE. They found that mentioning race or ethnicity in the instructions induced stereotype threat in African American students.[22] In contrast, a recent study eliminated performance gaps simply by highlighting a test's fairness within the instructions.[23]

There is also some evidence of stereotype threat's flip side, stereotype lift, in which a *privileged* group's knowledge of common stereotypes about intelligence elevates their self-worth, thereby boosting their test performance.[24] Taken together, this research helps explain why test score disparities may persist despite structural changes to the instrument and narrowing gaps on other academic indicators, such as grades. Scores capture qualities of test takers, to be sure, but also qualities of the environment in which the test is taken, including "threat[s] in the air" about how intellect will be judged. On average, test scores from historically privileged groups may therefore be persistently inflated, and those from historically marginalized groups somewhat depressed. To strengthen review and reduce inequities, the search for intelligent life needs to extend beyond these familiar forms of achievement. Reviewers need to attune their gaze to see intellectual strengths they may have previously failed to notice and potential in the discipline that can be nurtured through continued learning.[25] The thorough, open-minded, self-critical approach to evaluating writing samples that I observed in the philosophy programs encouraged me that such review is possible.

Across programs, many took for granted that an implicit task of admissions is to identify and select the brightest students in the pool. How can something as difficult to pin down as intelligence play so fundamental a role? An important part of the answer, I think, is that intelligence is homologous to the broader idea of merit. In both cases, faculty committees look for and weigh markers of a quality they struggle to define, whose meaning escapes consensus, and about which they have little research knowledge. Yet because merit and intelligence are central to excellence and to scholars' own sense of academic self-worth and belonging, the very act of striving for these interests brings legitimacy to the selection process, even if it is done in flawed ways. This striving means committees make many inferences and guesses based on limited evidence and the comforting, if spurious, precision of quantitative metrics. As Chapter 6 will emphasize, those inferences are especially tricky to make when evaluating across cultural contexts and when evaluating international applicants.

CHAPTER SIX

International Students and Ambiguities of Holistic Review

The way international applications work is that there is a cloud of random applications, but good applications come in pipelines.
—BIOLOGY ADMISSIONS CHAIR

GROWING DEMAND for American higher education from international students is a trend that spans fields of study, institutional types, and undergraduate, master's, and doctoral programs alike.[1] Between 1900 and 2000, the number of college-aged students enrolled in postsecondary education exploded from 500,000 to 100 million, a stunning 200-fold increase. Decolonization and the expansion of democracy and human rights help explain widening participation in higher education, along with economic, scientific, and technological development. In countries around the world, sociologists Evan Schofer and John Meyer argue, these broad trends have converged to institutionalize a new model of society in which elite classes established around "schooled knowledge" have replaced traditional landowning, business, political, and military elites. In the United States, adults with graduate degrees now comprise almost 50 percent of those in the top 5 percent of the wealth distribution, up from 28 percent in 1989.[2] Colleges and universities are organizational lynchpins to these trends, with the establishment of new universities around the world cultivating demand for well-trained faculty and U.S. doctoral programs providing that training ground for students from across the globe.

International students have driven rising applications, enrollment, and degrees awarded in U.S. graduate education. Overall first-time graduate enrollment has grown by an average of about 3 percent each year since 2001, largely due to international students, with Chinese students leading the

Table 7   Percent Change in International Offers of Admission by Country or
Region of Origin

	2010–2011	2011–2012	2012–2013	2013–2014
International Total	+9	+9	+9	+9
Country of Origin				
China	+21	+20	+5	0
India	+2	0	+27	+25
South Korea	−2	0	−10	−9
Taiwan	—	−4	−3	−6
Canada	—	+9	−1	+4
Mexico	—	+6	0	−1
Brazil	—	+6	+46	+98
Region of Origin				
Africa	—	+10	+7	+3
Europe	—	+2	0	+2
Middle East	+16	+17	+12	+9

Note: Prior to 2011, data were not collected for Taiwan, Canada, Mexico, Brazil, Africa, and Europe.
Source: Council of Graduate Schools, 2013.

way.[3] Of the 220,000 international students enrolled in U.S. graduate programs in 2013, 34 percent were from China alone. In the last four decades, the percentage of doctorates awarded in the United States to international students has more than doubled.[4] Table 7 reports the percentage change in offers of admission to international students from U.S. universities, including the years of data collection on this project.

International Students and Organizational Interests

Enrollment management is big business in higher education today, and for good reason. Colleges and universities use the composition of their student bodies to serve a variety of organizational interests and to signal their priorities to stakeholders. Yet pursuing one set of interests may require concessions on another, as illustrated in John Cheslock and Rick Kroc's analysis of the trade-offs for higher education institutions among fair access, containing costs, and strengthening academic profile.[5] In this vein, whether one sees rising international student enrollment as a positive trend for U.S. graduate programs may depend upon whether or not one's metric for quality is equitable access, financial security, or strength of academic profile.

International graduate students clearly benefit the United States as future "contributors to the U.S. economy as professors, researchers, and entrepreneurs." One recent calculation estimates that international student enrollment has brought $24.7 billion to the U.S. economy and turned U.S. higher education into a top service-sector export.[6] Colleges and universities often embrace the demand from international students, as well, both for financial and intellectual reasons. Public institutions in particular rely on tuition revenue from non-resident students to offset declining state appropriations, with few states capping tuition increases for out-of-state students and international students ineligible for most forms of federal and state financial aid. International students have also helped sustain faculty research in STEM disciplines amid the declining share of domestic students pursuing such majors. International students therefore fill important gaps in graduate education today.[7]

Faculty in highly ranked graduate programs may also see international student enrollment as a strategy for negotiating two pressures—increasing diversity and maintaining a strong academic profile. As I reported in Chapter 2, programs that struggled to recruit U.S.-born Latino, black, and Native American students with extremely high GRE scores would use well-credentialed international students in one of two ways. Some programs, such as economics and physics, elevated national origin to the level of race/ethnicity, gender, and socioeconomic status as a type of valued diversity. Doing so was consistent with those fields' disciplinary cultures, for the major research initiatives in high-energy physics today are deeply international endeavors and some of the most prestigious economists and economics programs are in Europe, not the United States. A strategy used in some other programs was to claim a strong commitment to racial/ethnic diversity, but downplay whether they were attaining that diversity through enrollment of domestic versus international students. In both scenarios, the program reframed how international students "counted" in programs' efforts to present a diverse and conventionally high-achieving image.

Especially in STEM fields, a commonly expressed concern is that international students may be crowding out domestic students. In 2012, 54.7 percent of international students enrolled in graduate programs in STEM fields compared to just 17.3 percent of U.S. students. Yet by controlling for self-selection into graduate study in various fields, research by higher education scholar Liang Zhang found more support in *non*-STEM fields for the displacement of domestic students. Some graduate programs try to avoid crowding out domestic students by giving special attention to international students whose applications indicate independent sources of funding for their education. Like institutional diversity fellowships for domestic students, independent funds for foreign nationals expand program capacity, allowing them to enroll more students than they anticipated and to avoid scaling back their support of U.S. students. Yet with whites composing a declining share of the national population, some scholars note that achieving diversity in U.S. postsecondary education by increasing international student enrollment does little to shift the needle on educational inequality in the United States. Higher education and law scholar Michael Olivas, for example, has argued that the trend to establish overseas branch campuses diverts attention from the needs of persistently underserved communities here in the United States.[8]

For graduate programs like those I studied, all of these countervailing forces converge to make rising demand from international students a bit of a conundrum for enrollment management. These programs are committed to admitting students with full funding and to maintaining extremely strong academic profiles. Many could fill their entire cohorts with conventional academic achievers from outside the United States. However, their values are to some degree symbolized by the backgrounds of their students, and central though it may be, conventional achievement is not their only value. They strive to create cohorts of students that are "balanced" on a variety of dimensions, and many feel obligated to take steps toward reducing racial inequalities. Every program is different, but under these conditions, I found that there are limits to the number of international students that most faculty feel they can legitimately admit.

Ambiguities of Reviewing International Student Applications

The swelling volume of applications from international students poses an additional challenge: How should they all be reviewed? Applications from foreign students for U.S. graduate programs have increased for nine straight years (by 10 percent in 2014), and overall applications to graduate programs in research universities have increased at an average annual rate of 5.3 percent for the last decade. For the typical admissions committee, this steady growth amounted to a daunting 72 percent more applications to review in 2011 compared to 2001.[9] The greater the volume of applications, the greater the strain it places on the system of holistic review. Evaluation can easily become routinized rather than reflective.

Internationalization also complicates how faculty interpret applicants' files because students come from widely varying cultural and national contexts whose distinctions are mostly unknown to faculty.[10] Should the metrics used to assess international applicants be the same or different from those used to assess American students? If different standards are warranted, should Canadian, Cambodian, and Chinese applicants' files also be read differently? Should faculty expect higher quantitative GRE scores from countries with deep cultures of test preparation? If so, how much higher should those scores be, and do the usual concerns about gender disparities apply? How well do indicators of English skills in an application correspond to practical fluency? Should a letter of recommendation that comes across as odd be understood as the product of different cultural norms or a red flag about the applicant? These are just a smattering of the many questions that faculty worry about in trying to construct an equitable process of review.

In this chapter I explore how faculty wrestle with a few of these ambiguities.[11] First I discuss the difficulties that faculty most frequently reported when tasked with reviewing applications from international students. Then, in light of previous research that suggests that ambiguities create conditions in which stereotypical views thrive,[12] and having shown that some common assumptions about Asian students correspond to the "model minority" paradigm, I offer a brief review of current research about test score validity and cheating among international students. It would be impossible to remove ambiguity from the admissions process. Nevertheless, having the best available information about circumstances in which it tends to crop up can keep us from succumbing to the stereotypes and cognitive biases that ambiguity tends to encourage.

A note about labels: Students from China accounted for 29 percent of all international applications to U.S. universities in 2011–2012, the second year of data collection in this project,[13] so it should come as no surprise that when faculty spoke about the difficulty of evaluating international applicants, they frequently referred to "Chinese applicants," often tying them to Taiwanese, Korean, and Japanese applicants under the label "East Asian." Unless mentioned otherwise, faculty narratives focus on applicants from this group.

Quantitative GRE Scores and Admissions Ethics

What should reviewers make of international students' quantitative GRE results? As I have discussed, faculty relied upon very high GRE scores as one of a few criteria that could reduce the pool to a size for which close reading of the application felt manageable. Using GRE scores to winnow the pool was convenient, and they treated it as a standardized signal of one's intelligence, belonging, and likelihood of success. However, they did not always see scores this way for international students, whose formal training in basic skills and test preparation might be different than American students'. "The educational infrastructure leading up to this test is not the same across countries," one physical scientist put it, "so we set the bar at different places depending on the country and gender." A social scientist born in Italy commented more specifically on the relative quality of test preparation that he believed to characterize different regions:

> European students tend to be pretty bad in performing in the standardized tests . . . They don't get exposed to this kind of test in their regular curriculum. For example, I'd never done a test in my life until I had to face the GRE . . . [So] we tend to underweigh the scores of students from South Asia for the very simple reason that we know that some of them actually go to school to do the GRE for months. There's not a lot of signal in the scores from South Asian students, especially students from China.

His perspective was hardly unique. A philosopher also shared, "There certainly is a kind of stereotypical *[Pauses, apparently catching himself]* Chinese student who will have astronomical test scores."

With a large pool of East and South Asian applicants who have high quantitative reasoning scores, many participants came to set higher GRE score expectations of Chinese, Korean, and Indian applicants than of American and European applicants. "If a kid from the PRC has not essentially . . . perfect scores on GRE exams," one linguist admitted, "they're regarded as probably brain dead." In a few fields, however, faculty read Chinese students' higher mean scores as a sign that the test was less useful for comparing them, to the point that some dismissed the scores entirely. Describing applicants from China, Japan, and Vietnam, a midcareer scientist who led his program's admissions effort noted:

> The scores on the standardized tests are just out-of-sight, just off the charts. So you can basically throw that out as a discriminator. They're all doing 90th percentile and above. The domestic students were all over the place so there was actually some spread, some dispersion . . . so you could use that more as one of the quantifiers.

Another, who had been born outside of the United States himself, said,

> To evaluate them [Chinese students] relative to Americans and Europeans is not so easy. The Americans will not push to take the prep on the GREs and sometimes do very poorly on them . . . If you had to admit them strictly on the basis of the GRE, we'd basically have . . . all the kids would be Chinese. There's no doubt about it.

His comments reflect a broader pattern of faculty attributing high scores from Asian students to a deep and powerful test-taking culture. This line of thinking branded students from China, in particular, as "trained to really achieve very high scores" and supported the notion that China's "test-preparation industry is second to none in the world," and a "well-developed machine."

Although standardized testing has a relatively short history in the United States, in China it dates back to the seventh century A.D. At that time, emperors created the Civil Service Examination to identify top performers and place them into high-ranking positions that bestowed "financial rewards, prestige, power, [and] fame." These highly consequential exams birthed an intense focus on rote memorization and test-taking skills, supported by a network of test-preparation schools and "test-coaching" books. As an informal system of shadow education, China's test preparatory infrastructure has evolved into a multimillion-dollar industry and a critical factor in students' process of applying to U.S. higher education programs.[14]

Thus, even as many professors had come to *expect* high scores of applicants from China, they also *distrusted* that those scores signaled the same things they stood for among American applicants. And without the weight of their associated cultural meanings, many faculty felt they must be taken with a grain of salt. Along with widespread questions about the amount of test preparation that went into producing student scores, participants openly expressed concern that GRE scores of students from China lacked credibility because "people game these things" and there may be cultural differences in what counts as fair test-taking, gaming the system, or outright cheating.

The suspicion that cheating may be quietly prevalent throughout China was a major concern for some reviewers. Lowering his spectacled eyes, one professor I interviewed asked me, "You *know* about the cheating, don't you?" I did in fact know a little about the recent cheating scandals, but because I also knew that his own research included some Chinese history, I applied the standard interviewing technique of feigning ignorance to keep him talking. In return for this bit of deception, I was treated to a brief history that dipped into the Civil Service Exam and *gao kao* (the National College Entrance Examination, or NCEE) as foundations of a culture in which students will push the boundaries of well-being and ethics to earn high scores.

During English-examination season, he said, it is not uncommon to find advertisements for "hired guns" (test takers) who charge students and their

families exorbitant prices to take the TOEFL exam or, in some cases, to provide answers in advance.[15] And in 2001 the Educational Testing Service,
which administers both the TOEFL and the GRE, filed a lawsuit against
China's largest and most profitable test preparation company for illegally
publishing ETS materials. Official correspondence from ETS notified graduate school deans across the United States of the situation.[16] The effect of
these scandals and others, he argued, has been to call into question *all* test
scores from Chinese applicants. In a system as competitive as this, when
"you're not 100 percent sure whether they are the person who took it,"
doubts about the trustworthiness of a test score could be used to discredit
the applicant in general.

Others distrusted the signaling value of the GRE for Asian applicants because it does not capture the work that they worry Asian students will
struggle with in graduate school: open-ended, creative scholarship. This pattern was exemplified in physics and astrophysics, two programs in which
most or all faculty expected strong performance on the GRE, especially the
Physics Subject test. William explained:

> If we let in all of the top GRE scores automatically, then we'd have all Chinese
> students, which aren't bad. But historically what's been found is that students
> from China tend to not succeed as well as their GRE scores would indicate
> since they've learned over the years to learn towards the test. This is a general-
> ization, but they generally don't perform as well as graduate students when it's
> more open-ended because they've learned—they've been trying to work towards
> a particular task their whole time in undergraduate. It's something that we look
> at, but we do a lot of talking about how it is an imperfect measure.

Another physicist discussed his perception of Chinese and Indian students'
scores in relation to the habits of mind that graduate school requires:

> It is incredibly rare for any American undergrad to score more than seventies
> or eighties in terms of percentile. Like 99th-percentile scores, invariably, are
> from China or India or something like that. But often the students aren't as
> successful, because what that proves is that they're really, really good at mem-
> orizing formulas and solving problems based on them. And the way physics is
> taught in—as I understand it from talking to people who went through that
> system in India and China—is, it is very rote . . . You will solve problems until
> you can solve them in your sleep . . . But if that's what you've been trained to
> do and you haven't been trained to think about things that aren't reducible to
> simple formulas, you'll have a lot of trouble in grad school.

A high GRE score might be earned through single-minded focus on rote
knowledge and by gaining familiarity with the type of questions the test
asks, but it offers no insight into the dispositions and skills that faculty as-

sociated with independent scholarship, nor the English-language skills they associated with real fluency.

In sum, the difficulty of disentangling test scores from the social context in which those scores were produced, combined with suspicions of fraud, made it difficult for faculty to trust Asian students' Quantitative GRE scores. One thing was clear: their scores must be interpreted differently than domestic students. Where many expressed worries that test preparation rendered Chinese students' scores suspect, not once did a respondent express similar concerns about formal test preparation courses convoluting the meaning of a wealthy American student's score. And although faculty emphasized the importance of interpreting GRE scores within a *national* context, most were reticent to interpret an African American's score differently than a European American's score, or a man's differently than a woman's.

The Search for Credible English Skills

Faculty also considered English-language fluency central to international students' academic preparation and potential, and many found it difficult to gauge the credibility of Chinese students' English skills using information contained within the application—namely, TOEFL and GRE scores and their personal statements. There was broad disciplinary variation in the reasons faculty gave for their concerns about English fluency. Physical scientists worried about student ability to teach undergraduate courses, whereas those in the social sciences and humanities wanted to avoid editing students' written work with a fine-toothed comb. A linguist recalled:

> A large proportion of our applicants are from other countries . . . We had a student like that who was really absolutely brilliant but who got here and wasn't successful because their English was not good enough. So with that kind of student, then, my primary concern is to make sure that their English is good enough, so that when they come to write their dissertation, they don't have to have somebody go over every sentence with them.

Remembering another student, a second linguist ruefully summarized, "He couldn't do *anything* because he couldn't speak English. It was awful. And you know, we only have four or five places, so it's awful to waste one on somebody who washed out in a year." A senior professor commented, "I get really tired of editing . . . so some people do get knocked because of their language." One person succinctly captured the ambivalence with which I heard many faculty describe Asian students. They tend to be "really bright and interested," she said, "but their English is just not good enough to keep up." As with their evaluations of domestic students, admissions committees hoped for students who would work hard, but not struggle too much, because struggling slows students down and drains faculty time and resources.

And like their interpretations of scores from the quantitative section of the GRE, some faculty admitted suspicions that Asian students' English skills were weaker than implied in the application because applicants had gamed or cheated the system, or had forged personal statements. One frankly put it, "I think there's something notorious out there. The TOEFL scores somehow can get jacked up." Like many of the assumptions I picked up on in our interviews, I probed respondents about what led them to believe this. Typically, they cited vague memories of publicity from the cheating scandals or memories of isolated instances in which students arrived on campus with subpar English skills. Several also discussed rumors of students contributing illegally to banks of GRE items after completing the exam or of hiring someone to stand in for them on the TOEFL or phone interviews. Recalling his experience at another university, a sociologist recounted:

> There were people applying from China who were getting 100 percent perfect scores on the verbal part. These are people for whom English is not only not their native language, but they don't live in an English-speaking country. And we found out later there apparently was all kinds of cheating going on.

Perfect TOEFL or GRE Verbal scores are simply not expected of Chinese students because of the context in which those students are growing up. Although the economics and physics committees liked to see extremely high or perfect Quantitative scores, none expected perfect Verbal or Writing GRE scores—even of American students. Therefore, when such scores showed up in the application of a U.S.-born student, it was a remarkable surprise, and when they appeared in a non-native English speaker's file, it was considered suspect. And, indeed, uncertainty about whether their GRE Verbal or TOEFL scores might be ethically tainted often cast doubt upon Chinese applicants' fluency, generally.

Those faculty who discussed efforts to gauge fluency from the application alone described it as an almost impossible task. In the sociology program, several faculty stated the perception that the best evidence for applicants from China was having studied in the United States, for having American transcripts and taken the GRE in the United States provided "a U.S. basis to judge them. They've done work in English." Some programs conducted video interviews with prospective international applicants to

Table 8   Patterns of Interviewing across Programs

Interviewed All Students on the Short List	Interviewed Only International Students on the Short List	No Interviews Conducted
Physics	Political Science	Economics
Astrophysics	Biology	Sociology
Linguistics	Philosophy	Classics

"deal with the paranoia" of admitting students with poor English fluency or inadequate research experience (see Table 8).

Portraits of Admissions Interviews

In two programs I had the chance to observe several of these interviews and the faculty debriefings that followed. For the first set I attended, three male professors of astrophysics huddled around a laptop in a nondescript conference room. They joked with one another that the time difference—which had students in China interviewing in the middle of the night—was a good test of interviewees' readiness for the rigors of graduate school. After connecting successfully, Victor, an associate professor born outside the United States, informally took the lead, and others only occasionally piped in. He congratulated the applicant—I will call her Chun—on making the short list, and gave her basic information about the number of applications they had received, the number they were interviewing, and what the selection process would be going forward. I noted that right from the beginning, the interview's tone was comfortable and conversational, like most interactions I had observed among this committee. The easygoing tone that Victor and the others set seemed to put Chun at ease.

Transitioning into the main topics of the interview, Victor said that the committee was "impressed" that she had worked with researchers in two major areas of the field. She responded that she was most "excited" about one of them, and spoke with some awe about just how much it was possible to know with recent advancements in methods and technology. What she may or may not have known was that the area she cited as a primary interest was far from the intellectual subject matter that two of the three committee members present examined. They asked her to talk about her research interests, and after briefly describing a line of inquiry, she added, a bit sheepishly, "I am open to learning anything in the first year." They assured her that they were not "expecting her to define a thesis," but by my read, they were looking for more detail than what she was giving.

I sat a few feet behind the committee members during the interview, and each time I looked up from the field notes I was taking, I could see she was wearing a wide grin. It appeared that she did not stop smiling from the moment the interview started until the time they disconnected from the video conference. I was reminded in the moment of William Tierney and Estela Bensimon's idea of "smile work," an impression management strategy that women sometimes employ to "fit into departments with a tradition of male dominance." Knowingly or unknowingly, women may present themselves as "pleasing and agreeable" in order to avoid being stereotyped as overly aggressive.[17] Her smiles were not lost on the committee. After finishing the interview and disconnecting, they leaned back to debrief. They discussed her "very nice personality," with one remarking that she was "glowing." One admitted he hoped that "she would go into greater detail" about her research, and in the only comment about language, another commented that she was "not the most articulate person we've interviewed."

"Good but not great . . . Maybe not as serious about us as some," the committee chair concluded, to nods from the others. My read of the debriefing was that they wanted to like Chun because she seemed so very likable, but that they did not see her as sufficiently professional, at least when compared with others whom they had interviewed. Interestingly, none of their comments related to her English skills, which they previously shared with me was a primary motivation for the video interviews, or other issues specific to her status as an international applicant.

Finishing up their conversation in the minutes before the next interview, two of the committee members commented on gender dynamics they had observed in interviews over the years. Victor said he felt women tended to give concise responses and "speak only when they know what they are talking about" whereas men will "just keep talking to convince you that they know what they're talking about." It was not clear whether they made these comments because I was in the room or because questions about the depth of Chun's responses hung in the air after her interview, but it was clear that the pattern they noted with women had been true of Chun. Similarly, the pattern they attributed to men was evident in the next interview, with Bradley, a male in his thirties.

The two other committee members joined the huddle to participate in Bradley's interview. They may have judged Chun "good, but not great" after her interview, but that was the general impression of Bradley held by two of the five before his interview began, largely because of an unconventional trajectory into the discipline (he had worked for several years in the arts) and his undergraduate education at a moderately selective public university. He had just barely made the short list, and they wanted to video interview him to gather more information about his background. The two skeptics wanted to be present to take a closer look, and the three who were already impressed wanted to attend out of curiosity—and to make sure the skeptics did not grill Bradley too harshly. By the end of the interview, however, he had completely won them all over with the story behind his unusual background (a triple major, including astrophysics and art), his obvious ease discussing his research in detail, and by the incisive questions he asked the committee. For example, whereas Chun's first question for the committee was "What is it like to live in your town?," Bradley's first question for the committee was, "It seems from the website like you distinguish your department in specific ways. Could you talk about your current priorities as a department?" He even went so far as to directly inquire about the committee's thoughts on a personal and legally protected characteristic that he disclosed in the personal statement, and which, indeed, one member of the committee had raised as a red flag in their last meeting. "We think it is worth something," one of them assured him. Victor added, "It's worth a lot."

In the closing back-and-forth comments between Bradley and the committee, the chair's tone and comments seemed to presume admission and enrollment, and in debriefing his interview after it finished, the committee displayed none of the ambivalence or equivocation that I heard after Chun's interview. Instead, discussion repeatedly included such words as "superb." It was clear that they wanted badly to attract him to their program, and indeed, at the end of the process he was one of the first to be added to their "admit" list. In the end, however, Bradley chose to enroll elsewhere.

I do not mean to imply that Chun's and Bradley's interviews represent how the committee judged women versus men or Chinese versus American students. This committee was thoughtful in their deliberations, and the conclusion to my field notes from that day includes the line, "If I could admit two of the four people interviewed today, I would select the two men." However, these interviews did draw out just how much more evaluation may take place in interviews than is formally communicated to students. As a professor in another department admitted to me, "That's what you're going to tell them, that you're going to screen them for language. But frankly, we think a little broader."

As with GRE scores, suspicions of fraud surfaced in respondents' stories to me about their interviews with students from China, South Korea, and Japan. Some faculty admitted that they would continue to be skeptical of international students' English skills until they arrived on campus. A member of the committee described above recalled the case of a recent South Korean applicant:

They interviewed him on the telephone. His English was fine, and he was very, you know, his credentials were good. We admitted him. But he couldn't talk English. I mean he couldn't understand what you said to him. He couldn't speak English. The only thing we could think was that he'd gotten a ringer to do the interview.

Only one person openly acknowledged that the widespread skepticism about Asian applicants' English skills "seems in some ways like racial profiling." Yet a posture of distrust was pervasive, and consistent with the contagiousness of stereotypes found in social psychological research. Stereotypes spread through rumors, storytelling, and innuendo as well as through firsthand experience.[18]

Cultural Distinction Work

Interviews were also important to many faculty in managing a third ambiguity: the perception that students from China are so similar to one another as to be essentially fungible. Given that the basic task of admissions evaluation is making relevant distinctions among applicants, faculty approached the short list with a desire to identify doctoral applicants' unique qualities and contributions. Some admitted to me in interviews, however, that they found this more difficult to do with Chinese applicants, especially using only the application materials. The chair of the physics program explained this in some detail:

> There will be awful, many, Chinese students that look very, very similar. They have similar scores from similar universities, similar everything. They all get stellar recommendations because that's the style of the Chinese recommenders. And how exactly do we tell the difference? Well, we interview. And that gives you much, much better sense, certainly. Each of these people that were just numbers and looked exactly the same, suddenly, they have different personalities and different interests and they become alive. So that's great. It really works very well and not restricting really strictly just to language screening.

Difficulties in seeing differences among students from China began with seeing their names on the applications. "How do you compare six students from China, who all have the same last name?" one humanities scholar wondered aloud to me. Although her comment overstated the pattern, it is true that the United States has a much wider distribution of surnames than China. The hundred most prevalent surnames in China account for 87 percent of its huge population, whereas only 17 percent in the United States have one of the hundred most common surnames. Li, Wang, and Zhang alone comprise 22.4 percent of the Chinese population, and the Chinese phrase "three Zhang, four Li" translates in English to "just anybody."[19]

Their expectation that Chinese students would have high quantitative GRE scores and weak English skills also reflected the troubling tendency to think of students from China not as individuals, but a profile of group averages.

To grasp individuality, several committees involved additional faculty members in the review process. A Chinese-born professor in one program, not a member of the committee, cross-checked ratings of Chinese applicants when there were specific ambiguities in an applicant's file or when readers gave widely divergent ratings. Two departments each informally dubbed one of their faculty members who had served on the admissions committee for several years their "China specialist" or "China expert." This role was thought to reflect significant social capital, with one described as "know[ing] pretty much all the top astrophysicists in China. He knows what all the good universities are." In one program, this expertise was instrumental in conducting what amounted to a separate evaluative process of the hundred or so applications they received each year from Chinese students.

Colleagues with special expertise would also aid committee members in sorting out letters of recommendation—a part of the application that holds promise for making distinctions but which can be an interpretive minefield without an understanding of how recommendation letters may vary across cultures. Faculty were divided on the utility and trustworthiness of letters of recommendation to inform judgments of international students. Paradoxically, letters were both the most frequently cited way that participants said they came to trust international applicants and the most frequently cited source of concern about applicant credibility. A close analysis of faculty comments on this issue revealed that this paradox can be explained in terms of how well an international student's letters of recommendations reflect American cultural norms.

When a letter of recommendation conformed to American norms, it could "speak to the record" of an international student or "compensate" for uncertainty about academic preparation. When letters failed to fit the American style, however, faculty declared them "pretty useless" and "basically worthless." One senior professor summarized, "Now, 15 to 20 percent of our letters are from Asia. If you've ever read them, you can't compare them with Americans. You basically have to ignore the letters." Another scholar summarized a series of cultural trends that I heard participants from various disciplines express:

> There's also a difference in culture in what the letters of recommendation look like. American letters of recommendation tend to be pretty descriptive. They tend to be pretty positive. Often European letters of recommendation are more reserved. Ones from China in particular are often extremely perfunctory. They tend to be one paragraph. "This is a good student. He is honest."

The most common concern faculty named about reading letters was how to interpret a less-than-exuberant *tone*. Could they safely use tone as a clue to the letter writer's feelings about the applicant? Or was it a function of cultural norms or the letter writer's personality? After tone, faculty struggled with how to make sense of *content,* especially in letters from scholars in China. Letters from China often emphasized applicant morality, when what faculty primarily wanted were hints about fit and the quality of their research experience. Also, what would the applicant be like as a junior colleague for five or more years? How did she or he compare to other students?[20] The chair of the economics committee described their general understanding of the situation: "Internationally, they [the committee] know the programs they trust, and there *are* some institutions producing very good economists, but their faculty don't know how to craft the kind of recommendation that at U.S. reader will find persuasive." Recognizing this tendency, he has made it a point to explain these norms to scholars he meets at international meetings and collaborations.

Like differences in the cultures of test preparation, cultural differences in letter-writing norms complicated faculty members' efforts to get to know individual applicants and their skills. Ultimately, that ambiguity prevented most Chinese applicants from receiving the same boost that a well-received letter could give students with nontraditional backgrounds.

Ambiguities Create Conditions in Which Stereotypes Thrive

Challenges of ambiguity in decision making have drawn scholars' attention for over fifty years, and recent experiments have found that decision makers are more likely to interpret ambiguous information using expectancies or stereotypes.[21] I found that the layers of ambiguity involved in evaluating international applicants created conditions under which stereotypes thrived. Reviewers leaned on what they knew (or thought they knew) about students from a particular group in order to manage the uncertainties. Most frequently, the ambiguities of evaluating students from China and other East Asian countries—what to make of their GRE scores, English skills, and individual differences—primed faculty to adopt elements of the "model minority" paradigm. For East Asian applicants to distinguish themselves therefore required evidence that refuted the stereotypes associated with this paradigm and suggested alignment with American norms.

The model minority paradigm portrays people of Asian[22] descent as conforming to a monolithic model of academic and economic success. It reduces the complex Asian and Asian American diaspora to a set of simplistic stereotypes[23] and emphasizes Confucian cultural values (assimilation, strong work ethic, deference to authority) and dissimilarity from American norms.[24] These stereotypes are rarely challenged in mainstream social discourse. For example, the popular media draw on model minority stereotypes in their typical portrayals of Asians and Asian Americans—as nerdy, passive, socially awkward, perpetual foreigners with poor English-language abilities, but who also are courteous, well-educated, overachieving, hardworking, and talented in math.[25] This mix of qualities takes on special meaning in the context of recent economic development in many Asian countries, the history of cheating scandals, Asian Americans' mean test scores advantages, and their representation in selective colleges. It paints Asian immigrants and Asian Americans as a threat to white America's "educational, economic, and political opportunities."[26] As such, the model minority stereotype is fundamentally one of ambivalence. As seen in the comments of so many faculty in the current study, views of Asians and Asian Americans often mix respect and resentment with a basic sense of distrust.

Scholars argue that because it focuses on cultural differences associated with race, rather than phenotypical characteristics, the model minority paradigm is an example of contemporary racism, or neoracism. The paradigm has been especially toxic to American race relations, pitting Asian Americans against other minority groups, and holding up their example as evidence that the United States must have an open, meritocratic opportunity structure in spite of its racialized history. Higher education scholars Samuel Museus and Peter Kiang have found that in higher education, the model minority stereotype manifests in assumptions that Asian American students are all the same, are not really minorities, are immune from negative experiences with race, and neither seek nor require academic resources and support.[27]

In addition to the specific racial stereotyping Asian students face, research has found that foreign graduate students in general may face stereotyping, such as the assumption that they are intellectually backward strangers to the community of science.[28] International students from Asia, India, Latin America, and the Middle East report proportionally more experiences with discrimination than students from Europe, including negative remarks about their home countries or cultures; hostility toward nonfluency in English; social exclusion; conflicts with professors, administrators, and classmates; and direct verbal insults or physical attacks.[29] For those whose experience of American higher education requires them to contend with model minority and foreigner stereotypes, the degree may come with a psychological price tag as high as the tuition bill.[30]

Decision makers need to be aware of the existence of these stereotypes because the nature of admissions review involves conditions under which stereotypes are easily activated. When trustworthy information is scant, individuals are being compared, and assessments are routinized rather than reflective, humans have a tendency to replace ambiguity and complexity with simpler explanations. In this sample, the composite stereotype that faculty held of Asian applicants was one of mathematically sophisticated test takers and status seekers with weak English skills, who are difficult to distinguish from one another. Thus, it makes sense that the international students whose applications impressed faculty had characteristics that contradicted this stereotype.

The effort to create broadly diverse departments compelled faculty to consider uniqueness and freshness of perspective when taking stock of the short list. Amid many conventional achievers, admissions committees sought applicants who were both demographically diverse as well as diverse in their personal backstories, personalities, and nonacademic interests. When faculty evaluated applicants who seemed demographically and academically similar, these latter types of personal uniqueness were especially salient. "That kind of stuff jumps off of the page," one physicist explained. "It sort of says, 'Hi, I'm a little bit different.' You're looking for something to distinguish all these great test scores."

I nonetheless observed striking patterns across disciplines in the personal qualities faculty considered desirable among applicants from China and Korea. One of the important interview questions I posed to each participant asked them to describe applicants—domestic or international—who fit the profiles of two "ideal types": *borderline students,* those about whose admissibility the committee disagreed, and *easy-to-admit students,* of whom the committee all thought highly. Among those whom participants described as easy to admit, seven happened to be from China, Korea, Taiwan, or Japan. Juxtaposing the descriptions of these individuals took me aback. They were remarkably similar to one another, and clearly contradicted the model minority stereotype.

Of the seven, Table 9 presents descriptors of "easy admits" from the four most lengthy profiles that participants provided. Not only mathematically skilled, three were recognized for artistic and creative pursuits, including two poets. In contrast to the image of a quiet student struggling with English, three were described as "communicators." Not only seeking status or opportunity for themselves, three of the four were identified for their academic and social engagement on behalf of others (activist, advocate, tutor). And breaking the stereotype that students from East Asian countries are indistinguishable from one another, three of the four were acknowledged

Table 9   Descriptors Used by Faculty in Profiles of "Easy to Admit" Students from China, South Korea, and Japan

Theme	Student 1	Student 2	Student 3	Student 4
Creative		Poet	Poet; Renaissance type	Photographer
Communication		Communicator	Communicator	Extremely good communicator
Outreach	Activist	Advocate; tutor	Tutor	
Unique	Original; interesting		Different; special	Broad interests; eclectic tastes
Engaged	Motivated	Excited; interested	Enthusiastic; genuinely interested	
Other	Talented; very good	Distinguished; genuine		Not poor, not super-rich

Note: Descriptors that faculty used in the other three profiles of "easy to admit" students from East Asian countries were "thoughtful," "knowledgeable," "really good," "very strong," "imaginative," and "independent."

for their uniqueness. In sum, stereotypes associated with the model minority paradigm informed faculty judgment, but when it came to reviewing the stack of outwardly "indistinguishable" Chinese applicants, those with the best chances of being admitted contradicted those stereotypes.

Conclusion

Under even the most straightforward conditions, admissions evaluation is work filled with uncertainty, but reviewing international students' files introduces specific ambiguities. Some of these may predispose faculty to default to model minority stereotypes. This possibility was exemplified in participants' expectations of Chinese students' GRE scores and English skills, and their perception that these students did not differ substantively from one another. Two forces seem to fuel the doubts cast on Chinese applicants as a group. Personal memories and departmental tales of admitted Chinese students who came to campus and confirmed negative stereotypes loomed large in faculty members' minds. There was also widespread skepticism about the credibility of Chinese students' applications. Some recalled the cheating scandals as if they were yesterday, and others believed the rumors that cheating, forgery, and other efforts to game the admissions system define all Chinese students' efforts to gain admission to American universities.

A natural question is: To what extent is there evidence for the types of assumptions that faculty held? On the question of whether TOEFL and GRE Verbal scores are valid indicators of English proficiency and student success, more than forty years of research have yielded few clear trends about the TOEFL's utility in predicting international students' academic performance. A recent study, which sampled 1,733 international students enrolled in U.S. graduate programs between 2005 and 2009 (22 percent of whom were Chinese), found that TOEFL scores did not predict graduate school academic performance. Other studies suggest that the TOEFL is a more useful metric in the humanities and social sciences than in the natural sciences and more effective in predicting academic performance of students with lower English proficiency. An interesting study of international graduate teaching assistants found that those who received negative teaching evaluations from students were also likely to have lower TOEFL and Verbal GRE scores. These mixed findings suggest that faculty should not count on the TOEFL alone to gauge students' fluency. When doubts are present, seeking additional information to assess applicant English proficiency appears to be a reasonable step.[31]

It is true that, on average, international students have higher GRE Quantitative scores than U.S. citizens, by 6 points in 2012. Chinese students have the highest mean GRE Quantitative scores in the world (162.9 points), more than 13 points higher than the mean for U.S. test takers.[32] However, Fu found that, among international students, GRE Verbal, GRE Quantitative, and undergraduate GPA *together* explained only 3.1 percent in the variance of first-year graduate school grade point average, less than half of that explained in an identical model with domestic students. She also found that GRE scores did not on their own significantly predict international students' graduate school GPA,[33] suggesting that reviewers had a point in not taking international students' scores too seriously. If the test's weakness for some U.S.-born African American and Latino students is that scores are susceptible to noise from stereotype threat, then for many Asian-born students, the weakness may be scores' sensitivity to large amounts of practice and preparation. Rather than reducing students to their performance on tests, faculty should weigh TOEFL and GRE scores as part of a holistic set of considerations about students.

Reliable evidence on the presence, nature, and extent of academic cheating is difficult to obtain, and to my knowledge there is no academic research on the topic of cheating in graduate school admissions.[34] Incidents of fraudulent TOEFL and GRE test taking in China seem to have reinforced the fundamental distrust with which many faculty regard applicants from that country, even though the incidents were thought to involve only a small proportion of applicants to U.S. graduate programs.[35] It is difficult to gain an understanding of cheating in China because the application process in China is decentralized through private consultants, and cultural norms vary in what should be considered to be cheating, gaming, or fair play. A white paper written by one such private consultant, Zinch China, claimed that parental pressure, aggressive private college counselors, and high schools' complicity all carry some responsibility for the pervasiveness of cheating in China. Admitting that the findings would be impossible to verify, Zinch's paper concluded that "the common refrain" from 250 interviews with students in top Chinese high schools and their parents (who were asked to ask their friends), as well as several agents, was, "Everybody cheats."[36]

Regardless of the reliability of evidence, the clear correspondence between judgments of students from China and a common racial stereotype is worth calling to mind when faculty assume that they are immune from implicit biases about other groups, whether women, LGBTQ (lesbian, gay, bisexual, transgender, and queer) students, those from southern states, or any other group. Perhaps because model minority stereotypes receive little challenge in American society—and because Asian success has been positioned as a threat not only to people of color but also to white America—participants were more vocal and candid about their distrust and ambivalence about this group than about any other single demographic group.

Finally, faculty members' review of applications from China clearly demonstrates some malleability to ideals about merit, a point that may be worth remembering when claims are made that a program should not take into account domestic students' previous contexts for learning. Rather than judging students against a uniform ideal of quality or as representatives of broader categories or identities, the aim of holistic review is to evaluate students as individuals, in the context of their own opportunities and potential.

Conclusion
Merit beyond the Mirror

My first thing about graduate admissions is that we do it as conscientiously as we can, but it is a crapshoot. It really is. We don't know who's going to blossom and who isn't. We have not found reliable predictors.

—Senior professor of classics

IT IS NO WONDER that issues surrounding admissions are among the country's most controversial topics. It's not only educational credentials, but where they are earned, that increasingly shapes professional opportunities, both in academia and in the broader labor market. Two recent studies have found that faculty hiring occurs within largely closed networks and that most of the faculty who are hired into tenure-track positions possess PhDs from a small set of institutions.[1] And in industry, firms in some sectors only seriously recruit from a very small set of "super-elite" undergraduate institutions, creating what sociologist Lauren Rivera called a "golden pipeline" into society's most lucrative positions.[2] In a system like this, the transparency of selection mechanisms into selective colleges and doctoral programs is critical for equity in the system. At both the undergraduate and the graduate level, however, the basis for any applicant's acceptance or rejection is usually opaque to applicants and admissions personnel alike. Uncertainty about what admission requires, combined with the sense that it will play a determining role in their life outcomes, raises the stakes and anxieties for applicants and their families. For those tasked with making admissions decisions, the process may be known, but the basis for individual outcomes may be just as difficult to articulate.

Summary

We know this much about how faculty evaluate prospective graduate students: Test scores, college grade point average, and college reputation play a formative role in the initial review of applications, which explains their relationship with the probability of admission, generally. From the current study, I learned that faculty conceive of "merit" at this point in review principally as a matter of conventional achievement, although scholars across the disciplines may vary in the sections of the GRE they weigh and in considering overall GPA versus grades earned within one's major. They do not interpret every student's scores the same way. Due to China's deep-rooted culture of test preparation and history of admissions fraud, for example, many faculty believe that students should have very high GRE and TOEFL scores but that those scores cannot be trusted to reliably predict student skills. Intriguingly, although it is standard practice to contextualize test scores by national origin, and grades by institutional prestige, most faculty do not contextualize test scores in light of their distributions by race, gender, and socioeconomic status. Just two respondents, an economist and a philosopher, actively encouraged consideration of diversity and/or students' social identities in the initial round of review.

Why the double standard? The most common explanation I heard was that such an interpretation would introduce diversity into the conversation too soon. As a sociologist in the study put it: "First you have to be above a bar, then we can ask the diversity question." Setting extremely high bars on GRE scores and college prestige, however, disproportionately excludes the very populations whom university websites and mission statements claim they wish to attract—and who are already underrepresented in many fields at the levels of doctoral education and the professoriate. For example, 16 percent of Asian American high school graduates enrolled in highly selective colleges and universities in 2004 compared to 2 percent of African American high school graduates. In the physical sciences, 82 percent of Asian and white students earned a 700 or above on the Quantitative section of the GRE, compared to 5.2 percent of underrepresented minority students.[3] The informal admission standards that elite doctoral programs have established in many fields therefore make it extremely difficult for people of color to gain access.

As a matter of procedure, committees commonly maximize efficiency and minimize conflict by discussing only the cases in which initial ratings diverge from each other. As long as committee members rate an applicant similarly, the average rating can serve as a proxy for "the collective assessment of the committee." Through this process, they can quickly eliminate a large share of the pool using common, academic criteria. But deliberations about borderline applicants are handled quite differently; these decisions often come down to hair splitting or making subtle distinctions between applicants based on novel criteria that were not considered relevant to the assessments of other candidates.

Academic preparation is just the tip of the iceberg when it comes to "merit," because faculty judge many more students smart and competent than their doctoral programs have capacity to accommodate. For the small number whose applications survive to receive full review, judgments are thus holistic, complex, and unpredictable. When comparing generally qualified students, seemingly small matters may matter very much to an applicant's chances because of the layers of inference involved. In the words of one tenured philosopher, "We are in the business of making fine distinctions." A single, ambiguous line in a letter of recommendation; the appeal of a writing sample's introduction; the poor reputation of a letter writer for speaking too highly of too many students; an applicant's weekend hobby or hometown—reviewers may read meanings and value judgments into each of these, in ways that can spell the difference between a candidate's admission or rejection. With few cases discussed and evaluations subject to a myriad of considerations, pinning down what counts as merit late in the process is more difficult than it is earlier in review, when a few key criteria go a long way in shaping ratings. "Everything matters, and nothing matters most," as one faculty member commented.

In this type of situation, *any* basis for comparing applicants can have the effect of a "preference." The individualistic analyses that are inherent to holistic review can elevate opportunities for one student in spite of reducing chances of another with different, albeit also desirable, qualities. When a small program like classics admitted one of two applicants from rural New England because a committee member envisioned it as a "pastoral" place for early socialization in classics, it impinged on opportunities for many applicants whose geographic origins were not perceived as salient. In political science, when a student with mediocre grades was admitted in part because a committee member thought it was "cool" that she wrote for an online magazine, it came at the cost of another borderline applicant who had written a book. Committees in several disciplines admitted applicants from China who disclosed creative hobbies over dozens of their fellow Chinese nationals who did not. What counts as merit when comparing borderline cases sometimes comes down to details that appear idiosyncratic and far afield from conventional achievement.[4]

Many of the grounds for judgment late in the review process are specific to one or two applicants rather than applied to the entire pool, but those evaluations are all part of an effort to shape the future of their programs and disciplines. Leaving behind the focus on conventional achievement in most cases, deliberations revolved around how applicants "fit" with the program in the present and their idealized academic communities of the future. They sought students who offered fresh perspectives and strong grounding in discipline-specific research dispositions and skills. Diversity, broadly defined, was integral to the fresh perspectives they sought, and a majority strived to construct "balanced" cohorts of students. Rarely, however, did they discuss race, gender, or socioeconomic status in explicit or substantive ways. In contrast to the state of affairs that some worry about, in which race considerations drive admissions in ways that compromise the fairness of the entire process and its outcomes, I was more taken aback by the almost complete silence on these topics in the meetings that I observed.

Explaining the Gap between Principles and Practice

This observation returns us to the questions that motivated my research. With problems of inequality widely known, why do so many faculty rely upon selection criteria that obstruct access for women and underrepresented minorities? If they value diversity, why are they loathe to make racial diversity part of the conversation? I investigated the culture of faculty decision making in elite doctoral programs as a root cause. From there, the answers depend in part on the data and in part on the lenses through which we read it. I will synthesize my findings from three theoretical perspectives before turning to their implications for admissions practice.

Multiple Interests, Multiple Contexts

Assessments of the sort that happen in admissions committees are by nature an elaborate compromise, according to Luc Boltanski and Laurent Thévenot's theory of situated judgment.[5] Graduate programs choose their next cohorts of students with many social goods in mind—student success, prestige, and diversity, to name a few—and each of these will be more or less salient for a particular discipline, program, committee, or reviewer. Practically speaking, admissions decision making consists of negotiating multiple hierarchies of priorities (a heterarchy) that emerge from disciplinary logics, program values, committee dynamics, and personal identities. This perspective would argue that because faculty are trying to satisfy perceived demands of multiple evaluative contexts that it is rare for any one interest or criterion to consistently hold up as decisive or determinative across reviewers and rounds of review. Only those interests constructed as core *across* contexts are likely to withstand the layers of compromise. A situated judgment angle on my data would conclude that diversity may be one in a constellation of interests that faculty would like to maximize, but especially with respect to race, it has not yet attained the status of a major priority when faculty are thinking about their own values, and those of their programs, committees, and disciplines. Here, it helps to contrast the role of diversity in admissions with that of prestige, an even more well-institutionalized interest.

Prestige. The powerful influence of pedigree and prestige can be understood from two related angles. Pierre Bourdieu's perspective argues that the power of pedigree reflects a broader tendency for elite educational institutions to organize their activities and define quality in ways that preserve their status in the field.[6] Because institutional reputation ("peer assessment") and enrolled doctoral students' mean GRE scores and grade point averages contribute to popular university-ranking systems, prestige-oriented graduate programs use admissions to boost their academic profile.[7] Often this enrollment management decision comes at significant cost to other espoused priorities, such as broadening access for underrepresented groups.

However, status competition does not explain the many individual preferences that also shape admissions judgments. These more complicated patterns signal locally defined—even self-defined—ideas about quality and the tendency for faculty to judge prospective students in the same domains they judge themselves.[8] Michèle Lamont explains how drawing such identity-based boundaries can contribute to social reproduction:

> Exclusion is often the unintended consequence or latent effect of the definition by the upper middle class of its values and indirectly of its group identity and its nature as a community . . . Only when boundaries are widely agreed upon (i.e., only when people agree that some traits are better than others) can symbolic boundaries take on a widely constraining (or structural) character and pattern social interaction in an important way.[9]

I observed faculty using informal conversation to express shared tastes, identities, and goals, thereby constructing symbolic boundaries that guided their assessments of fit and belonging. The student from a politically conservative, religious college was debated as a possible "nutcase." The student with a strong but conventional file was mockingly compared to a Ford. In physics, a lack of research experience was called the "kiss of death."

Prestige thus drives graduate admissions in programs like these because it helps them maintain their status and because it is central to their identity. More than admitting a group whose average characteristics preserve the program's position in nationally defined status orders, it helps graduate programs create the sort of community they feel they are and aspire to be. For such organizations, which already see themselves as successful, the status quo therefore represents a powerful default. This is particularly the case, as I will discuss, if changing the basis for admission may require some soul searching about flaws in their collective identity or goals, and if admission already requires more time and effort than is desirable.

Diversity. In contrast to prestige, diversity is relatively new among admissions priorities. How has it emerged as an interest at all? According to the organizational theory of institutionalism, organizations survive by adapting their practices and priorities to changes in the institutional and political environment. Shifting values in society can bring about new policy in organizations like colleges and universities by motivating changes that might otherwise have been avoided.[10] This institutionalist angle helps explain why educational equity came to be recognized as a social imperative during the Civil Rights Movement, and why diversity has come to be viewed as a practical interest for higher education today.[11]

A very brief history can situate the current state of diversity as an interest for higher education stakeholders. Civil Rights protests changed the political environment in the 1950s and 1960s to support demands for improved access to higher education and employment for African Americans, Latinos, Native Americans, and, in spaces where they were still excluded, white women. The Civil Rights Act of 1964 and executive orders for affirmative action under Presidents Lyndon Johnson and Richard Nixon made these shifting values visible, and they presented them to the public as means of redressing the effects of long-standing policies of segregation, discrimination, and exclusion. These macro-level influences, coupled with acute pressures that campus-based student movements placed on university administrators, compelled the adoption and diffusion of race-conscious admissions policies by selective colleges and universities across the country.

The difference that scholars and institutional researchers found diversity to make for student learning and development provided an empirical foundation for another affirmative action rationale—the educational benefits of diversity. Proponents sought to broaden the appeal of affirmative action by emphasizing its benefits for all students' development, namely white students, not only for those who bore the "present effects of past injustice." Thus, whereas universities implemented affirmative action due to changes in the political environment, university efforts since the 1970s have been to protect the legitimacy of race-conscious admissions by elevating the rationale with the widest public support.

Institutions have also focused on diversity's educational benefits because the courts have established narrow parameters for the constitutionality of race-conscious admissions. In 1978 in *Regents of the University of California v. Bakke* the U.S. Supreme Court ruled racial quotas unconstitutional, and in 2003 in *Gratz v. Bollinger* it also struck down the awarding of "automatic, predetermined point allocations" to underrepresented students.[12] Justice Lewis Powell's controlling opinion in *Bakke* ruled consideration of race permissible as a "plus factor" in admissions and financial aid decisions, but this consideration requires narrow tailoring to a compelling state interest.[13] What counts as a compelling state interest? In *Bakke,* whose precedent has been upheld in such recent decisions as *Fisher v. University of Texas,* the Court rejected three of the four interests in affirmative action asserted by the University of California–Davis Medical School. However, Powell's opinion affirmed the educational benefits of diversity, broadly defined, citing promotion of diversity in higher education as a "compelling governmental interest." Powell also upheld educational institutions' discretion to determine the selection procedures that best suit their needs, associating it with academic freedom and the First Amendment.[14] In the years since *Bakke,* voters have banned affirmative action through ballot initiatives in Arizona, California, Michigan, Nebraska, Oklahoma, and Washington, and the legislature and governor passed anti-affirmative policies in New Hampshire and Florida. These bans are responsible for declining racial/ethnic diversity in selective undergraduate institutions and in many graduate fields of study, amid increasing racial and ethnic diversity in the population.[15] For academic institutions in the other forty-two states, however, principles from Powell's opinion are still the law of the land, and are important for those engaged in admissions to know. A brief from the Civil Rights Project at UCLA summarizes them:

1. Reserving seats or proportions of seats specifically for underrepresented students is not permissible.
2. Reviewers should use a common process of review for all applicants.
3. Race should be one of several individual characteristics assessed as a plus factor in the effort to promote diversity.
4. Every applicant should be evaluated as an individual, and should not be assumed to represent a broader identity category.
5. Programs should not single out specific racial/ethnic groups, but consider the contribution that all groups make to diversity.[16]

Bakke focused on admission to medical school and *Grutter* on law school, but the Supreme Court has not specifically examined graduate school admissions among the arts and sciences. However, economists, psychologists, sociologists, as well as higher education and legal scholars have all advised that selection processes and their rationales be tied to educational mission.[17] In addition to ethical and economic rationales, the distinct mission of doctoral education may therefore elicit interests in equity and diversity that are distinct from those in undergraduate and professional education. As discussed earlier, research by teams possessing diverse social identities is associated with core characteristics of scholarly quality. Heterogeneous research teams have demonstrated advantages in creativity and problem solving, and publications that result from ethnically and gender diverse research collaborations are cited more often.[18] Relatively few people I interviewed associated increasing social diversity with intellectual excellence or the health of their fields. Important new analyses also assert that, if reducing inequities in higher education is the goal, then "diversity" itself merits critical evaluation as a rhetorical strategy for organizational behavior.[19]

From the perspective of situated judgment, what counts in practice as merit is as an institutionalized compromise across multiple interests associated with the multiple social contexts that decision makers represent. Professors strive to simultaneously maximize individual, committee, program, and disciplinary interests, and to uphold their personal values, interpersonal relations, and institutional and wider policy. Prestige and diversity may both be organizational interests, but only if something is conceived as a core interest *across* those contexts will it be likely to survive as a priority in the negotiation process. We can explain continuing inequality in spite of diversity's institutionalization through (1) the entrenched value that status and prestige hold for organizations and participants like the ones in this study, (2) the more tenuous place that diversity holds (legally, politically, and discursively) as a value in their disciplines, programs, committees, and for many of the individual reviewers, and (3) evaluative scripts that associate very high GRE scores and attending elite institutions with intelligence and belonging (two additional shared values) in prestigious communities like theirs, and that construe lower GRE scores or less selective college enrollment as a trade-off with excellence. However, same deliberative processes by which faculty collectively define merit can be used to diversify what counts as merit. Decision makers may encourage alternative interpretations of common criteria, for example, or use admissions and hiring to encourage new perspectives or collective goals.

Preferences Imply Aversions

Decision theory offers a second perspective from which to interpret this study's findings. Although research and public debate about admissions often revolve around the justice and necessity of specific evaluation criteria, a contribution of this research is to show that decision-making processes are also implicated in ongoing reliance on pedigree and GRE scores. Specifically, participants' preference for a *process* that reduces uncertainties and preserves collegiality revealed their shared aversions to ambiguity, risk, and conflict.

Ambiguity aversion. The complexity of comparing hundreds of applicants who come from different national, institutional, and personal backgrounds makes faculty *ambiguity averse*. Faced with a "cloud of random applicants," professors hunger for clarity and conviction about which ones are likely to thrive as scholars and bring vitality to their departments and disciplines. From this standpoint, reliance upon test scores is not exclusively about what they signal, but instead about how they make it easy to compare applicants. Participants associated GRE scores with convenience because their apparent standardization, precision, and clarity seem to cut through all of the apples-to-oranges comparison that evaluating students' letters of recommendation, essays, and writing samples requires.

Professors in the humanities were both more thoughtful about and less averse to the subjectivity inherent in judging and comparing their applicants. Yet they too ultimately quantified their judgments to bring closure to deliberations, and they were especially likely to do so for the sake of expediency. Though fallible, "the numbers" provided something on which humanities faculty felt they could stand. By contrast, in the physical sciences, greater trust in numbers engendered trust in the validity of distributions of test scores and average ratings. In both cases, quantifying differences in perceived admissibility was a hallmark of deliberative bureaucracy, one that increased efficiency by masking perceived ambiguities. For busy professors, the GRE's appeal was in no small part the possibility that it would simplify their work.

Risk aversion. There is also abundant evidence that faculty in these prestigious programs engaged with admissions work from a posture of risk aversion. This tendency, paired with the specific assumptions about risk that they frequently made help clarify why they favored criteria that undermine increased racial diversity. Many respondents associated less selective undergraduate institutions and lower test scores and grades with less preparation and intelligence, and they associated less preparation and intelligence with a higher risk of academic struggle or failure. This risk aversion script pervaded ratings and deliberations at *all* stages of review. Risk aversion also provided a bottom-line basis for rejecting well-pedigreed individuals who had personality red flags, research interests that aligned only marginally with faculty expertise, or letters of recommendation that raised eyebrows.

Organizational theorist James March has found that a propensity to risk aversion is common in high-status organizations' decision-making processes.[20] In this case, faculty rationalized risk aversion as an organizational luxury, a matter of financial prudence, and a foundation of responsible decision making. They knew they could *afford* to be risk averse because their highly ranked programs attracted so many qualified candidates. Further, they convinced themselves they *should* be risk averse in light of the financial investment involved and what admitted students represent—namely, the program, discipline, and university's quality, status, and future.[21]

High-status organizations are also more prone to fundamental attribution error—the tendency to attribute the outcomes of their members to intention and skill rather than to the conditions in the environment. Under these conditions, high-status organizations often simply exclude prospects perceived as risky rather than measuring the risk and making a decision on that basis.[22] This point highlights a critical detail about the risk aversion I observed—that it was almost always grounded in perceptions of risk rather than generalizable evidence or calculations of it.

Availability bias offers a third way of understanding risk aversion in terms of cognitive biases. Trusting the reliability and validity of the limited information that is currently available to decision makers can lead them to overestimate the likelihood of rare but memorable events. Availability bias facilitates group-based stereotyping, and I observed it to be a process by which racism was subtly institutionalized in the admissions process. For example, a number of faculty regarded African American, Latino, or Native American applicants from less selective colleges or non-native English speakers from East Asian countries as admissions risks because their programs did not enroll many of these students and recollections of one or two students who had enrolled and struggled were hard to shake from their memories. Several participants admitted that they felt "spooked"—three using this particular word—when reading applications from students whose profiles reminded them of individuals who did not graduate.

Availability bias is especially dangerous when combined with fundamental attribution error. The combination of these two biases locks in faulty assumptions about who is successful and why, and then uses those faulty assumptions as a basis for distributing future opportunities. First, attribution errors blind academic departments to how the climate and culture that they create may contribute to students' successes and struggles. Then, availability bias encourages extrapolation of a few students' struggles (which resulted in part from organizational conditions the department could change) to a larger category of students as a basis for evaluating their future potential, and thus their deservingness for opportunities. Taking steps to actively check the natural tendency toward these biases can prevent the experiences of a few individuals from becoming the basis for judging whole categories of future applicants as risks. It also highlights the importance of encouraging faculty mindfulness about their own role in shaping student success.[23]

Conflict aversion. Quantification also suppresses conflict among faculty. Conflict aversion is the flip side of the deeply rooted professional norm of faculty collegiality. Admissions committee members felt that quantifying their judgment—whether through test scores, individual ratings, or average ratings—provided more uniform interpretation than the many understandings that the committee might generate about individuals and their relative admissibility. With a few keystrokes, numbers could be sorted into a single ranked list, obviating the need for difficult negotiations about who should be deemed more or less admissible. Most departments viewed some deliberation as prerequisite to legitimate admissions decisions. However, committee members preferred not to argue with each other, especially about matters that were rooted in deeply held epistemological differences, such as the validity of statistical inferences about GRE scores. As such, two key elements to the deliberative bureaucracy decision making model that I observed included careful committee appointments and substituting potentially controversial discussion of applicants with relatively uncontroversial discussion of admissions procedure. The formal task of admissions may be to identify applicants with the most impressive achievements and greatest potential, but the process of collective selection was one of political compromise and avoiding uncomfortable conversations.

Resistance to Change, Ambivalence about Diversity

By combining elements from the first two theoretical perspectives— inconsistencies across context in how faculty weigh diversity and the important role of aversions in shaping faculty decision making—we can also interpret deference to entrenched evaluation criteria as a matter of resistance to change. An entire scholarly literature has developed around resistance and ambivalence to organizational change, with Louis Menand going so far as to argue that twenty-first-century American professors are trying their best to maintain a nineteenth-century system. They want to make a better world through their research and teaching, but often eschew making change in their own ranks to help bring it about. Among the admissions committee chairs I interviewed, outright resistance to change did not seem to be the problem. Indeed, three of them welcomed me to observe their admissions committees to learn how their systems could be improved. However, their colleagues were in many cases more ambivalent—about changing admissions, generally, and about rethinking their applicant pools and diversity, specifically.

Why is it that faculty might stand by equity and diversity in principle, but feel ambivalent about practical efforts to achieve them? For one thing, many thought of these as obligations dictated by social norms and for their pragmatic benefits, not as conditions that demonstrably improved their work or their community. Faculty typically build their careers on the visions of academic excellence they inherit from their academic forebears, and for most, diversity is not yet integral to that vision.

Thus, in political science, linguistics, astrophysics, and philosophy, faculty supported their *colleagues'* advocacy for a small number of borderline applicants with nontraditional profiles, but they were reticent to take on such students as their *own* advisees. They expressed concerns about the additional mentoring investment that might be required. The self-trained philosopher from the Deep South, the astrophysicist born in the Himalayas, and the political scientist with unusually low GRE scores each received admissions offers, for example, but only after extended debate and assurance that someone else would take responsibility for their supervision.[24] Most faculty could be persuaded to admit specific individuals in the name of diversity, but I observed little evidence that diversity was either understood to be a collective responsibility or enacted as a shared value in the day-to-day of department life.

Postracial discourse in American society may also contribute to ambivalence about reform. For one, claims that racism is a problem of America's past undermine attention to continued structural inequalities and everyday biases.[25] Constraints on affirmative action reflect postracial sensibilities, and I learned that regardless of whether or not a program was subject to specific legal constrains, that bans, rumors of bans, and worries about lawsuits all made faculty reticent to discuss race at all with respect to recruitment and admissions.

However, like the other factors I have discussed, uncertainty about options for equity-based reform must be read as an explanation, not an excuse.

Research by Roger Worthington and colleagues found that "colorblind-ness" and personal privilege predispose those within higher education to an overly rosy view of the status quo on their campuses.[26] Most faculty in the ivory tower—especially in elite institutions—are distanced and well sheltered from the struggles with exclusion, marginalization, and discrimination that have historically compelled equity-minded reform efforts in higher education. I found that, with the exception of some sociologists and a handful of others, most participants in this study did not see equity or diversity as *their* issues, or the students admitted under these banners as *their* students. I did not collect data to measure implicit bias against women and students of color, but we must not cast aside the evidence of this pattern uncovered in prior research. Faculty judgments of many applicants from China were consistent with model minority stereotypes, providing a window into the likely presence of other identity-based biases of which faculty may have been unaware or more careful to conceal.

Finally, organizational change tests collegiality, especially when it occurs through democratic processes. It can be costly in time and effort, two scarce resources for faculty operating in a reward system that privileges research productivity over student development or improving departmental struc-tures. Were faculty to receive rewards or incentives for time spent strength-ening admissions, not to mention student mentoring, maybe the gap between expressed and enacted commitments would not be quite so wide.

With myriad social forces acting upon faculty as they select and discuss applicants, we need to think systemically when we think about improving admissions. Faculty members' ambivalence about admissions reform has several dimensions, and must, itself, be understood as one among several explanations for continued inequality. Shared aversions to ambiguity, risk, and conflict shape the work of decision making in powerful ways, and pres-tige often trumps other organizational interests when faculty seek shared values to which they can collectively defer. In addition, the perceived costs of admitting more diverse cohorts, a lack of awareness about compelling alternatives to affirmative action, satisfaction with the way things are, priv-ilege and personal distancing from equity-related issues, and a changing sociopolitical context each stand as barriers to change.

From this angle, the slow pace of change is hardly a surprise, because change is needed on many fronts. There are no silver bullets, easy answers, or quick fixes to systemic problems. Faculty may be so reluctant to wrestle with the complexity of diversity and inequality that they avoid altogether the conversations required to get the process started. Comments from Jonathan, a white male associate professor, summarize these points perfectly:

It's uncomfortable to be reminded that I'm part of the problem. What I don't want are things that will feel unnatural, take 300 percent more time, or that my colleagues will fight. I want to keep my sanity as a professional, and I don't want admissions work to consume me. What I want are straightforward ideas that help me be part of the solution.

Implications for Practice

With this idea and Jonathan's quote in mind, I turn now to discuss the implications of this research for graduate admissions practice. "Admissions decisions are actionable choices," as higher education scholars Rachelle Winkle-Wagner and Angela Locks wrote, and although professors may inherit their colleagues' approach to admissions, they also have autonomy in most universities to change the way things are done. My research was not designed to encourage policy prescription, but integrating its findings with those of other recent research studies is useful for sketching a framework for structural changes needed in many fields and programs. Within this framework, graduate programs can craft and evaluate practices that suit their own unique needs.

Revisit Admissions Routines and Make Them Explicit

All but two of the graduate programs in my sample would have benefited from taking a fresh look at their routines for recruitment, admissions, and awarding financial aid. For example, developing a thorough list of the many steps in admissions that involve subjective judgments may aid faculty in checking themselves for implicit biases. Which email inquiries a professor chooses to follow up on with a phone conversation, which colleges a graduate program chooses to visit for recruitment, who should be awarded financial aid packages as a recruitment tool—each of these procedural decisions involves a degree of subjectivity.

Also, considering the important role of initial reviewer ratings, many graduate programs can improve admissions generally by improving the review of individual files. Like selection criteria, approaches to evaluating files come with benefits and drawbacks, and each program must decide for itself what the optimal review process is, in light of what they are trying to accomplish. I will describe here some benefits and drawbacks of two models for evaluating files.

Open, holistic review incorporates into evaluation all available information about students. One strength of a holistic approach is that students

Table 10 Example Rubric

Rating	Academic Preparation	Potential for Scholarship	Contributions to Dept., Cohort, Discipline	*[Insert additional evaluation standards]*	Basis for Ratings
	Weak-Acceptable-Strong	Weak-Acceptable-Strong	Weak-Acceptable-Strong	Weak-Acceptable-Strong	
Applicant 1					
Applicant 2					
Applicant 3					
. . . and so forth					

are easily assessed in the context of their individual trajectories and opportunities. Open-ended review can lack transparency, however, putting the applicant in the position of playing a game whose rules are unknowable. This opacity maximizes institutional discretion, but it can also allow unseemly preferences and biases to enter the review process.

More structured approaches to review define in advance the criteria on which every application will be assessed. The National Science Foundation's ADVANCE program has developed rubrics and other evaluation tools that codify and define selection criteria and ask reviewers to provide a rationale for their ratings. Table 10 presents a very basic skeleton of a rubric that departments could customize. Rubric-based evaluation raises transparency and does not preclude reviewers from contextualizing applicant characteristics or attending to underlying rationales. Rubrics can also be designed to note desirable qualities that come along so rarely that it makes little sense to include them in evaluations of everyone.[27] Using a rubric increases *equity,* by comparing all applicants using the same criteria, and *efficiency,* by focusing reviewer attention on key information. Rubrics do raise the stakes associated with each criterion, so they need to be chosen with care.[28]

Strengthen Recruitment and Align It with Admissions

The need to strengthen outreach and recruitment early in the admissions cycle was an almost universal pattern across the ten programs. Two programs had experimental outreach efforts in place to build the diversity of their applicant pools, but weak coordination with admissions committees undercut those initiatives' efficacy. The problem in the other eight programs, however, was that early recruitment strategies were virtually nonexistent, consisting of little more than email responses to inquiries from prospective applicants. Departments looking to build a more diverse applicant pool have several options, including developing relationships with sister departments in institutions whose undergraduate alumni of color frequently go on to earn doctoral degrees. A recent study examined the baccalaureate origins of African American, Latino, and Asian/Pacific Islander doctoral degree recipients, and assembled lists of the colleges and universities that produce the most doctorates of color for each racial/ethnic group. Table 11 lists these institutions, many of which are minority-serving institutions (MSIs).[29] Graduate school administrators and diversity officers could assist academic programs in developing discipline-specific lists of this sort, which would enable faculty to recruit where students are, rather than waiting for students to approach them.

Table 11 Top 30 Institutions Producing African American, Latina/o, and Asian/Pacific Islander PhDs

	Top 10 African American	Top 10 Latina/o	Top 10 Asian/Pacific Islander
1	Howard University	University of Puerto Rico–Piedras	University of California–Berkeley
2	Spelman College	University of Puerto Rico–Mayaguez	University of California–Los Angeles
3	Florida A&M University	University of California–Los Angeles	Massachusetts Institute of Technology
4	Hampton University	University of Texas–Austin	Harvard University
5	Southern University A&M College	Florida International University	University of California–San Diego
6	Jackson State University	University of Texas–El Paso	Cornell University
7	Morehouse College	Harvard University	Stanford University
8	University of Michigan–Ann Arbor	University of Florida	University of Hawaii–Manoa
9	North Carolina A&T University	University of New Mexico	University of Michigan–Ann Arbor
10	University of California–Berkeley	University of Arizona	University of California–Davis

Sources: Lundy-Wagner, Vultaggio, and Gasman 2013, 158, citing Survey of Earned Doctorates 2009.

Informal recruitment relationships can become institutionalized over time, such as the Fisk-Vanderbilt Masters-to-PhD Bridge Program. This respected multidisciplinary program identifies promising undergraduates from Fisk University who would like additional preparation or research experience before beginning a PhD. Students enroll in a master's degree program at Vanderbilt, which subsequently offers them "fast-track admission" to participating doctoral programs there.[30] Bridge programs are growing in popularity as a means of broadening access to doctoral education, especially in STEM fields, and the National Science Foundation regularly fields calls for proposals for institutions that would like to develop them.

Undergraduate research programs also develop students who are interested in and qualified for doctoral study. Faculty-supervised research experience has long been promoted as a nonremedial strategy to encourage the success of undergraduates from underrepresented backgrounds. Among the studies that find positive outcomes of undergraduate research participation, scholars at UCLA's Higher Education Research Institute recently concluded through a rigorous quantitative methodology that it increases black, Latino, and Native American students' participation in graduate education.[31]

Other research, using qualitative methods, indicates that student research promotes continuation to graduate education through mutually reinforcing processes: (1) attracting students by solidifying aspirations and providing early socialization, and (2) making applicants, especially with less conventional profiles, more attractive to faculty in the admissions process. Through extended engagement with research, students cultivate forms of cultural capital deemed valuable in doctoral education and the academy, including fluency with disciplinary jargon, ease in discussing technical details and the significance of one's research, and national presentations or publications.[32] I found in this study that professors make critical inferences about prospective students from their research experiences, such as how they might contribute to the future of the discipline. As with many admissions criteria that involve some subjectivity, decision makers may want to set norms before they review files about how they will evaluate research experience, rather than allowing themselves to be impressed by students with the most prominent research experiences.

Finally, I want to offer a few comments about a common recruitment dilemma. Graduate programs striving to increase their enrollment of a particular group often find themselves stuck in a negative feedback loop: For admitted students from the underrepresented group debating whether or not to enroll, an absence of individuals who share their identity can raise red flags about what the quality of their experience will be. This uncertainty may contribute to their decision to matriculate elsewhere, which perpetuates the group's underrepresentation. Breaking this cycle requires strong leadership and evidence that diversity is, for the program, more than a platitude. Those in recruitment roles should be ready to initiate honest conversations about how and why diversity matters, what it means for their scholarly work, what students from underrepresented backgrounds will gain from and offer to the program, and what the climate is like for students from that group in the program, campus, and broader community. Especially for people from privileged backgrounds, it can be hard to speak frankly about these issues because they are always works in progress. However, developing the proficiency to do so in recruitment, admissions, mentoring, and instructional contexts is part of the change process itself.

Examine Assumptions about Merit

Perhaps the most fundamental implication of this study is the need to reframe relationships among fundamental principles like excellence, merit, and diversity. Diversity was one dimension of merit when faculty assessed applicants on the short list, but many spoke about "diversity with excellence" as well—as if these are independent entities accompanying one another. The Association of American Colleges and Universities recommends educational institutions work toward a culture of inclusive excellence, which

> integrate[s] diversity, equity, and educational quality efforts into their missions and institutional operations . . . The action of making excellence inclusive requires that we uncover inequities in student success, identify effective educational practices, and build such practices organically for sustained institutional change.[33]

In admissions, inclusive excellence means broadening recruitment efforts beyond the relatively small network of colleges and universities through which opportunities tend to flow, reassessing assumptions about what it means to be qualified (and what the grounds are for those assessments), and tracking the equity implications of current selection practices and any proposed reforms.[34]

Making excellence inclusive also means recognizing that common performance metrics do not tell the full story about underrepresented students' potential.[35] Research is needed to refine measures and assess their predictive validity, but there is a growing movement to formally assess students' noncognitive strengths as part of a holistic definition of what it means to be qualified for doctoral education.[36] For example, the Fisk-Vanderbilt Master's-to-PhD Bridge Program added an interview to their selection process that assesses students' grit and resilience. It asks them to reflect upon their interest in science, how they persevered through challenges, and the resources and relationships to which they turn in struggles. Their outcomes have been impressive. Since 2004, 81 percent of its entrants have continued on to doctoral studies, which flips a national trend in which 80 percent of students of color with STEM bachelor's degrees do not continue to graduate school.[37] Raising the profile of promising alternatives to current educational and selection models has value when a dearth of alternatives is often presented in defense of the status quo.

Stop Misusing Standardized Test Scores

For some faculty, meeting a standard of fairness in admissions will require that they learn more about the proper interpretation and limits of standardized test scores (GRE, TOEFL, GMAT, others) and reassess their use in the admissions process. Documentation from ETS, for instance, indicates that the GRE measures skills. It advises that raw scores and percentiles should not be used as sole or primary admissions considerations, and that score thresholds should not be applied.[38] However, decision makers in these programs routinely used scores as a primary consideration in the first round of review. About half thought of scores as signaling intelligence, and it was common practice to assess applicants against formal or informal score or percentile thresholds. Simply put, they misused the GRE.

The appeal of simple metrics is undeniable. Indeed, anything that makes this complicated review process more convenient is hard to ignore. However, the patterns I observed both run contrary to the psychometric properties of the test and put already underrepresented populations at a disadvantage. By failing to read scores in context, reviewers made overly simplistic comparisons about students' relative potential. Many had a general awareness that GRE scores have patterns associated with race, gender, and first-year graduate school GPA. Fewer knew that research studies have come to very different conclusions about the strength of the correlation between test scores and longer-term academic outcomes, or that stereotype threat helps explain group-level disparities.[39] Professors thus need better knowledge of ETS guidelines, of research about the full scope of factors that test performance can reflect, as well as its validity for different groups of students and for short- versus long-term outcomes. With this knowledge, admissions leaders can come to more thoughtful decisions about whether to require the test and, if they choose to do so, how to appropriately use and interpret its results.[40]

Awareness of the many problems with standardized test scores—that they are more complicated than they appear, that reliance on them can undermine equity efforts, that they do not reliably predict students' long-term success—has led some higher education institutions to reduce their reliance on these measures or eliminate their requirement entirely. As of summer 2014, the National Center for Fair and Open Testing reported that 103 selective colleges and universities had implemented test-optional admissions processes. At the graduate level, doctoral programs in at least thirty-two different fields have eliminated their GRE requirement, including ones at Columbia University, University of Pennsylvania, Johns Hopkins University, and the University of Michigan.[41] Research is needed about the effects of going test optional, both at the undergraduate and graduate levels. In one study, results indicated that making standardized test scores optional resulted in an increase in the enrollment of women, students of color, and international students, without changing the institution's mean GPA or graduation rate. But in another study, researchers found that going test-optional did not on its own increase diversity, but instead increased selectivity because only the applicants with higher scores submitted theirs.[42] If increasing the enrollment of students of color is specifically a goal, making GRE scores optional or declining to review them are options that should be on the table. However, they will be more successful as part of a coordinated set of efforts.[43]

Seek Small Wins in Admissions as Part of a Multifaceted Change Process

Changing culture and confronting inequality can seem daunting prospects, and that may be part of the problem. According to organizational theorist Karl Weick's idea of "small wins," how we define long-term challenges affects the chances of making progress on them, because when social problems are conceived at large scales, people become immobilized from taking action and they perform more poorly when they try. "When the magnitude of problems is scaled upward in the interest of mobilizing action," he writes, "the quality of thought and action declines, because processes such as frustration, arousal, and helplessness are activated." Weick therefore recommends that organizations approach major challenges by "identify[ing] a series of controllable opportunities of modest size that produce visible results," particularly in how they interpret and classify problems, which shapes the scope of possible solutions.[44] Among the examples of small wins that Weick cites is Alcoholics Anonymous conceptualizing sobriety as a goal that is achieved one day—even one hour—at a time.

Improving admissions is a small win relative to systemic problems of inequality in academia and society. Yet to bring the scale down to something even more manageable, admissions itself holds possibilities for small wins because the work is replete with classification. The endgame, of course, is to classify a subset of the applicant pool as admitted, but along the way decision makers employ an elaborate mental classification system when they infer complex qualities like intelligence and potential from the application. Counterscripts—alternative interpretations of common criteria—serve as a small win by systematically shifting how decision makers mentally classify students. By focusing on engrained assumptions, small wins can build consensus and create sustainable change.[45] By shifting discourse they help shift conventional wisdom, motivating change as they signal that such change is already under way.[46]

The field of philosophy offers an excellent case of how small wins in admissions can be part of a broader strategy for equity-minded change, in their case, with respect to gender. In one of the two the committees I observed, female members and male allies actively challenged their colleagues on misinterpretation of GRE scores, and they offered counterscripts about how to read undergraduate college prestige. On the latter, they introduced into the deliberations some of the reasons other than talent (such as financial barriers, family commitments, or opting out of the prestige chase) that students attend less-selective institutions. The support of a critical mass for these counterscripts shifted the dominant narratives about at least three borderline applicants. Instead of playing a determinative role, scores and affiliations counted as two among many considerations.

In addition to broadening the meanings attributed to GRE scores and college prestige, individual faculty, graduate students, and small groups in both of the philosophy departments I worked with are engaged in other departmental and national efforts to increase women's participation. At the department level, they are hosting coffee hours and dinners for aspiring female philosophers, and creating structures through which individuals can safely report experiences of discrimination or harassment. At the national level, female faculty in these departments are working through formal and informal collectives and campaigns.[47] There are active networks promoting equity and opportunity for women through the American Philosophical Association's Committee on the Status of Women (APACSW) and the Women in in Philosophy Task Force, for example. One recent APACSW campaign gathered and posted online information from master's and PhD programs about their enrollment, retention, and job placement rates by gender, as well as comments about each one's efforts and achievements to increase women's participation. Another popular campaign compiled photos of more than 200 women in philosophy into posters with the line "Philosophy. Got women?" There are also anonymous, cooperatively published websites (titled "Feminist Philosophers" and "What is it like to be a woman in philosophy?") that provide a public forum for speaking out and sharing experiences. As philosophers work to change the culture of philosophy, changing the assumptions that decision makers bring to admissions evaluations is just one part of their efforts.

Conclusion

I have argued that judgments of the "best" graduate programs in the country and the "best" applicants in the pool come about only by negotiating across priorities associated with specific social contexts. Thus, there is wisdom in my colleague Paul Courant's admonition to "beware the tyranny of best practices." The best practices for admission to a department's doctoral program may be different from those used to admit master's-level students, who may have different professional goals. What is best for recruiting graduate students to New York or Los Angeles may be different from what it takes to draw students to Madison or Boulder. From this perspective, a final implication of this study is not the need for a specific set of practices, but rather for faculty to approach their gatekeeping work with a different state of mind. Instead of proceeding by default or adopting a specific checklist of procedures developed for some other program's needs or goals, admissions decision makers need to approach gatekeeping with mindfulness of their own situation and needs. When evaluation and selection happen by default rather than intention, the social consequences of decision making may be misrecognized as the normal course of events—the way things *should* be rather than the way things ended up. And over time those outcomes can be thought of as natural rather than deliberate, for the more deeply held a belief is, the more likely it is to keep a person from seeing things any other way.

Today's faculty choose students on the basis of an array of perceptions that only sometimes have a strong evidentiary basis. In a process so competitive that the mere *presence* of doubt can seal an applicant's fate, perceptions often carry the weight of truth. They drive decision makers to act—to rate and advocate, to admit and reject—as if perception were reality. As the theorem made famous by sociologists William and Dorothy Thomas puts it: "If men define situations as real, they are real in their consequences."

Context and circumstance will always establish broad parameters within which we make choices. Yet social constructionism teaches us that the social world is as we perceive it to be because we act upon our perceptions.[48] Admissions judgments are socially situated; they result from inference upon inference, and from filters associated with organizational contexts and goals. The benefit of research like this study, which puts participant interpretations at the center of analysis, is in uncovering these taken-for-granted filters, for it is only by stepping outside of and analyzing them that we can understand their power. Like the prisoners in Plato's cave, misled to believe that shadows on the wall were reality, scholars may not even realize that the way they have been conditioned to see excellence in themselves and others is not natural, but constructed to serve specific ends. Yet unlike the prisoners, scholars can shape the social contexts in which their judgment is situated. In doing so, they refine the lenses through which their own understanding—and that of their colleagues and students—will be filtered.

Indeed, one of the great values of understanding an organization's gatekeeping systems is that it lays bare cultural values that drive policy, which are often so engrained as to be taken for granted. Too often our preferences and aversions go unspoken—even unrealized at a conscious level—so that misguided assumptions and implicit biases are never challenged and continue to shape the outcomes of review. Honest dialogue about the values and norms that shape interpretations of scholars' records is therefore needed, not only in admissions, but across the disciplines and the range of gatekeeping processes the academy employs. These conversations are relevant to how we admit students; how we hire postdoctoral researchers and faculty; how we select individuals for awards, grants, and fellowships; how we advance students to candidacy; and how we assess faculty scholarship for tenure and promotion. Each of these evaluation processes is fundamentally an activity of defining and monitoring organizational boundaries, of determining the grounds for membership, belonging, and recognition.

The faculty I spoke with want their students to succeed, and they like the idea of increasing diversity of many sorts. They carry out gatekeeping activities consistent with field-level norms and with those of their own training. Yet having mostly graduated from selective doctoral programs themselves, and with limited exposure to other models, their inclination may be to so strongly associate their own training with "quality" training that they recreate its selection process and the educational gauntlet in the interest of preserving what they see to be the purity of the discipline and excellence of the program.

However, society is changing. The labor market for PhDs is changing. And higher education is changing, too, both intellectually and demographically. If doctoral education and our means of identifying talent do not change with them, it will be doctoral education and the professoriate that fail by falling behind, not our students. Re-creating academic programs and disciplines in our own image may be the natural tendency, but in a changing world—one that is more diverse, more collaborative, more interdisciplinary— stewardship of our disciplines' futures means being flexible to recognize what the world needs from our fields of study and adapting our ideals of excellence accordingly.

Methodological Appendix

Research design follows from one's research questions, and the two questions that guided my design were straightforward: How do faculty members individually judge and collectively select prospective doctoral students? How do disciplines shape judgments of admissibility? I could have answered these questions through a number of methods but opted to design an ethnographic comparative case study after weighing several options. I could have statistically inferred faculty priorities from the characteristics of students that they admitted, but I wanted to explore reasons for the apparent contradiction between diversity as an institutionalized value and continuing inequalities in higher education. I also wanted to see how admissions negotiations unfolded over multiple rounds of review—knowing from previous research that there were likely to be differences between how reviewers approached the pool as a whole compared to how they approached the short list.[1] Third, quantitative research only picks up patterns present across many people, and many of the reasons that individuals are selected for graduate programs may be idiosyncratic to committees, programs, disciplines, or specific applicant pools. Thus, the benefits of greater generalizability that might have come from findings of a quantitative study would have come at the cost of capturing the very complexities that make it a socially important, and intriguing, phenomenon.

My own conceptualization of faculty evaluation also suggested the need for naturalistic research. I think of evaluation as an activity situated in, and thus shaped by, social forces associated with multiple organizational contexts, whose priorities may or may not align. I therefore sought to be closely engaged with the phenomenon as it was happening, where it was happening. Observations would also help triangulate what the evaluative scripts in use were, per methods used in Goffman's

Table 12　Overview of Sample and Data Collection

Discipline	Subject Matter	Year	University	Interviews	Observations
Astrophysics	Natural Science	1	B	X	X
Biology	Natural Science	2	C	X	
Physics	Natural Science	2	C	X	
Philosophy 1	Humanities	1	A	X	X
Philosophy 2	Humanities	2	C	X	X
Linguistics	Humanities	2	C	X	X
Classics	Humanities	2	C	X	X
Economics	Social Science	1	A	X	
Political Science	Social Science	2	C	X	X
Sociology	Social Science	1	A	X	

initial work on scripts, Garfinkel's ethnomethodological tradition, and more recent organizational and institutional scholarship.[2] I knew that observational data would also be useful in drawing out aspects of decision making that are important for outcomes but that faculty may take for granted as routine. Finally, collecting and analyzing data at multiple levels of analysis would facilitate theory elaboration, which is often an implicit aim in inductive, comparative case studies.[3]

After weighing these considerations, I conducted comparative ethnographic case studies of the PhD admissions cycle in ten departments that represented disciplines in the humanities, social sciences, and natural/physical sciences. They were located in three research universities with very high research activity, and data collection took place over two admissions cycles (2010–2011 and 2011–2012). See Table 12 for details.

Case Study as a Methodology

Merriam defines case study as "in-depth description and analysis of a bounded system."[4] This definition has four critical elements: depth, description, analysis, and bounded system. Case study methodologists strive to illuminate a particular phenomenon by learning as much as possible about the particulars of one or a handful of cases rather than learning a few things about a very large sample.[5] Cases are carefully selected for how they are likely to reveal the phenomenon of interest.

Description and analysis are the researcher's means of revealing the case. "Thick description" uses details of what is immediately observable to take readers *beyond* the immediately observable into the realm of deeper social meanings. In his famous article on the topic, Clifford Geertz illustrates thick description by considering the difference between an eye twitching and winking.[6] Thin description would note muscle contraction in one eye, but miss whether it was involuntary (a twitch) or conspiratorial (a wink) because this distinction may also require detail about the actors, setting, other communication, and circumstances. Description along these latter dimensions ensures that the meaning of a socially important moment is not lost. Small matters—the lighting in a conference room, the order in which applicants are reviewed, the topics of side conversations preceding the "real" conversation—may matter much as cultural insights, and through describing such details I have tried to capture the social and organizational complexity of faculty evaluation.

Case study methodology does not prescribe specific analytic methods, but weaving together a case narrative that both accounts for details and sorts out participants' signification structures is empirical, interpretive work.[7] To make sense of the voluminous data typically collected for case studies, the researcher's meaning-making is a key intellectual activity of analysis.

The final element in Merriam's definition is the case itself—the object of study—as a bounded system. The case can be an instance of a population or of a conceptual class, but either way it may be thought of as the phenomenon *in context*.[8] I strove to capture individual and collective faculty judgment in situ, so my case boundaries were organizational (highly selective PhD-granting programs) and temporal (the admissions cycle from application to yield). Case selection often takes place by selecting on the dependent variable (identifying a case or cases that maximize the phenomenon of interest). In a regression this sampling approach is understood to produce selection bias, but comparative case study researchers make no assumptions about broad generalizability from the case. Instead, their goal and intellectual contribution is deep understanding, including capturing necessary (versus sufficient) conditions.[9] For case study researchers, it is more important to gain a rich picture of a phenomenon in a meaningful context.

Sampling

Rather than generalizing from their small n's to broader populations, case study scholars hope that the theoretical leverage obtained through thick description and in-depth analysis generates understanding that can illuminate similar cases. Case study sampling involves selection decisions at two levels: (1) the case, which serves as the primary unit of analysis, and (2) subjects within the case, whose perspectives help the researcher craft a holistic depiction.[10] At both levels I used criterion sampling, in which the researcher chooses cases that meet a predetermined criterion or set of criteria.[11]

Because the majority of doctoral degrees are awarded in research-focused universities, I focused on programs within three universities that have the Carnegie classification Research Universities–Very high research activity (RU/VH). Two are public and one is private, and they are located in two regions of the United States. Both for participant and program confidentiality and because institutional details are less salient to my analysis than details of the departments, programs, and disciplines, I do not discuss in the results the names or other identifying details of the universities in which data were collected. Initially I was disappointed by the Institutional Review Board's constraint on discussing the details of the universities in which I collected data. However, as my time in the field went on, I came to see that the universities varied more in their yield—the ability to draw admitted students—than in their selection processes, which was my focus.

Table 12 summarizes the sampling design. Within each university, I sampled PhD-granting programs representing disciplines in humanities, social sciences, and physical/natural sciences. I expected that such programs would evince disciplinary influences more clearly than applied or interdisciplinary programs. I also narrowed my choice of institutions to those in which the fields of interest maintain programs ranked in the top fifteen in their field.[12] In these contexts, many qualified individuals apply; therefore, the competing demands of selection come into sharper focus. Although I initially hoped to study the same departments at multiple universities, there was only one instance in which I could gain access from a second department that was also ranked in the top fifteen in the discipline. The exception to this is philosophy, in which I collected data at two of the three universities. However, within the humanities, social sciences, and natural/physical sciences, I sampled at least one higher-consensus discipline (such as classics, economics, or physics) and one lower-consensus discipline (such as linguistics, political science, or biology), which has lent structure and intellectual focus to my cross-case comparison.

My sample in each of the ten programs consisted of the chair of the department and/or admissions, members on the admissions committee, and one emeritus professor. Where this group totaled fewer than six people due to a small committee size or a small proportion of the committee who consented to be interviewed, I interviewed additional faculty members. The astrophysics, linguistics, and political science departments each included one to three graduate students on the admissions committee as well, for a total of six graduate student participants. I wanted to create a picture of admissions as it is currently practiced in these departments, and therefore I did not oversample by race/ethnicity or gender. As a result, my sample reflects the same problems of underrepresentation by female and domestic faculty of color that the U.S. professoriate does.

Recruitment

Sensitive to the ethical and reputational implications of this research for the programs and individuals who participated, I tried to design and write it in ways that protected them, and to make it as easy as possible for prospective participants to feel comfortable in our early interactions. In the initial contact, I framed my study as a matter of decision making and the challenge of balancing multiple interests. Although I probed for issues around diversity throughout data collection, I saved the protocol questions about diversity for the end of interviews, after some rapport and the beginnings of trust had been established. Also, I outlined in both the initial email and the informed consent document the measures I took to ensure confidentiality. In summary, although the nature of the research undoubtedly deterred some from participating, I made a concerted effort to minimize the risks to participants and maximize their anonymity.

With a target sample of four to six programs per year, I initiated contact via email with seventeen programs in the first year of data collection and eighteen programs in the second year. My first contact with each was an email message in September to the department chair or program director in qualifying programs at prospective universities. I requested a thirty-minute informational interview to discuss their program's approach to admissions. The department chair referred me in most cases to the admissions committee chair for this interview. Ten and nine programs agreed to informational interviews in the first and second years, respectively. I continued the recruitment process during those interviews by explaining the research study design, but I encouraged the chair to consult others in the department before making a decision. In a few cases, general consent to conduct the departmental case study was immediately provided or declined at the informational interview, but more often this occurred via subsequent email communication. We agreed in all cases that individuals would each have the opportunity to consent or decline participation, and that if any faculty member on the admissions committee preferred for me not to observe, that I would not observe that department's committee.

Once general consent to conduct the case studies was provided, I requested an official approval letter to file with the IRB, printed on department letterhead and signed by the department chair. I also requested from the admissions chair a list of their committee members for the year and the names of one or two emeritus faculty whom I might recruit for an oral history of the department and its admissions practices. Then, using an email template similar to that used with department chairs, I emailed each committee member an invitation to be interviewed for the study. As described above, in departments with small committees or where fewer than six committee members and emeriti agreed to be interviewed, I used snowball sampling within each department to develop a list of individuals with few and many years of admissions experience whom I could also recruit to participate.

Data Collection

To achieve deep and holistic understanding of a case, leaders in case study research advise using all three of the common qualitative data collection techniques—interviews, observation, and artifact analysis.[13] In this study, data collection consisted of observations, interviews, and collection and analysis of department websites and participants' curricula vitae. In the first year, I collected data from one program at one university and three more at another university. Then, in the second year, I collected data from six programs at one university.

Observation. Observation of admissions committee meetings in six of the ten programs was a crucial complement to the interview data by laying bare the priorities and preferences that shaped admissions outcomes in practice. I feel privileged to have had access to this invaluable source of knowledge, which also highlighted similarities and differences across disciplines in how faculty make admissions decisions.

I conducted observations in four types of events over the two years of data collection: admissions committee meetings, faculty training workshops at two universities, Skype interviews of applicants in two programs, and campus visit weekend events in one program. Every member of the admissions committee in six of the ten departments kindly consented for me to attend their admissions committee meetings, for a total of ten meetings observed overall. The shortest meeting was eighty minutes and longest was three hours and fifteen minutes (both in the political science department), for a total of twenty-one hours of meeting observations. I took structured field notes longhand to document the following:

1. The frequency with which various criteria and applicant traits were mentioned
2. The patterns of participation and interaction among faculty
3. How faculty discussed issues of merit and diversity
4. Which members of the committee appeared to have power or to be marginalized
5. How applicants were compared with one another and with external standards
6. Examples of consensus and conflict and how these were reached/handled
7. The physical setting and participants' nonverbal communication in the setting

The astrophysics committee also added me to their email list, so that I could observe their email interactions.

In addition, I received permission from administrators in two of the three universities to attend admission workshops conducted by their graduate schools for admissions committee chairs and faculty members throughout the university. These training events were one and two hours long, respectively. The astrophysics and physics departments also offered to have me sit in the room during select Skype interviews they planned with prospective students. Over two hours, I sat in on a total of four such interviews—two with domestic students and two with students from China—as well as the subsequent debriefing faculty had with one another following the interviews. Finally, the astrophysics department invited me to sit in on the two-hour introductory session of their campus visit weekend hosted for admitted students. I took open-ended field notes in these settings.

Insider status presents decided advantages in interview settings, but when it comes to observation, being an outsider has clear benefits, assuming that access to the group is permitted and group members do not make significant changes to their language or behavior. Chief among the benefits is that outsiders are able to notice what has become routine to or taken for granted.[14] For all observations, I sat in the back of the room or in a corner to minimize my obtrusiveness, and within twenty-four hours I transcribed the field notes into electronic format and composed memos/reflections. According to Gold's classic typology of observers' stances toward the observed, I was an "observer as participant."[15] That is, the group knew my activities and research aims, but did not count me as one of its members or invite me into the activities I observed. There were moments early in a few meetings where those around the table commented on my presence or seemed to self-monitor, but the many times faculty spoke in ways that were socially undesirable led me to believe that I was seeing more than a performance of their best behavior.

Interviews. I conducted eighty-six interviews ranging from twenty-three to eighty-five minutes in length with four groups: department and/or admissions committee chairs, other committee members, additional faculty, and faculty emeriti. As described above, recruitment for the study involved thirty- to sixty-minute semistructured informational interviews with program chairs and/or admissions committee chairs in prospective programs. These unrecorded interviews in faculty offices inquired into details of the department's admissions process and assessed interest in further participation in the study. Of the seventeen informational interviews I conducted, eleven resulted in approval for me to interview other department faculty; however, I opted out of one because only one other committee member in their program was willing to be interviewed. The final sample therefore includes ten departments. Of these, eight of the ten chairs also agreed to an unstructured follow-up interview after final offers were made. In some of the most candid interviews of the study, we discussed their reflections on how the admissions process went, admissions challenges, and deliberations about applicants on whom it was difficult to find consensus.

The initial research design proposed two thirty-minute interviews with each committee member—one before and one after file review. However, in the first year of data collection, many participants expressed concern about the scheduling difficulties this would pose, so I proposed as an alternative a single, longer interview. That approach proved much more appealing and resulted in response rates in excess of 70 percent. In the second year I made the single, longer interview the norm for non-chairs, and had almost 100 percent participation from all six committees. Consistent with a semistructured approach, these interviews varied somewhat, depending on when in the admissions process the interviews were conducted.

Standard faculty interviews began with faculty providing a brief narrative of their route to the professoriate, emphasizing their personal experience with graduate admissions so that I might ascertain any personal factors that might prove salient to their admissions work in the present. We also discussed important criteria and the meanings and signals they carry; perceptions and challenges of committee deliberations; profiles of easily admitted, easily rejected, and borderline cases; and how traits of highly valued faculty candidates compare to those of compelling PhD program applicants. These interviews averaged approximately fifty minutes each, and all but one took place in faculty/student offices. Upon my request in the informed consent document, all but three consented to have the interviews audiotaped and transcribed. Consistent with principles of emergent design in qualitative research, I adapted the interview protocol in response to unexpected themes that emerged in early interviewing. Most importantly, after the first five interviews in the first year of data collection, it became apparent that a common quality that participants sought in applicants was intelligence, but that their beliefs about what this meant varied widely. In response, I added a question to the interview asking them to reflect on the meaning of intelligence in their discipline and how they try to recognize it in applicants.

Finally, to contextualize current admissions practice in these programs, I interviewed an emeritus professor in each program to gain an oral history of developments in the department and discipline, and to probe for connections between the discipline's epistemology and selection criteria. These audiotaped interviews averaged just over sixty minutes each, and took place in either their homes or campus offices, per the participant's preference.

I developed the interview protocols using principles advocated by Robert Weiss in *Learning from Strangers: The Art and Method of Qualitative Interview Studies* and Herbert and Irene Rubin in *Qualitative Interviewing: The Art of Hearing Data*.[16] Asking main questions was intended to "elicit the overall experiences and understandings" of participants, while follow-up questions clarified responses and probes encouraged the participant to provide detail that could produce a more complete narrative.[17] A number of the questions had been used in or revised from a small-scale study I conducted in the winter and spring of 2009 on merit and diversity in graduate admissions. Using interview strategies employed in studies by William Tierney and Estela Bensimon, Stephen Barley, and Michéle Lamont, a set of important questions inquires into "ideal types" of applicants.[18] First advocated by Weber as a research technique, understanding ideal (and less than ideal) types of applicants is useful, not because they represent typical applicants or individuals who are admitted, but because they clarify symbolic boundaries and serve as models or heuristics to guide our thinking about social phenomena.[19] By integrating the observational and interview data, I have tried to outline common scripts of merit and other decision pathways.

Audio-recorded interviews were transcribed verbatim. I personally transcribed 25 percent of the interviews to aid in reflecting on the quality of my interviewing and the effectiveness of the interview protocol. Personal transcription also enabled me to remain mindful that transcripts do more than put talk in print; they re-present discourse, including both what is said and not said.[20] Transcripts thus noted the relative length of pauses, verbal pauses, events that interrupt the flow of conversation, laughter, in addition to words spoken. I augmented select transcripts with researcher memos as a forum for reflexivity, or self-critique about my work and self as researcher and instrument of research.[21]

History, place, and thick description. Understanding contemporary social and educational phenomena requires us to consider how they are situated spatially and temporally.[22] Present events and prevailing logics constitute "the signature of history."[23] Details of space and setting similarly shape social phenomena. What may appear to be background details are more than local color, for the dimensions of time and space create dependencies and contingencies that help explain how and why a case plays out as it does under our analysis. Howard Becker describes such detail as "the *environing conditions* under which the things we stud[y]—the relationships we uncover, the general social processes whose discovery we want to brag about— exist."[24] While rigorously adhering to the standards of confidentiality that human subjects policy and informed consent agreements demanded, my analysis involved careful observation, investigation, chronicling, and sifting of details about the settings and histories of the programs, disciplines, and universities to draw out context-specific variation and provide rich case descriptions.

Data Management

Case studies are notorious for the amount of data they generate, and I knew that my ability to craft a meaningful narrative would depend partly on its overall organization and the accessibility of individual bits of data. My first step in managing the data was creating an inventory, for which I maintained a comprehensive Excel workbook. To organize the field notes, interview transcripts, documents, and memos, I utilized NVivo 9.2. NVivo was also a critical tool for me in data analysis.

Data Analysis

The aims of case study—to "uncover patterns, determine meanings, construct con-clusions, and build theory"—provided a guide to selecting appropriate analytic methods.[25] Techniques from the grounded theory tradition provided a systematic means of capturing patterns and meanings and of developing conclusions and theoretical contributions. Grounded theory's constant comparative method is prev-alent across various qualitative research traditions, including case studies.[26] I drew, in particular, from Strauss and Corbin's approach, which involves three stages of coding (that is, seeking patterns in the data).[27] Data collection and analysis occurred simultaneously to facilitate ongoing reflection on the data and adjustments to my interviewing and observations. However, analysis continued long after data collec-tion concluded. I initially analyzed the data one department at a time and used those analyses to write cases of each department. Then I conducted a cross-case analysis in which I compiled all of the cases into a new NVivo project and interpreted case similarities and differences by disciplinary type and paradigm strength using the same micro-level analytic steps described below. Analysis was iterative, alternating between aggregated data from specific cases, cases themselves, and the sample as a whole.

Analysis at the micro level proceeded according to the three stages of coding rec-ommended in grounded theory: open, axial, and selective. During the initial open coding phase, I stayed close to my original research questions, looking for themes in faculty members' decision making processes, the meanings they associated with common criteria, and evidence of disciplinary cultures. However, the second round of open coding was more inductive, and through this I developed a variety of ad-ditional codes including homophily, bureaucracy, aversions, intelligence, and many more. For the purposes of an ethnographic case study, I think of axial coding as data-driven theory generation and of selective coding as an opportunity that case study presents to intersect theory generation with thick description. It was through selective coding that I developed a narrative that accounts for the relationship of the codes to one another and to critical details of the case. By interrelating the data and themes across levels of analysis and abstraction, my findings include a combi-nation of description and interpretation at both the individual level and the case level.

Case Development and Cross-Case Analysis

In the months following each admissions cycle and my initial analysis of data from programs studied that year, I composed cases of each program. Most were between five and fifteen pages, single-spaced. Writing these cases was a substantial task due to the number of departments I had studied and the amount of data I had gener-ated about each. Cases were understandably shorter in the programs where I con-ducted only interviews, and longer in the departments where I also observed ad-missions meetings and other events. My goal in composing each case was to represent what the results of the study might have been if I had sampled only that case. I devel-oped and utilized a case template that was organized around answering the research questions and reconstructing specific episodes in which faculty negotiated questions of merit, diversity, and equity (either the equity of their choices or the equity of their process). The goal of cross-case analysis was to answer the research questions in a rigorous way that would enable me to make broader theoretical propositions.[28]

Protecting Participant Confidentiality

Protecting participant confidentiality ranked high on my list of concerns in this study, as did protecting the anonymity of any student applicants discussed by the committees. Among the several items in the suite of protections, I masked or gave pseudonyms to all information that might be personally identifiable. In referring to specific institutions, I sought to balance the need to ensure anonymity with the need to convey a real-world sense of the institutional strata in which these programs are located. Therefore, when the need arose to name specific universities including the data collection sites, I randomly drew from a list of fifteen institutions in the same tier of program rankings for that discipline. This means that the actual university in which data was collected could have potentially been named due to chance, but readers should be no more able to recognize that institution as being the data collection site than any other, similarly ranked institution.

Trustworthiness and Reliability

I engaged in a number of practices to increase the trustworthiness and reliability of the findings. These include data triangulation across interviews and observations, thick description, reflexive researcher memos, member checking, and searching for disconfirming evidence. Member checking is rooted in the idea that the qualitative researcher's role is not to impose one's own voice on those of participants, but rather to get inside of participants' perspectives and give voice to their concerns. Practically, member checking consists of consulting research participants to learn "whether the data analysis is congruent with the participants' experiences."[29] My objective was to discuss whether and how preliminary findings about each department resonated with the respective admissions committee chairs, who had practical, professional knowledge of the processes I was trying to capture.

I circulated a draft of each program's case to its respective admissions chair and offered to exchange feedback in person or via email. Most opted for face-to-face conversations, and I did not receive any negative responses about the credibility or clarity of the findings; however, not everyone *liked* what they read about their colleagues and their own practice. One department chair provided me with some additional organizational history that helped me make sense of a gap in the data. Another explained how their interpretation of test scores has changed in the transition to the new version of the GRE. In several cases, the admissions chairs with whom I met also asked for my recommendations about specific changes they might make to improve the department's admissions process.

With respect to falsifiability, Popper advocated an approach to knowledge production in which progress is measured not only by the volume of evidence that can be amassed in support of a theory, but by its ability to withstand a search for disconfirming evidence.[30] Lareau supports this view.[31] In the name of presenting apparently clean results, she argues that contemporary qualitative researchers in sociology and education too frequently sacrifice the rigor of searching for and responding to disconfirming evidence. Therefore, a late stage of data analysis in my study involved an additional round of analysis for disconfirming evidence of the prevailing themes and propositions. Patterns in disconfirming evidence or alternative interpretations are presented before the conclusion section in most chapters of findings.

Limitations

The principal limitations of this study concern data imbalances across departments and demographic groups. Female, African American, or Latino faculty are underrepresented in the highly ranked departments I partnered with and on the committees I studied; their voices are therefore underrepresented in my sample. Although this means that my results capture prevailing viewpoints in these departments (and thus, I hope, cultural dynamics that help sustain structural inequality), the results do downplay the alternative viewpoints that individuals from these backgrounds may contribute.

Another limitation is that I have interview data from all ten programs, but observational data from only seven. Seven of the ten permitted observation, and one of these (physics) does not convene for traditional admissions committee meetings. Though I observed two Skype interviews of applicants in physics, I am unable to provide concrete examples from deliberations in four departments: biology, economics, physics, and sociology.

Also, the committee sizes and response rates for consent to be interviewed varied widely across departments. In an extreme case, although the admissions chair was eager for my involvement with his committee, only one other member consented to be interviewed; therefore, I withdrew this case from the set of cases (for a final total of ten). On the other end, in astrophysics, each member of the five-person committee was willing to be interviewed multiple times. In several departments the committee consisted of fewer than six individuals or not every member of the committee consented to be interviewed; in these departments, I recruited faculty to interview from outside the committee, using snowball sampling starting with the admissions chair.

Researcher's Role and Establishing Rapport

Origins of this research. My interest in graduate admissions began in the course of working from 2003 to 2007 with the McNair Scholars Program at the University of Northern Colorado. McNair is a federally funded TRiO program that facilitates research opportunities for low-income, first-generation, and underrepresented minority students, with an eye toward long-term improvement in faculty diversity. I taught introductory research design courses, advised them in working with their faculty mentors, and supported those who elected to continue their education through the graduate school admissions process. Each summer, program staff facilitated GRE preparation workshops, and we invited a graduate admissions consultant for

a two-day seminar. Then, each fall, I worked one-on-one with students as they selected prospective graduate programs, initiated contact with prospective advisors,
wrote their personal statements, solicited letters of recommendation, and managed
the myriad of details, deadlines, and emotions that the process requires and creates.

Through this work, I became interested in several aspects of graduate admissions.
As mentioned in the Preface, I struggled to find cross-disciplinary, empirical studies
that could inform my advising work, and thought this absence of research was
curious considering how much has been published on undergraduate admissions.
The similarities between doctoral admissions and faculty hiring processes also
became striking to me, including the role that research potential and establishing institutional fit play in perceived merit. When I decided to pursue a PhD myself, it
was with an interest in building knowledge about the current structure of access to
graduate education.

Positionality and building rapport. I began the research as an outsider to these departments, disciplines, and the professoriate itself. According to Jorgensen, a major
strength of the ethnographic approach is that long-term involvement allows time for
the building of insider perspective and, with it, trust in the researchers.[32] Conversely,
where trust is low, the risks are higher that participants will withhold or distort information, act out their roles differently than usual, or provide socially desirable
answers to interview questions.[33] Thus, it came as no surprise that I encountered a
wide range of comfort and candor levels from participants. Five participants of the
eighty-six who consented to be interviewed projected a clear sense of guardedness
throughout the interviews. These interviews were also relatively short. The other respondents thawed over the first fifteen minutes of the interview or displayed ease
from the beginning and an interest in co-constructing bridges of rapport.

Rapport was demonstrated in ways including but not limited to: socially undesirable and politically incorrect responses (which I probed), an offer to provide me
with an office within the department for my work (which never panned out due
to space limits), an invitation to have our families meet for a playdate (which I
declined), requests for additional conversations about the department's admissions
reform efforts (which I agreed to), and expressions of emotion such as tears, excla-
mations, and laughter (which I noted with gratitude).

Although it was impossible to know how forthcoming any research participant
was being, the faculty I interviewed seemed to be especially direct with me when
interviews took place after I had already observed an admissions meeting in that
department. Having seen them involved in this difficult work, they spoke with the
honesty that one has when there is nothing left to hide. Interviews with emeritus
faculty were also rich, and often entertaining as they passionately recounted to me
the tides of change and currents of stability in their careers and the lives of their
departments and disciplines. Faculty emeriti, I learned, have not only a wealth of
knowledge about the politics and "dirty laundry" of their departments and disciplines. Unlike graduate students and untenured professors, they have little to lose
in disclosing it. I also learned they have a deep, emotional appreciation for their
work and the academic communities who have supported them.

Reflecting on this rapport, I brought a few characteristics to the research relationships that may have unexpectedly worked in my favor in cultivating trust or candor. My having been a graduate student may have led professors to view opening up to me as less threatening than if I were a professor, for example.[34] Furthermore, informational interviews suggested that my affiliation with the University of Michigan brand lent credibility, and that my ability and interest in establishing a yearlong relationship with the departments rather than swooping in for a one-time interview may have helped build rapport. Finally, with a sample that was 82 percent male and 85 percent white, my identity as a white woman undoubtedly affected the majority of participants' comfort and candor during interviews. I came to realize in the course of the first year of data collection that when I presented in stereotypically female ways—such as wearing pink or wearing lipstick—male interviewees were often more candid with me. Though it never sat well with my feminist sensibilities, I kept my one pink shirt in regular rotation for the sake of the research and bought another mid-year off of the clearance rack. Interview-based research is hardly immune from the social forces that affect everyday interactions.

Conclusion

Each experience one has for research is an opportunity for continued learning, both about one's subject matter and the research process. Although I am unable to share the original data from this study with others due to my agreements with participants and the Institutional Review Board, I would be pleased to discuss further details of the research methodology or findings with readers who are interested.

Notes

Introduction

1. All faculty, applicant, and university names, as well as other personally identifiable information, have been changed or masked to protect participant confidentiality.

2. My first thought when I scoped out the room was that I must be in the wrong place. "Come to the conference room off of the copier room," my email instructions from the committee chair had read. The only such room I could find, however, was about 10 feet by 10 feet, with walls on three sides covered with storage units and filing cabinets. In the middle was a table for four—but which could seat six if you were willing to get cozy. I walked the hallways to see if there might be another copier room for the department. By the time I made my way back I found three of the committee members seated at the table, and concluded that this tiny space must be it after all.

3. These numbers refer specifically to admission/rejection in doctoral programs in research universities with very high research activity. For this and other statistics about admission rates in master's and doctoral programs in universities with additional Carnegie classifications, see Allum, Bell, and Sowell 2012, 5.

4. Other correlates of admission include college curriculum and grade point average, stated religion, and perceptions of professional competency and interpersonal and intrapersonal problems (Campbell 2009; Brear, Dorrian, and Luscri 2008; Attiyeh and Attiyeh 1997; Gartner 1986).

5. For a few of the explanations behind rising graduate degree pursuit, see Collins 2002, Labaree 1997, Pappano 2011, Walker et al. 2008, and Wulff et al. 2004.

6. Schmidt 2010; Schofer and Meyer 2005. For detailed trend data about U.S. doctorates in the twentieth century, see Thurgood, Golladay, and Hill 2006. Findings from the Council of Graduate Schools' annual International Graduate Admissions Survey offer useful information about trends in application, admission, and enrollment across countries, regions of origin, and fields of study. For example, Chinese nationals comprised 34 percent of international students enrolled in American graduate programs in 2014. See J. Allum et al. 2014.

7. Torche 2011.

8. U.S. Department of Education, National Center for Education Statistics 2012.

9. Gonzales, Allum, and Sowell 2013. Note that across racial/ethnic groups, women comprised the majority attaining doctoral degrees in 2010 if first professional doctoral degrees (e.g., MD, JD, DDS) are included in the calculation (U.S. Department of Education, National Center for Education Statistics 2012).

10. Bell 2010. In 2012, U.S. universities awarded just 102 new PhDs to Native Americans (Patel 2014).

11. Leslie et al. 2015; Attiyeh and Attiyeh 1997.

12. National Science Foundation 2010.

13. Gonzales et al. 2013.

14. On rising pursuit of the PhD, see Jones 2003, Gibney 2012, and Cyranoski et al. 2011.

15. Nettles and Millett 2006, 101.

16. Schillebeeckx, Maricque, and Lewis 2013;Cassuto 2015. Recent attention in the popular press to the academic job market in the humanities includes a forum in the *New York Times* ("Room for Debate" 2013) and an article by Michael Bérubé (2013) in the *Chronicle of Higher Education*.

17. Cassuto 2015; Kezar and Sam 2010.

18. James 1903.

19. To maintain a clear focus, this research excluded from analysis professional doctoral degree programs (e.g., MD, JD) because processes of admissions to such programs are unique in several ways. Professional staff often review applications, and criteria emphasize experience with and potential for practice. Notwithstanding the range of careers those with a PhD may pursue, PhD programs continue to emphasize research training over (or in addition to) training for professional practice. Different standardized tests are also used for professional admissions, and scores on those tests are more heavily weighted in admissions decisions than in most PhD programs.

20. APA-accredited clinical psychology programs—arguably among the most elite in the discipline—offered admission to only 10.5 percent of the nearly 19,000 applicants in 2002 (Landrum and Clump 2004). Within and across the disciplines, admissions selectivity and overall doctoral program enrollment explain large proportions of reputational scores used to calculate the 1995 National Research Council rankings (Grunig 1997) and the 2008 U.S. News and World Report rankings (Sweitzer and Volkwein 2009). The exception to this trend is in education, where average admissions test scores for graduate programs are not significantly associated with program reputation (Sweitzer and Volkwein 2009). Nevertheless, Vanderbilt University's Peabody College of Education, the

highest-ranked college of education nationally in 2010, admitted just 6.5 percent of its PhD applicants in 2009 (K. Tanner, personal communication, August 24, 2010).

21. Jaschik 2009.

22. Frank and Cook 1995, 3.

23. Collins (2002) examines the implications of credential inflation in the labor market for the future of higher education. Mitchell Stevens (2007) finds in a study of undergraduate admissions that quality is also a moving target in the review process because decision makers often judge applicants not according to a specific set of standards but relative to the characteristics of others in the pool.

24. Beneath the debates over these questions are fundamental debates about what our standards of fairness should be, and whose standards of fairness should carry the day.

25. For some of the earliest research on graduate admissions, see Cureton, Cureton, and Bishop 1949; Borg 1963; Newman 1968; Madaus and Walsh 1965; and Lannholm 1968.

26. Sternberg and Williams 1997, 630.

27. See, for example, Kuncel and Hezlett 2007.

28. Pennock-Roman 1986, 252.

29. Further, the methods most scholars have used do not allow for causal inference at all; they have been almost exclusively correlational and meta-analytic, with few controls for confounding variables. Predictive validity research typically samples admitted students, not the applicant pool, restricting the range of observations to the right tail and therefore producing attenuated correlation coefficients. If samples were to include the outcomes of rejected students who enroll elsewhere, a broader range of GRE scores would be available for analysis and GRE scores would be more likely to predict academic outcomes. Further, the covariance structure of admissions variables consists of negative correlations because admissions decision-making is usually a holistic process in which there are a large number of practical considerations, whose relative importance varies widely from person to person (Dawes 1971, 180).

30. Kuncel and Hezlett 2007. For two examples of meta-analyses, see Kuncel, Hezlett, and Ones 2001; and Morrison and Morrison 1995. For examples of single-discipline predictive validity studies, see Grove, Dutkowsky, and Grodner 2007; Ruscingno 2006; and Wilkerson 2007. Through meta-analysis in several disciplines, Kuncel, Hezlett, and Ones (2001) concluded that the GRE is a generalizably valid predictor of passing comprehensive examinations. This finding holds in a separate study of economics students, although the GRE does not predict completion of the PhD itself (Grove, Dutkowsky, and Grodner 2007). In Morrison and Morrison's 1995 meta-analysis, there is no significant correlation between GRE scores and first-year GPA.

31. See Educational Testing Service, 2014a for ETS guidelines on the appropriate interpretation of scores.

32. Stevens (2007) found a similar pattern in his ethnographic study of undergraduate admissions in a liberal arts college. As economist Robert Klitgaard put it,

highly ranked universities and graduate programs within them tend to receive applications from many students who fall in the "right tail of the distribution of talent" (Klitgaard 1985, 12).

33. A few scholars have noted how environmental characteristics shape the relationship between academic admissions criteria and student outcomes, such as Walters, Lee, and Trapani, 2004. Organization-level characteristics, such as those of the test center (e.g., ethnic match between test proctor and test-taker), graduate program (e.g., number of same-gender peers in a graduate program), or university (e.g., perceptions of climate) may also explain the relationship between applicant criteria and later outcomes. Regression analyses that fail to control for organizational-level factors will produce upwardly biased estimates about the strength of the relationship between an admissions criterion and later measures of success.

34. For examples of research on higher education that examines the use of hiring and admission to encourage broader organizational goals, see Birnbaum 1988, Klitgaard 1985, Killgore 2009, Nivet 2011.

35. Stevens 2007.

36. Lamont 2012.

37. The organizational perspective on merit that I propose draws upon ideas from the sociology of evaluation and sociocultural research on undergraduate admissions and the professoriate. See, for example, Karabel 2005, Kahlenberg 1996, and Karen 1990. In higher education research, specifically, sociocultural scholars approach selection and promotion in higher education as contextualized and socially constructed. See Tierney 1988, and Peterson and Spencer 1990, 13. Beginning with Burton Clark (1960) sociocultural paradigms have been used to study process-based phenomena such as socialization and tenure (Tierney and Bensimon 1996) and the institutionalization of interdisciplinarity (Lattuca 2001). Stevens 2007, Birnbaum 1988, Twombly 1992, and Lamont 2009 all bring sociocultural sensibilities to bear on selection in higher education. I also thank Janet Weiss and Andrew Kinney for their insights into this angle on merit.

38. Cassuto 2015; Guinier 2015.

39. Wechsler 1977, 244. See also Stevens 2007 and Stampnitzky 2006 for institutional accounts about the production of preferences in undergraduate admissions.

40. A narrow definition of diversity is heterogeneity based on individual characteristics such ethnicity, race, gender, gender identity, sexual orientation, class, religion, geography, experience, and viewpoint. Beyond this narrow framing, which Daryl Smith calls "the laundry list approach," the pursuit of diversity through graduate admissions may encompass a wide range of important considerations about the nature of the knowledge produced, the unique strengths and weaknesses that prospective cohort members hold, the representation of historically marginalized groups in an increasingly multiethnic society, and the place of justice and opportunity among an organization's aims (National Center for Institutional Diversity 2011).

41. Attiyeh and Attiyeh 1997; Karabel 2005; Grodsky 2007; Stevens 2007; Lamont 2009. Inequalities in graduate education condition the equity in the labor

market, and indeed, women and people of color are underrepresented in many corners of academia, especially tenured faculty positions and selective colleges and universities. For example, women constitute just 21 percent of the population of employed philosophers (Crasnow 2007).

42. Attiyeh and Attiyeh 1997; Klitgaard 1985; Grodsky, Warren, and Felts 2008; Campbell 2009.

43. According to Educational Testing Service (2013a), among U.S. citizens who took the GRE in 2012, men had higher scores than women on both the verbal and the quantitative reasoning sections. Including international students, men had higher scores only on the quantitative section of the test. Among the racial/ethnic classifications that ETS uses, whites and Asians earned the highest scores on the verbal and quantitative sections of the test, respectively. There are just three studies that point to how faculty actually use test scores or other criteria in graduate admissions decisions. In a 1984 ETS-sponsored study of 333 faculty members, participants claimed that their most important admissions criterion is grade point average, followed by letters of recommendation, and then GRE scores. However, as the authors admit, "We are dealing with self-reports and not observed actions" (Oltman and Hartnett 1984, 7). A decade later, Landrum, Jeglum, and Cashin (1994) found that GRE scores were the second most important criterion in psychology admissions outcomes, and Attiyeh and Attiyeh (1997) found GRE scores the strongest predictor of admission.

44. Moss-Racusin et al. 2012.

45. Milkman, Akinola, and Chugh 2014.

46. That I did not find evidence of discrimination does not mean it does not occur, but I designed the research as an open-ended inquiry into possible explanations for inequality rather than as a specific test for prejudicial behavior.

47. See Roithmayr 2014 for a description of the ways in which white privilege is reproduced through everyday choices, including in college admissions.

48. Tilly 1998.

49. See Bonilla-Silva 2010, 8, on colorblind racism and how contemporary social scientists may unwittingly reinforce racial hierarchy by describing racial inequalities without explaining the processes that create those inequalities.

50. DiMaggio and Powell 1983; Stevens 2007.

51. Findings from research like these cannot be used to directly *prescribe* policy, but they can be used to inform a more thoughtful approach to policy formation.

52. Sociologists such as Lyn Spillman call the uncovering of mechanisms and concepts through thick description "theoretical generalization." See her excellent 2014 paper in *Qualitative Sociology* for an example.

1. Decision Making as Deliberative Bureaucracy

1. Gutmann and Thompson 2004, 3–7.

2. Ibid. For examples of other settings in which deliberative democracy has relevance, see Fishkin 2009, Hess and Posselt 2002, Ryfe 2002, and Schoem and Hurtado 2001.

3. Salthouse, McKeachie, and Lin 1978; Twombly 1992; Jackson 2006.

4. Weber 1978b; Wilson 1989.

5. Weber 1978b.

6. Ibid., 974.

7. Morrison 2006, 226.

8. Some of the departments in this study conduct admissions differently for their MA/MS vs. PhD programs. Given my focus here on doctoral education, I use the language of "program" rather than "department;" however, some respondents used these words interchangeably.

9. Walker et al. 2008, 22.

10. See Geiger 1986 and Clark 1987 for helpful histories and analyses of academic departments as organizations, and Gumport 1993 for an excellent treatment of the central role that sponsored research plays in American graduate education.

11. Analyses by Twombly (1992) and Salthouse, McKeachie, and Lin (1978) discuss committee-based selection of students and faculty. Landrum et al. (1994) claim that "a wide range of studies have examined the decision-making process within graduate admissions committees" (240), but this claim is quite a semantic stretch. The studies they cite do not focus on the work of decision making or consider the process itself, but rather develop prediction models to approximate the likely *outcome* of decision-making processes. Landrum et al. (1994) come closest by asking fifty-five department chairs to describe, in writing, their department's decision-making processes and then conducting a content analysis of the answers.

12. Baseline program demographics surely contributed to the absence of racial/ethnic diversity on most committees as well.

13. Wilson 1989.

14. Meyer and Rowan 1977; March, Simon, and Guetzkow 1958.

15. In the other two programs, the department chair was a voting member of the admissions committee.

16. Through follow-up interviews, I gathered that the faculty and administrative committee members' biggest concern with this episode was not about the charge of cherry picking, which they dismissed as unfounded to begin with, but with Will's inserting himself into "their" process. They felt his involvement violated the bureaucratic procedures that lend legitimacy and efficiency to their work. Strong feelings motivated Will's challenge, and they also provoked strong feelings among other participants. Participants saw the challenges and the associated feelings as corrupting influences on an otherwise orderly and objective process.

17. Lemann 2000, 18.

18. Stevens 2007; Espeland and Stevens 2009; Porter 1996.

19. Educational Testing Service (ETS), which administers the GRE, recommends against this practice.

20. Espeland and Stevens (1998) define commensuration as "the transformation of different qualities into a common metric" (314). If two things are incommensurable, it implies they are sufficiently distinctive that they should not be considered in relation to the other.

21. In linguistics, the only program that does not assign numerical ratings, individual faculty members commensurate their judgment into a yes/no vote for each applicant.
22. Porter 1996, 6.
23. Judgment is quantified in other ways as well, but not as consistently across programs. For example, in biology the faculty developed a system for rating along several dimensions the applicants whom they interview. Summary scores from those evaluations are averaged and tabulated to develop a rank-ordered list that drives the final round of decision making.
24. Only in political science and physics were faculty formally asked to provide written comments to justify their ratings.
25. I thank Michael Bastedo for this insight.
26. Indeed, their discussion did not only reveal differences in interpretation about what a rating of 1, 2, or 3 means. It turned out that one committee member had used the three-point scale as three categories and others on the committee had regarded the numbers as ordinals.
27. Griffin and Muñiz 2011.
28. Heimer 2001.
29. Ibid.; Stevens 2007.
30. Porter 1996, 5.
31. Klitgaard 1985, 13.
32. Fisher v. University of Texas, 570 U.S. 11-345 (2013).
33. Gartner 1986.
34. Wilson 1989.
35. Thucydides (trans. Crawley) 1951, 105–106.
36. Birnbaum 1988; Twombly 1992.

2. Meanings of Merit and Diversity

1. By the standards of disparate impact law, "facially neutral" hiring practices (those that appear to be race-neutral) that have adverse effects on opportunities for specific populations may be judged discriminatory. Disparate impact has been ruled constitutional only when "business necessity" motivates the discriminatory action. In *Smith v. City of Jackson,* police officers over forty years old brought suit against the city for granting larger raises to junior officers. Because the city offered the raises to achieve parity with "comparable positions in the market," the basis for age discrimination was ruled a matter of business necessity, and therefore constitutional in spite of the negative, disparate impact it had on more senior officers (Smith v. City of Jackson [03–1160] 544 U.S. 228, 2005).
2. Fisher v. University of Texas, 570 U.S. 11-345 (2013).
3. Association of American Colleges and Universities 2014.
4. Guinier 2015.
5. Milem, Chang, and Antonio 2005, v.
6. Lamont 2009; Goffman 1959.

7. Lamont 2009. Note that evaluative scripts are distinct from interaction scripts qua Barley: "outlines of recurrent patterns of interaction that define in observable and behavioral terms, the essence of actors' roles" (Barley 1986, 83).

8. Birnbaum 1988, 498.

9. Birnbaum 1988; Brink 1999; Klitgaard 1985; Twombly 1992.

10. Chapter 3 examines how these trends play out in specific disciplines.

11. March 1994; Karen 1990.

12. Espeland and Sauder 2007; Bourdieu 1984; Attiyeh and Attiyeh 1997; Hersch 2014.

13. When I reviewed my findings with the chair of economics (i.e., what qualitative research methodologists call member-checking), he mentioned that he now pulls applications from black and Latino students to ensure a diverse pool in later rounds of review. He reported that they have relaxed the GRE score threshold since the test's 2011 revision, which he believes "nicely distinguishes among highly qualified people."

14. Klitgaard 1985, 32.

15. Their devaluing of unknown institutions is consistent with previous research on status judgments of organizations, such as that by Bitekine (2011).

16. Zimmerman and Zeitz 2002, 416.

17. Bowen, Rudenstine, and Sosa's (1992, 11) study of doctoral education in ten institutions found that graduate programs with small cohorts had higher completion rates and shorter time to degree that those with larger entering cohorts.

18. March 1994, 38. Just two programs among the ten in this study had been collecting data on applicant characteristics in relation to students' academic and professional outcomes. Neither used the data to inform current admissions practice.

19. ETS does not claim that the GRE measures intelligence. For guidance on interpreting scores on tests taken after August 2011, see ETS 2014a.

20. Bourdieu 1988; Lamont 2009.

21. Mitchell Stevens (2007) called this phase "coarse sorting" in his study of undergraduate admissions.

22. Although my study was not designed to assess alternative approaches to using the GRE, there are a number of possibilities, including interpreting scores in light of known disparities, waiting to consider GRE scores until the rest of the application has been reviewed, or cutting the GRE from their considerations entirely.

23. Walker et al. 2008, 11.

24. For a thoughtful discussion of drawbacks to a "laundry list" approach to diversity in higher education, see Smith 2009.

25. For a few of the many studies on the benefits of educational diversity for undergraduates, see, for example, Bowen and Bok 1998; Chang, Astin, and Kim 2004; Gurin et al. 2002; and Jayakumar 2008. Some studies have found that educational experiences with diversity can strengthen professional preparation and research innovation; these include Page 2008 and Harvey and Allard 2012.

26. For studies that examine how colleges and universities strive to present themselves as diverse, see Osei-Kofi, Torres, and Lui 2013; regarding admissions

viewbooks, see Stevens and Roksa 2011; regarding mission statements, see Morphew and Hartley 2006. Stevens and Roksa argue for a "metrical" understanding of diversity as an indicator of organizational excellence in higher education today.

27. Two respondents in philosophy noted that women have better representation in ethics and the history of philosophy than they do in other subdisciplines.

28. In an interesting example of how one's own identity may frame conceptualizations of diversity, I found that the majority of people who counted national origin among salient dimensions of diversity had, themselves, been born outside of the United States. Similarly, individuals in two programs who had grown up in Appalachian states defended the importance of regional diversity.

29. Garces 2012.

30. Smith et al. 1996.

31. Beutel and Nelson 2005; Kulis, Chong, and Shaw 1999; Olivas 1994; Smith et al. 1996; Trower and Chait 2002.

32. Smith 2009, 149.

33. Haro 1995, 196; Danowitz Sagaria 2002, 689.

34. Garces 2014; Marichal 2009; Smith, 2009.

35. Brief for Columbia University, Harvard University, Stanford University, and the University of Pennsylvania as Amici Curiae at 3, Regents of the University of California v. Bakke, 438 U.S. 265 (1978) (No. 76–811).

36. Smith 2009; Garces 2014.

37. It was unclear from these comments whether the faculty assumed that the courses the students had taken signaled their "intellectual capacity," whether some committee members were concerned about preparation and others about capacity, or whether Peter was just uncomfortable describing their rationale for eliminating these two individuals and so spoke in apparent contradictions.

38. Kahneman 2011.

39. Bastedo and Jaquette 2011; Bielby et al. 2014; Posselt et al. 2012; Rojstaczer and Healy 2012.

40. For data on group differences in GRE scores and ETS recommendations for the appropriate use of GRE scores in the review process, see ETS 2013a and 2014a; Fischer, Schult, and Hell 2013; and Miller 2013.

41. See, for example, Fischer, Schult, and Bell 2013; Young and Kobrin 2001. In the most recent study of differential predictive validity on college admissions exams by gender, meta-analysis by Fischer, Schult, and Bell (2013) found that the problem of performance underprediction is worse for undergraduate admissions tests than for the GRE. Like all meta-analyses, however, the findings are only as generalizable as the data from which the studies' findings are drawn. Often in the research on graduate admissions, studies disproportionately examine student scores in psychology, which may not generalize to other disciplines.

42. ETS, 2014a.

43. Berrey 2015, 3.

44. Dowd and Bensimon 2014, 58.

45. Stevens (2007) noted that diversity has become an informal "index of prestige" (182) among selective liberal arts colleges.

46. Park (2013) highlighted the power of intentionality for meaningful diversity in her analysis of the racial reconciliation efforts of a religious student organization at a California university affected by Proposition 209, the state's ban on affirmative action.

3. Disciplinary Logics

1. Walker et al. 2008, xi.
2. The findings of the Carnegie Initiative on the Doctorate, described in full in Walker et al., *The Formation of Scholars* (2008), borrowed imagery and ideas from the training of clergy to promote an ideal of doctoral education that includes developing "stewards" of the discipline. See also Abbott 2001, Austin 2002, Thelin 2004, and Wulff et al. 2004 on doctoral education as credentialing and socialization for the professoriate.
3. Becher 1981; Clark 1987; Hermanowicz 2005.
4. Johnson (2008) discussed increasing divergence in the approaches to scholarship used by linguists.
5. It would have been convenient to defer to the disciplinary classification schemes developed through Hagstrom's (1964) or Biglan's (1973) analyses of disciplinary consensus or that of Lodahl and Gordon (1972) based on paradigm development. However, their classifications are forty or more years old, and disciplinary changes during this time period make adoption of previous scholars' assessments of paradigm strength a spurious task (Pfeffer 1993). Therefore, I adopted a historical approach to categorizing each discipline as high-, moderate-, or low- consensus relative to others within their respective subject area of humanities, social sciences, or natural sciences. To do so, I used (a) surveys of the history of the disciplines from secondary sources, (b) interviews with emeritus members of each department, and (c) member-checking with admissions committee chairs. Given what we know about the dynamics of change in disciplines, these classifications should be interpreted, not as static, enduring, or absolute, but rather as reflections of assessment in the context of the fields' historical trajectories.
6. Ioannides and Nielsen 2007, 1; Wolfers 2015.
7. For brief overviews of economics as a discipline, see Becker 1978, Skousen 2009, and Harvey and Garnett 2006.
8. March 1994.
9. Under the GRE's previous scoring rubric, the mean quantitative reasoning score of students enrolled in the top six economics programs in 2002 was 785, and 765 in the programs ranked 15–30 (Stock, Finnegan, and Siegfried 2006).
10. Russell 1972; Durant 2012.
11. Biglan 1973.
12. Durant 2012.
13. In classics, the department chair said that ratings were a "guide to the feelings that people have about candidates," but this was not established as the norm for the entire committee.
14. Knorr-Cetina 1999; Lamont 2009.
15. See, for example, Clark 1987 and Hermanowicz 2005.

16. Pfeffer 1993.
17. These findings could also be due to less consensus motivating more deliberation and, with it, challenges to be explicit about the basis for their ratings.
18. Snow 1959.
19. Indeed, if Abbott's (2001) argument about the fractal nature of knowledge within disciplines is true, then even high-consensus fields have considerable intellectual diversity.
20. For discussion and analysis of relationship between disciplinary cultures and evaluation, see Becher and Trowler 1989, Knorr-Cetina 1999, Lamont 2009, and Swales 2004.
21. The study in question (Sternberg and Williams 1997) analyzed GRE scores in relation to a number of academic outcomes and other admissions criteria for 167 current and recently graduated psychology students at Yale University. They found that the median correlation coefficient of GRE scores in four areas (Verbal, Quantitative, Analytical, and Subject) in predicting first-year grades was 0.17, with the Subject test (not the Quantitative reasoning) bearing the strongest relationship. GRE scores only weakly predicted "other aspects of graduate performance: ratings of analytical, creative, practical, research, and teaching abilities by primary advisers and ratings of dissertation quality by faculty readers." The authors noted "substantial" standard deviations and score ranges of 550, 520, 400, and 360 points (Sternberg and Williams 1997, 636–637).
22. See the conclusion section of Chapter 6 for a more complete discussion of stereotype threat research in relation to graduate admissions tests.
23. For one example of Barack Obama's personal characterization of his "improbable journey," see the transcript to his July 24, 2008 speech in Berlin, Germany, available at http://edition.cnn.com/2008/POLITICS/07/24/obama.words/.

4. Mirror, Mirror

1. McPherson, Smith-Lovin, and Cook 2001, 416.
2. Kanter 1977; Karabel 2005; Rivera 2012b.
3. DiMaggio 1992.
4. This tendency would be defensible if faculty were selecting students to be apprentices of their own, since it would be hard for a professor to advise a student in areas of research far afield from one's own. However, in the committees I observed, the committee members' task was to select a cohort of students for the department as a whole.
5. I began to notice it in the course of analyzing how disciplinary context shapes personal preferences, and how personal preferences affect admissions outcomes. I noted that preferences for self-similarity seemed especially prevalent in low-consensus disciplines, the very fields in which personal tastes often played an especially important role in evaluation, generally. Realizing that individual level preferences for particular types of students could not, in many cases, be divorced from reviewer backgrounds, the four types of homophily that I observed most frequently were by and for pedigreed, cool, socially mobile, and international scholars. This chapter focuses on the first three.

6. This finding could be due to the absence of individuals from these backgrounds in high-consensus disciplines (i.e., a selection effect) or the absence of a common disciplinary logic, making personal tastes more salient (i.e., a disciplinary effect).

7. Rivera 2011b.

8. What I observed is a perfect example of Pierre Bourdieu's description of elite reproduction through education. He noted that selection processes in elite French educational institutions treat elite social connections and cultural knowledge as forms of capital on par with financial resources. Social and cultural capital operate as arbitrary, and ultimately exclusionary, bases for selection that reproduce existing structures of privilege.

9. Given the small range in grades typically assigned for graduate courses, small increments carry greater meaning—both to the faculty to assign the grades and to the students who receive them.

10. Bourdieu 1984; Khan 2011; Lamont and Lareau 1988.

11. Patton 2013.

12. Professors may not be cool by society's standards, but signature frames may be a way some scholars try to express style while owning their intellectual status.

13. Lamont, 2009.

14. In this case, I do not mention disciplines to protect anonymity.

15. "Death match" can be thought of as the opposite of an undergraduate admissions model of "building" (Bastedo 2012), in which reviewers assess and collect applicants' strengths as grounds for moving an individual forward in the process.

16. Kanter 1977, 965.

17. McPherson et al. 2001.

18. Rivera 2012b.

19. Rivera 2011b.

20. Correll, Benard, and Paik 2007; Benard and Correll 2010. Benard and Correll argue that the judgments of likeability have to do as much with the importance of likeability on the job as the perception that professionally successful women have betrayed their proper gender role. The perceptions of mothers that Correll and colleagues have found can skew how opportunities and rewards are allocated. They also risk pigeonholing women—or other groups about whom there are strong moral overtones to their social roles—into persistently second-class status by nudging them to self-select out of careers and fields where their success may be negatively judged.

21. Sellers et al. 1998.

22. Martin 1992, 9–10. Such complexity might help explain trends that statistical research has represented as either weak or broad preferences (i.e., what sociologists have dubbed cultural omnivorism).

5. The Search for Intelligent Life

1. Crocker, Sommers, and Luhtanen 2002.

2. On the self as defined in relation to others, see Oyserman, Elmore, and Smith 2012; Tajfel 2010; and Zerubavel 1993. On the centrality of intelligence to

academics' self-concept, see Bourdieu 1988; Crocker, Sommers, and Luhtanen 2002; and Lamont 2009.

3. Robert Sternberg, one of the most highly published scholars of intelligence in his generation, argued that "how we should conceive of intelligence" was his research community's most fundamental matter of debate (Sternberg 2003, 4).

4. For discussions of socially constructed ideas of intelligence, see Hatt 2012, Lamont 1992, and Oakes et al. 2008. Yang and Sternberg 1997 conducted the cited study of ideas about intelligence in Taiwan, and Azuma and Kashiwagi 1987 published the study of Japanese college students' and their parents' ideas of intelligence. Furnham 2001 offers a review of differences in appraisals of intelligence across gender and national context.

5. Lamont 2009; Becher and Trowler 1989, 102.

6. Research by Rebecca Zwick (2002) finds that simple practice is the primary mechanism by which standardized test scores increase, and that official test-prep courses contribute less to score changes than is commonly assumed (as illustrated through the quote here).

7. It was within a sociohistorical context of racial hierarchy and striving for meritocratic college admissions that, after World War I, eugenicist Carl Campbell Brigham and colleagues tweaked the Army IQ test into the SAT. So initially entwined were the two tests' underlying factors that Brigham developed an algorithm for translating SAT into IQ scores (Lemann 2000). By the time he actively promoted the SAT to colleges and universities, however, he had come to distrust the notion that IQ tests measured an innate trait, and eventually he renounced his landmark study, *A Study of American Intelligence*. In 1934 he wrote,

> The test movement came to this country some twenty-five or thirty years ago accompanied by one of the most glorious fallacies in the history of science, namely, that the test measured "native intelligence" purely and simply without regard to training or schooling. I hope nobody believes that now. The test scores very definitely are a composite including schooling, family background, familiarity with English, and everything else, relevant and irrelevant. *The "native intelligence" hypothesis is dead* (quoted in Lemann 2000, 34, emphasis in original).

8. ETS 2014a.

9. Zwick 2002. The ACT's core areas are English, Science, Math, and Reading, for example, and the MCAT focuses on knowledge of Chemistry, Physics, and Biology.

10. Ibid., 32–33.

11. Neumann 2009, 54–55.

12. Ibid., 54–55.

13. Comments from Bruce Cole, former chair of the National Endowment for the Humanities, suggest that writing quality and cognitive clarity are inseparable in the humanities. He said, "Writing is thinking. To write well is to think clearly" (National Endowment for the Humanities 2002).

14. Gumport 1993, 226.

15. Walker et al. 2008.

16. My thanks to Elizabeth Knoll for this insight.

17. Leslie, Cimpian, Meyer, and Freeland 2015.

18. Mindful of higher education's democratic mission, Guinier (2003) urges admissions policymakers and decision makers to ask themselves whether test scores, intelligence, *or* first-year grades are robust conceptions of excellence for a democratic society.

19. For details of the revised general test, see ETS 2014b.

20. Goffman, 1959.

21. Wendler and Bridgeman 2014. ETS has released a compendium of research about the GRE that will be worthwhile for readers interested in learning more about the details of the test's validity. Most of the research was conducted before implementation of the revised GRE General Test.

22. Steele and Aronson 1995. For an excellent narrative about the results of stereotype threat research and the development of this line of scholarship, also see Claude Steele's accessible 2010 volume, *Whistling Vivaldi: How Stereotypes Affect Us and What We Can Do about It.*

23. See Logel et al. 2012 pp. 46–49 for additional recommendations about making college learning environments stereotype-safe. The 2008 field experiment by Catherine Good, Joshua Aronson, and Jayne Ann Harder revealed that stereotype threat can shape outcomes in a common STEM gatekeeping course, but that highlighting a test's fairness could eliminate performance gaps. They manipulated the instructions that students in a college calculus class received on a test with items similar to those on the GRE. To half of the class, the researchers described the test as diagnostic of mathematical ability; instructions to the other half stated, "This mathematics test has not shown any gender differences in performance or mathematics ability." The researchers found no significant gender differences in either group's final course grades and or in the test scores of students in the stereotype-inducing condition. However, women's performance in the stereotype-safe condition exceeded that of men's, implying that stereotype-neutralizing test instructions make a difference (Good, Aronson, and Harder 2008).

24. Gregory Walton and Geoffery Cohen's 2002 meta-analysis estimated that stereotype lift gives white males a bump of about 50 points on the SAT (Walton and Cohen 2003, 456).

25. Like the call to preserve democratic deliberation, this recommendation may seem to some a stumbling block on the already rocky path to decision making. But, hopefully, it will compel those with gatekeeping roles to growing in the definition of intelligence that literary critic Barbara Christian (1987) articulated: "a tuned sensitivity to that which is alive and therefore cannot be known until it is known."

6. International Students and Ambiguities of Holistic Review

1. I am indebted to Kimberly Reyes and Kelly Slay in equal measure for their support with the data analyses and review of literature that brought about this chapter.

2. For discussion of the trends that contribute to rising enrollment of international students, see, for example, Schofer and Meyer 2005 and Schmidt 2010. For the

share of adults on the top end of the wealth distribution with graduate degrees, see Thompson 2013.

3. Applications from Chinese students dipped 3 percent in 2012 and 1 percent in 2013, after increasing by 21 percent in 2010 and 19 percent in 2011 (Allum et al. 2014, 7).

4. For the proportion of the adult population, by gender, with graduate degrees, see Torche 2011. See Gonzales, Allum, and Sowell 2013 for statistics on international students in U.S. graduate education. Tracing the pathways from students' countries of origin to U.S. doctoral programs, as well as growth of foreign enrollments in U.S. doctoral programs and trends by educational development in the country of origin, Blanchard, Bound, and Turner (2009) found that students from countries with well-developed higher education systems typically come to the United States for doctoral degrees only when highly ranked programs admit them, in contrast to countries with fewer doctoral programs, which send students to lower-ranked U.S. doctoral programs as well. Their findings support a broader pattern of international students' strong preference for highly ranked universities. Fischer 2013 cites a study by IDP Education, a firm that facilitates study abroad opportunities, that found that no fewer than 85 percent of international students reported prestige to be an important consideration in their college choice process, and one-third said it was their top priority.

5. On trade-offs among enrollment management goals, see Cheslock and Kroc 2012. For the use of admissions and student body composition to signal priorities to stakeholders, see, for example Karen 1990 and Karabel 2005.

6. For rates of growth in first-time graduate school enrollment, see Gonzales, Allum, and Sowell 2013. For national economic benefits of international student enrollment, see National Foundation for American Policy (NFAP) 2013, Roach 2013, and Institute of International Education 2013.

7. See David 2012, Jaquette and Curs 2015, Rizzo and Ehrenberg 2004, for the role of nonresident student tuition in offsetting state appropriations. See Redden 2013 for the role of international students in sustaining STEM faculty research. See NFAP 2013 for the role of international students in filling gaps.

8. Olivas 2009.

9. Allum et al. 2014; Allum, Bell, and Sowell 2012.

10. Interestingly, they worried less about their ability to judge across American applicants' diverse institutional, geographic, and personal contexts.

11. In 1961, economist Daniel Ellsberg classically defined ambiguity as a type of uncertainty present "in situations where available information is scant or obviously unreliable or highly conflicting; or where expressed expectations of different individuals vary widely; or where expressed confidence in estimates tends to be low" (Ellsberg 1961, 660–661).

12. See Epley and Krueger 2005 for an example of research into how ambiguities create conditions for stereotyping.

13. Gonzales, Remington, and Allum 2013.

14. For the quotation about the Civil Service Exam, see Suen and Yu 2006, 48. For more about China's test preparation apparatus, see Golden 2011, Magnier 2006, Özturgut 2011, Xueqin 2011, and Zhao 2001.

15. Larmer and Lin-Liu 2002; Montlake 2006; Mooney 2005.
16. Chang 2001; Xu 2001; Zwick 2002.
17. For more on "smile work," see Tierney and Bensimon 1996, 83.
18. Epley and Kruger 2005.
19. Fish 2013.
20. An exception to this seems to be French philosophers, who, in the words of one participant in philosophy, are "very explicit about how they're ranking *{laughs}* the various people."
21. Epley and Krueger 2005, 419.
22. In this context, "Asian" refers to both Asian immigrant and Asian international populations.
23. According to the United States Census, more than 30 ethnic groups are represented in the Asian American category alone (Iwamoto and Liu 2010).
24. Chou 2008; Lee 1994; Osajima 2005.
25. Taylor and Stern 1997; Suzuki 2002; Zhang 2010.
26. Maddux et al. 2008, 86.
27. These stereotypes have implications for higher education research, as well as for the educational policies and practices that are informed by that research (Museus 2008; Museus and Kiang 2009; Nadal et al. 2010; Ng, Lee, and Pak 2007; Teranishi et al. 2009). In their critical review of educational literature on Asian Americans, for example, Ng, Lee, and Pak (2007) argue that even existing higher education scholarship is tainted by the model minority stereotype. The literature not only represents Asian American faculty as hardworking, nonconfrontational individuals incapable of departmental leadership, it also overlooks Asian American students' multiple social identities and their relevance to student support service needs and campus climate concerns (Ng, Lee, and Pak 2007).
28. Beoku-Betts 2004; Iwamoto and Liu 2010.
29. Lee and Rice 2007; Hanassab 2006.
30. Clearly detrimental, these experiences are expressed in higher reports of discomfort, stress, and homesickness; lower self-esteem; self-segregation from domestic students; and suppression of feelings of depression (Poyrazli and Lopez 2007; Schmitt, Spears, and Branscombe 2003; Trice 2004; Wadsworth, Hecht, and Jung 2008; Wei et al. 2008).
31. For studies on the TOEFL's validity, see Fu 2012; Wait and Gressel 2009; Light, Xu, and Mossop 1987; Johnson 1988; Yule and Hoffman 1990.
32. ETS 2013a.
33. Fu 2012, 105.
34. There is a growing body of creative scholarship on administrative pressure and K–12 teachers' efforts to game or cheat high-stakes standardized tests. See developing work by Hibel and Penn, as well as by Maloney, for example.
35. Chang 2001; Xu 2001.
36. Melcher 2010, 3.

Conclusion

1. See Clauset, Arbesman, and Larremore 2015; Fowler, Grofman, and Masuoka 2007.
2. See Rivera 2011b and 2012a on professional investment firms' consideration of elite college status for entry-level hiring. It's important to note that sorting out which colleges deserve "elite" status has become a national preoccupation, and simply gaining admission to the ones so deemed is now a veritable status symbol for both the young adults who attend them and their families. A growing share of families organize their children's time and very lives to put them on a trajectory toward one of these selective institutions. They do so because, to many, admission to elite colleges not only symbolizes status achieved. It also represents a gateway to status and a hope for inoculation from the financial stresses that plague so many Americans today. Graduate school is among the subsequent opportunities that may follow from attending an elite college, and attending graduate school is on the minds of young people from as early as tenth grade. A recent study I conducted with Matthew Holsapple found that U.S. tenth-graders who aspired to a graduate degree or who thought a college's graduate school placement rate was "very important" had higher odds of enrolling at one of *U.S. News and World Report's* top 100 colleges and universities (Holsapple and Posselt 2010).
3. For racial inequalities in selective college enrollment from 1972 to 2004, see Posselt et al. 2012, p. 1091. For percentage of women, men, underrepresented minority, and other ethnic groups earning scores of 700 or above, see Miller and Stassun 2014.
4. For an excellent analysis of trade-offs and opportunity costs in admissions, see Espenshade and Chung 2005. An important and related point is this: When a program fixes the number of students they will admit, they create a zero-sum game. Trade-offs for access and opportunity are inherent to these kinds of competitions, so the question is not whether there will be trade-offs, but what they will be, how they will be determined, and what their implications are. As we saw in affirmative action lawsuits by Abigail Fisher and Jennifer Gratz, controversy can erupt when a student denied admission assumes that she would have been admitted next if some preference or another had not been in play. Like other external sources of student financial support, institutional diversity fellowships for graduate students may therefore be most powerful as an incentive for increasing diversity when they *increase* program capacity, because it changes the very nature of the admissions competition.
5. Boltanski and Thévenot 2000.
6. Bourdieu 1984; Bourdieu 1988.
7. For details of the methodology behind the National Research Council's assessment of research doctoral programs, see http://www.nap.edu/catalog.php?record_id=12676#toc. For details of the U.S. News Best Graduate School Rankings, see http://www.usnews.com/education/best-graduate-schools/articles/2014/03/10/how-us-news-calculated-the-2015-best-graduate-schools-rankings.

8. Research context (French postsecondary vs. U.S. doctoral education) could also explain the insufficiency of Bourdieu's theory to capture the trends I observed. In the United States, cultural boundaries are fuzzier (Lamont 1992), elite tastes are more omnivorous (Bryson 1996), and institutionally valued cultural objects are defined by intersections of race, class, and gender rather than class alone (Yosso 2006).

9. Lamont 1992, 178.

10. Scott 2008.

11. Smith 2009; Stevens and Roksa 2011.

12. Regents of the University of California v. Bakke, 438 U.S. 265 (1978); Gratz v. Bollinger, 539 U.S. 244 (2003).

13. Narrow tailoring and compelling state interests are the two primary hurdles required to pass the legal test of strict scrutiny.

14. See Garces 2014 for an excellent history of legal developments shaping affirmative action in graduate admissions. Garces notes that introducing the test of strict scrutiny was a turning point in this history because it "equated efforts to promote access to education for racial minorities with discriminatory practice against whites" (460).

15. Ibid.

16. Civil Rights Project 2002.

17. Tienda 2013; Guinier 2003; Klitgaard 1985; Gurin et al. 2002.

18. Two studies have found that diversity on research teams has advantages for creativity and problem solving (Committee on Equal Opportunities in Science and Engineering 2013; Page 2008). Two studies that have found diverse teams' papers are cited more frequently (Campbell et al. 2013; Freeman and Huang 2014). A limitation of the citation analysis studies is that they rely upon the researchers' judgments of author gender and ethnicity from names alone, rather than on authors' self-reported gender and ethnicity.

19. Ahmed 2012; Berrey 2015; Dowd and Bensimon 2014.

20. March 1994.

21. Hagedorn and Nora 1996, 31.

22. March 1994.

23. Research using experimental, survey, and qualitative methodologies finds significant costs to the quality of intergroup relations and to students of color who experience racial isolation in the classroom. For example, Deo (2011) writes that graduate students of color are less likely to contribute to discussion in classes in which they feel tokenized, compromising their learning experience and the spirit of the broader group's discussion.

24. Some of this may have to do with a skewed knowledge base. Faculty were more aware of racial and gender gaps on standardized tests and other educational outcomes than they were of the research evidence that professors' own actions and learning environments contribute to student outcomes or that social diversity supports excellence in research.

25. See Bonilla-Silva 2006 and Carter and Tuitt 2013 for excellent discussions of colorblind racism and postracial discourse in U.S. education and society.

26. Worthington et al. 2008; Garces 2014.

27. Neglecting context is what Kahneman (2011) calls narrow framing, and it causes reviewers to misread the justifiable reasons some applicants might be weaker or stronger than expected on a desired criterion.

28. An extreme version of structured review is "policy capturing," which a small group of scholars recommended in the 1970s (Dawes 1971). Using the characteristics of recent cohorts to reveal a department's preferences, policy capturing would replace human judgment in admissions with regression models that measure an applicant's admissibility.

29. Lundy-Wagner, Vultaggio, and Gasman 2013.

30. See Fisk-Vanderbilt (2014) for a full description of the Fisk-Vanderbilt Masters-to-PhD Bridge Program. A similar bridge program links Spelman and Georgia Tech. Others using the bridge label offer the master's degree at a research university as a bridge to doctoral program admission, but do not recruit solely from an MSI.

31. Eagan et al. 2013.

32. Nagda et al. 1998; Posselt and Black 2012. Through the National Science Foundation's Research Experiences for Undergraduates program and the Department of Education's Ronald E. McNair Postbaccalaureate Achievement Program, the federal government has financially invested in student research as a means of diversifying graduate education and the professoriate. There are institution-specific programs, such as the successful Meyerhoff Scholars Program at the University of Maryland–Baltimore County, as well as multi-university efforts such as the Summer Research Opportunities Program, administered through a cooperative effort of Big Ten universities and the University of Chicago. The mission of programs like these is to develop professional interest in and commitment to research among underrepresented populations, but their participants may also be attractive recruits for graduate programs.

33. Association of American Colleges and Universities 2014.

34. Hersch 2014. See Rogers and Molina 2006 for research into the qualities of psychology doctoral programs that have been especially successful in recruiting and retaining students of color.

35. Rather than assume risk associated with metrics like college grades, TOEFL, or GRE scores, some leaders may want to start by measuring the probability of specific outcomes for students in their program relative to specific student characteristics. To do this well, though, there are a few measurement issues to take into account. For programs that have historically enrolled few people from a specific group (e.g., women, international students with lower TOEFL scores, students from less selective colleges), the validity of analyses may be hampered by small sample sizes. Also, measures concentrated in a small range, like enrolled students' college GPA, may produce downwardly biased estimates of correlations with the outcome (researchers call this attenuation bias). Finally, because student success is the product of a complex interplay of student inputs and the learning environments faculty create, such analyses would need to account not only for characteristics of students, but also for characteristics of the environment that shape student performance (e.g., perceptions of climate and/or stereotypes, proportion of same-identity individuals in one's cohort). Hierarchical

linear modeling is well suited to analyses of this sort. See Walters, Lee, and Trapani 2004 for a fine example.

36. Among the noncognitive characteristics that scholars have proposed for graduate admissions, Sedlacek (2004) has developed measures for the following: Positive self-concept, Realistic self-appraisal, Successfully handling the system, Preference for long-term goals, Availability of a strong support person, Leadership experience, Community involvement, Knowledge acquired in a field. The ETS Personal Potential Index provides opportunity for those writing letters of recommendation to assess the following qualities of applicants: Knowledge, Creativity, Communication skills, Teamwork, Resilience, Planning and organization, Ethics and integrity (Kyllonen 2008).

37. Powell 2013; Miller and Stassun 2014.

38. ETS 2014a.

39. For analyses of white and African American students' scores in relation to background characteristics, ethnic match with test proctors, and characteristics of the GRE test center, see Walters, Lee, and Trapani 2004. An interesting finding of this study, one that the authors argue contradicts a trend toward stereotype threat, is that a match between student ethnicity and proctor ethnicity is significantly associated with test scores for white students, but not for African American or Hispanic students.

40. ETS (2013b) promoted the most recent GRE overhaul as a "friendlier, more flexible test-taking experience." Among other changes, they have reduced the amount of rote vocabulary knowledge required for high scores on the Verbal section.

41. For the list of colleges and universities that have test-optional policies, see National Center for Fair and Open Testing 2014. For a list of PhD programs that do not require the GRE see http://ainsleydiduca.com/phd-programs-no-gre-required/.

42. For findings about the effects of going test-optional at the undergraduate level, see Hiss and Neupane 2004; Belasco, Rosinger, and Hearn 2015.

43. About test-optional undergraduate admissions, Belasco et al. (2015) wrote, "Arguably, institutions that fail to reach a majority of underrepresented students through recruitment or other outreach initiatives, will find it difficult to improve diversity in meaningful and significant ways, regardless of their admissions criteria" (219).

44. Weick 1984, 40. There are physiological explanations for freezing up in the face of significant challenges, such as overarousal in the limbic system, with observable physiological effects such as an inability to concentrate.

45. For doctoral programs that choose to require GRE scores, for example, another small win would be more nuanced classification of "high" and "low" scores. If, when reviewers sit down with files, they are provided with some discipline- or institution-specific data about the current distributions of GRE scores by national origin, race/ethnicity, and gender, they might interpret scores differently. One of the three graduate schools with which I worked already shares similar information in their admissions workshop for faculty, providing institutional data about the wide racial disparities in the number of students who score above 700 on each section of the test.

46. Weick 1984, 41.
47. Tilly 2005; Rojas 2007.
48. Berger and Luckmann 1966.

Methodological Appendix

1. Stevens 2007.
2. Goffman 1959; Garfinkel 1967; Lamont 2009.
3. Vaughan 1992; Eisenhardt 1989.
4. Merriam 2009, 39.
5. Stake 2005, 448.
6. Geertz 1973.
7. Charmaz, Denzin, and Lincoln 2000; Stake 2005; Yin 1994; Cronbach 1975; Geertz 1973.
8. Abbott 1992; Miles and Huberman 1994; Merriam 2009; Smith 1978.
9. Dion 1998.
10. Merriam 2009.
11. Patton 2002.
12. National Research Council 2010; "Best Graduate School Rankings" 2010.
13. Merriam 2009; Yin 1994.
14. Merriam 2009.
15. Gold 1958.
16. Weiss 1995; Rubin and Rubin 2009.
17. Rubin and Rubin 2009, 152–153.
18. Tierney and Bensimon 1996; Barley 1990, 1996; Lamont 1992, 2009.
19. Lamont 2009; Barley 1996.
20. Green, Franquiz, and Dixon 1997; Scheurich 1995.
21. Lincoln and Guba 2000.
22. Gieryn 2000; Clark 1987.
23. Gould 1990, 283.
24. Becker 2008, 54, emphasis in original.
25. Patton and Appelbaum 2003, 67.
26. Glaser and Strauss 1967, 22, 25, 101–116.
27. Strauss and Corbin 1998.
28. Rubin and Rubin 2009, 201.
29. Curtin and Fossey 2007, 92.
30. Popper 1959.
31. Lareau 2010.
32. Jorgensen 1989.
33. LeCompte and Schensul 1999.
34. Michéle Lamont, personal communication, 2010.

References

Abbott, A. 1992. What do cases do? Some notes on activity in sociological analysis. In C. C. Ragin and H. S. Becker, eds., *What is a case? Exploring the foundations of social inquiry*. New York: Cambridge University Press.

————. 2001. *Chaos of disciplines*. Chicago: University of Chicago Press.

Ahmed, S. 2012. *On being included: Racism and diversity in institutional life*. Durham, NC: Duke University Press.

Allum, J., et al. 2014. *Findings from the 2014 CGS International Graduate Admissions Survey: Phase II: Final applications and initial offers of admission*. Washington, DC: Council of Graduate Schools.

Allum, J. R., N. E. Bell, and R. S. Sowell. 2012. *Graduate enrollment and degrees: 2001–2011*. Washington, DC: Council of Graduate Schools. http://www.cgsnet .org/graduate-enrollment-and-degrees-2001-2011.

Association of American Colleges and Universities. 2014. *Making excellence inclusive*. http://www.aacu.org/compass/inclusive_excellence.cfm.

Attiyeh, G., and R. Attiyeh. 1997. Testing for bias in graduate school admissions. *Journal of Human Resources* 32 (3): 524–548.

Aud, S., M. A. Fox, and A. Kewal-Ramani. 2010. *Status and trends in the education of racial and ethnic groups (NCES 2010-015)*. U.S. Department of Education, National Center for Education Statistics. http://nces.ed.gov/pubs2010 /2010015.pdf.

Austin, A. E. 2002. Preparing the next generation of faculty: Graduate school as socialization to the academic career. *Journal of Higher Education* 73 (1): 94–122.

Austin, A. E., and M. McDaniels. 2006. Preparing the professoriate of the future: Graduate student socialization for faculty roles. In J. C. Smart, ed., *Higher education: Handbook of theory and research,* vol. 21, 397–456. Dordrecht: Springer.

Azuma, H., and K. Kashiwagi. 1987. Descriptors for an intelligent person: A Japanese study. *Japanese Psychological Research* 29 (1): 17–26.

Barley, S. R. 1986. Technology as an occasion for structuring: Evidence from observations of CT scanners and the social order of radiology departments. *Administrative Science Quarterly* 31 (1): 78–108.

———. 1990. Images of imaging: Notes on doing longitudinal field work. *Organization Science* 1:220–247.

———. 1996. Technicians in the workplace: Ethnographic evidence for bringing work in to organizational studies. *Administrative Science Quarterly* 41 (3): 404–441.

Barley, S. R., and P. S. Tolbert. 1997. Institutionalization and structuration: Studying the links between action and institution. *Organization Studies* 18 (1): 93–117.

Bastedo, M. N. 2009. Convergent institutional logics in public higher education: State policymaking and governing board activism. *Review of Higher Education* 32 (2): 209–234.

———. 2012. Cognitive repairs in the admissions office. Unpublished paper presented at the annual meeting of the Association for the Study of Higher Education, Las Vegas.

Bastedo, M. N., and O. Jaquette. 2011. Running in place: Low-income students and the dynamics of higher education stratification. *Educational Evaluation and Policy Analysis* 33 (3): 318–339.

Becher, T. 1981. Towards a definition of disciplinary cultures. *Studies in Higher Education* 6 (2): 109–122.

Becher, T., and P. Trowler. 1989. *Academic tribes and territories.* Columbus, OH: Open University Press.

Becker, G. S. 1978. *The economic approach to human behavior.* Chicago: University of Chicago Press.

Becker, H. S. 2008. *Tricks of the trade: How to think about your research while you're doing it.* Chicago: University of Chicago Press.

Belasco, A. S., K. O. Rosinger, and J. C. Hearn. 2015. The test-optional movement at America's selective liberal arts colleges a boon for equity or something else? *Educational Evaluation and Policy Analysis* 37 (2): 206–223.

Bell, N. E. 2010. *Graduate enrollment and degrees: 1999 to 2009.* Washington, DC: Council of Graduate Schools. http://www.cgsnet.org/ckfinder/userfiles/files/R_ED2009.pdf.

———. 2012. *Findings from the 2012 CGS International Graduate Admissions Survey, phase I: Applications.* Washington, DC: Council of Graduate Schools. http://www.cgsnet.org/ckfinder/userfiles/files/R_IntlApps12_I.pdf.

Benard, S., and S. J. Correll. 2010. Normative discrimination and the motherhood penalty. *Gender & Society* 24 (5): 616–646.

Beoku-Betts, J. A. 2004. African women pursuing graduate studies in the sciences: Racism, gender bias, and third world marginality. *NWSA Journal* 16 (1): 116–135.

Berger, P. L., and T. Luckmann. 1966. *The social construction of reality: A treatise in the sociology of knowledge.* New York: Anchor Books.

Berrey, E. 2015. *The enigma of diversity: The language of race and the limits of racial justice.* Chicago: University of Chicago Press.

Bérubé, M. 2013. The humanities, unraveled. *Chronicle of Higher Education,* February 18. http://chronicle.com/article/Humanities-Unraveled/137291/.

Best graduate schools rankings. 2010. *U.S. News & World Report.* http://grad-schools.usnews.rankingsandreviews.com/best-graduate-schools.

Beutel, A. M., and D. J. Nelson. 2005. Gender and race-ethnicity of faculty in top science and engineering research departments. *Journal of Women and Minorities in Science and Engineering* 11:389–403.

Bielby, R., J. Posselt, O. Jaquette, and M. Bastedo. 2014. Why are women underrepresented in elite universities? A non-linear decomposition analysis. *Research in Higher Education* 55 (8): 735–760.

Biglan, A. 1973. The characteristics of subject matter in different academic areas. *Journal of Applied Psychology* 58:195–203.

Birnbaum, R. 1988. Presidential searches and the discovery of organizational goals. *Journal of Higher Education* 59 (5): 489–509.

Bitekine, A. 2011. Toward a theory of social judgments in organizations: The case of legitimacy, reputation, and status. *Academy of Management Review* 36 (1): 151–179.

Blanchard, E., J. Bound, and S. Turner. 2009. Opening (and closing) doors: Country-specific shocks in U.S. doctoral education. In R. G. Ehrenberg and C. V. Kuh, eds., *Doctoral education and the faculty of the future,* 224–248. Ithaca, NY: Cornell University Press.

Bleske-Rechek, A., and K. Browne. 2014. Trends in GRE scores and graduate enrollments by gender and ethnicity. *Intelligence* 46:25–34.

Bobo, L., J. R. Kluegel, and R. A. Smith. 1997. Laissez-faire racism: The crystallization of a kinder, gentler, antiblack ideology. In S. A. Tuch and J. K. Martin, eds., *Racial attitudes in the 1990s: Continuity and change,* 15–42. Westport, CT: Praeger Press.

Boltanski, L., and L. Thévenot. 2006. *On justification: Economies of worth.* Princeton, NJ: Princeton University Press.

Bonilla-Silva, E. 2006. *Racism without racists: Color-blind racism and the persistence of racial inequality in the United States.* Lanham, MD: Rowman and Littlefield.

Borg, W. R. 1963. GRE aptitude scores as predictors of GPA for graduate students in education. *Educational and Psychological Measurement* 23 (2): 379–382.

Bourdieu, P. 1977. *Outline of a theory of practice.* Cambridge: Cambridge University Press.

———. 1984. *Distinction: A social critique of the judgment of taste.* Cambridge, MA: Harvard University Press.

———. 1988. *Homo academicus.* Stanford, CA: Stanford University Press.

Bourdieu, P., and J. C. Passeron. 1977. *Reproduction in education, society, and culture.* Thousand Oaks, CA: Sage.

Bourdieu, P., and L. J. Wacquant. 1992. *An invitation to reflexive sociology.* Chicago: University of Chicago Press.

Bowen, W., and D. Bok. 1998. *The shape of the river.* Princeton, NJ: Princeton University Press.

Bowen, W. G., N. L. Rudenstine, and J. A. Sosa. 1992. *In pursuit of the PhD.* Princeton, NJ: Princeton University Press.

Braxton, J. M., and L. L. Hargens. 1996. Variations among academic disciplines: Analytical frameworks and research. In J. C. Smart, ed., *Higher education: Handbook of theory and research,* vol. 11. New York: Agathon Press.

Brear, P., J. Dorrian, and G. Luscri. 2008. Preparing our future counselling professionals: Gatekeeping and the implications for research. *Counselling and Psychotherapy Research* 8 (2): 93–101.

Brink, W. J. 1999. Selecting graduate students. *Journal of Higher Education* 70 (5): 517–523.

Bryson, B. 1996. "Anything but heavy metal": Symbolic exclusion and musical dislikes. *American Sociological Review* 61 (5): 884–899.

Burris, V. 2004. The academic caste system: Prestige hierarchies in PhD exchange networks. *American Sociological Review* 69 (2): 239–264.

Campbell, J. 2009. Attitudes and beliefs of counselor educators toward gatekeeping. Unpublished doctoral dissertation, Old Dominion University.

Campbell, L. G., S. Mehtani, M. E. Dozier, and J. Rinehart. 2013. Gender-heterogeneous working groups produce higher quality science. *PLoS ONE* 8 (10): e79147.

Cantwell, B., M. Canche, J. Milem, and F. Sutton. 2010. Do data support the discourse? Assessing holistic review as an admissions process to promote diversity at a US medical school. Unpublished paper presented at the annual meeting of the Association for the Study of Higher Education, Charlotte, NC.

Carter, D. J., and F. Tuitt. 2013. *Contesting the myth of a "post-racial" era: The continued significance of race in U.S. education.* New York: Peter Lang International Academic.

Cassuto, L. 2015. *The graduate school mess.* Cambridge, MA: Harvard University Press.

Chang, L. 2001. Greater China: Cheating allegations anger Chinese; Row over TOEFL, GRE exams reveals cultural, educational, legal chasm; Students fear their scores now have no credibility with U.S. schools. *Asian Wall Street Journal,* February 21.

Chang, M. J. 2002. Preservation or transformation: Where's the real educational discourse on diversity? *Review of Higher Education* 25 (2): 125–140.

Chang, M. J., A. W. Astin, and D. Kim. 2004. Cross-racial interaction among undergraduates: Some consequences, causes, and patterns. *Research in Higher Education* 45 (5): 529–553.

Charmaz, K., N. K. Denzin, and Y. S. Lincoln. 2000. *Handbook of qualitative research.* Thousand Oaks, CA: Sage.

Cheslock, J. J., and R. Kroc. 2012. Enrollment management. In R. Howard, B. Knight, and G. McLaughlin, eds., *The handbook for institutional researchers,* 221–236. San Francisco: Jossey-Bass.

Chou, C. C. 2008. Critique on the notion of model minority: An alternative racism to Asian American? *Asian Ethnicity* 9 (3): 219–229.

Christian, B. 1987. The race for theory. *Cultural Critique* 56 (6): 51–63.

Civil Rights Project. 2002. *Constitutional requirements for affirmative action in higher education admissions and financial aid.* http://civilrightsproject.ucla.edu /legal-developments/legal-memos/constitutional-requirements-for-affirmative -action-in-higher-education-admissions-and-financial-aid/constitutional -affirmative-action-financial-aid.pdf.

Clark, B. R. 1960. *The open door college: A case study.* New York: McGraw-Hill.

———. 1987. *The academic profession: National, disciplinary, and institutional settings.* Berkeley: University of California Press.

Clauset, A., S. Arbesman, and D. B. Larremore. 2015. Systematic inequality and hierarchy in faculty hiring networks. *Science Advances* 1 (1): e1400005.

Collins, R. 2002. Credential inflation and the future of universities. In S. Brint, ed., *The future of the city of intellect: The changing American university,* 23–46. Stanford, CA: Stanford University Press.

Committee on Equal Opportunities in Science and Engineering (CEOSE). 2013. *2011–2012 biennial report to Congress: Broadening participation in America's STEM workforce.* CEOSE 13–01. Arlington, VA: National Science Foundation. http://www.nsf.gov/od/iia/activities/ceose/reports/Full_2011–2012_CEOSE _Report_to_Congress_Final_01–28–2014.pdf.

Correll, S. J., I. S. Benard, and Paik. 2007. Getting a job: Is there a motherhood penalty? *American Journal of Sociology* 112 (5): 1297–1339.

Council of Graduate Schools (CGS). 2009. *Graduate enrollment and degrees: 1999 to 2009.* http://www.cgsnet.org/portals/0/pdf/R_ED2009.pdf.

———. 2013. Press release: First-time enrollment of international graduate students up 10 percent. Council of Graduate Schools. http://www.cgsnet.org/sites/default /files/Intl_III_2013_release_final_0.pdf.

Crasnow, S. 2007. Report on the APA Status of Women. Paper presented at the annual meeting of the Central Division American Philosophical Association, Chicago.

Crocker, J., S. R. Sommers, and R. K. Luhtanen. 2002. Hopes dashed and dreams fulfilled: Contingencies of self-worth and graduate school admissions. *Personality and Social Psychology Bulletin* 28 (9): 1275–1286.

Cronbach, L. J. 1975. Beyond the two disciplines of scientific psychology. *American Psychologist* 12 (11): 116–127.

Cureton, E. E., L. W. Cureton, and R. Bishop. 1949. Predictions of success in graduate study at the University of Tennessee. *American Psychologist* 4:361–362.

Curtin, M., and E. Fossey. 2007. Appraising the trustworthiness of qualitative studies, *Australian Occupational Therapy Journal* 54 (2): 88–94.

Cyranoski, D., N. Gilbert, H. Ledford, A. Nayar, and M. Yahia. 2011. Education: The PhD factory. *Nature* 472:276–279.

Danowitz Sagaria, M. A. 2002. An exploratory model of filtering in administrative searches: Toward counter-hegemonic discourses. *Journal of Higher Education* 73 (6): 677–711.

David, J. 2012. Michigan colleges welcome Chinese students. *Detroit Free Press,* March 6.

Dawes, R. M. 1971. A case study of graduate admissions: Application of three principles of human decision making. *American Psychologist* 26 (2): 180–188.

———. 1975. Graduate admission variables and future success. *Science* 187 (4178): 721–723.

Deo, M. 2011. The promise of *Grutter*: Diverse interactions at the University of Michigan Law School. *Michigan Journal of Race & Law* 17 (1): 63.

DiMaggio, P. 1987. Classification in art. *American Sociological Review* 52 (4): 440–455.

———. 1992. Nadel's paradox revisited: Relational and cultural aspects of social structure. In N. Nohria and R. Eccles, eds., *Networks and organizations: Structure, form and action,* 118–142. Boston: Harvard Business School Press.

———. 1997. Culture and cognition. *Annual Review of Sociology* 23 (1): 263–287.

DiMaggio, P. J., and W. W. Powell. 1983. The iron cage revisited: Institutional isomorphism and collective rationality in organizational fields. *American Sociological Review* 48 (2): 147–160.

———, eds. 1991. *New institutionalism in organizational analysis.* Chicago: University of Chicago Press.

Dion, D. 1998. Evidence and inference in the comparative case study. *Comparative Politics* 30 (2): 127–145.

Dowd, A. C. and E. M. Bensimon. 2014. *Engaging the "race question": Accountability and equity in US higher education.* New York: Teachers College Press.

Duguid, M. M., D. L. Loyd, and P. S. Tolbert. 2012. The impact of categorical status, numeric representation, and work group prestige on preference for demographically similar others: A value threat approach. *Organization Science* 23 (2): 386–401.

Durant, W. 2012. *The story of philosophy.* New York: Pocket Books.

Eagan, M. K., S. Hurtado, M. J. Chang, G. A. Garcia, F. A. Herrera, and J. C. Garibay. 2013. Making a difference in science education: The impact of undergraduate research programs. *American Educational Research Journal* 50 (4): 683–713.

Educational Testing Service (ETS). 2013a. A snapshot of the individuals who took the GRE Revised General Test. http://www.ets.org/s/gre/pdf/snapshot_test _taker_data.pdf.

———. 2013b. Test content and structure. https://www.ets.org/gre/revised_general /about/content/.

———. 2014a. GRE: Guide to the use of scores. http://www.ets.org/s/gre/pdf/gre _guide.pdf.

———. 2014b. Test content and structure. https://www.ets.org/gre/revised_general /about/content/.

Eide, E., D. Brewer, and R. Ehrenberg. 1998. Does it pay to attend an elite private college? Evidence on the effects of undergraduate college quality on graduate school attendance. *Economics of Education Review* 17 (4): 371–376.

Eisenhardt, K. M. 1989. Building theories from case study research. *Academy of Management Review* 14 (4): 532–550.

Ellsberg, D. 1961. Risk, ambiguity, and the Savage axioms. *Quarterly Journal of Economics* 75 (4): 643–669.

Epley, N., and J. Kruger. 2005. When what you type isn't what they read: The perseverance of stereotypes and expectancies over e-mail. *Journal of Experimental Social Psychology* 41 (4): 414–422.

Espeland, W. N., and M. Sauder. 2007. Rankings and reactivity: How public measures recreate social worlds. *American Journal of Sociology* 113 (1): 1–40.

Espeland, W. N., and M. L. Stevens. 1998. Commensuration as a social process. *Annual Review of Sociology* 24 (1): 313–343.

———. 2009. A sociology of quantification. *European Journal of Sociology* 49 (3): 401–436.

Espenshade, T. J., and C. Y. Chung. 2005. The opportunity cost of admission preferences at elite universities. *Social Science Quarterly* 86 (2): 293–305.

Feldman, M. S., and B. T. Pentland. 2003. Reconceptualizing organizational routines as a source of flexibility and change. *Administrative Science Quarterly* 48 (1): 94–118.

Fischer, F. T., J. Schult, and B. Hell. 2013. Sex-specific differential prediction of college admission tests: A meta-analysis. *Journal of Educational Psychology* 105 (2): 478.

Fischer, K. 2013. American universities yawn at global rankings. *Chronicle of Higher Education.* http://chronicle.com/article/American-Universities-Yawn-at /141947.

Fish, I. S. 2013. Why do so many Chinese people share the same names? *Foreign Policy,* April 26. http://blog.foreignpolicy.com/posts/2013/04/26/why_do_so _many_chinese_people_share_the_same_name.

Fisher v. University of Texas at Austin. 2013. 570 U.S. 11–345.

Fishkin, J. 2009. *When the people speak: Deliberative democracy and public consultation.* Oxford: Oxford University Press.

Fisk-Vanderbilt. 2014. Fisk-Vanderbilt Masters-to-PhD Bridge Program. http://www .vanderbilt.edu/gradschool/bridge/descript.htm.

Fowler, J. H., B. Grofman, and N. Masuoka. 2007. Social networks in political science: Hiring and placement of PhDs, 1960–2002. *PS: Political Science & Politics* 40 (4): 729–739.

Fox, C. R., and A. Tversky. 1995. Ambiguity aversion and comparative ignorance. *Quarterly Journal of Economics* 110 (3): 585–603.

Frank, R. H., and P. J. Cook. 1995. *The winner-take-all society.* New York: Free Press.

Freeman, R. B., and W. Huang. 2014. Collaborating with people like me: Ethnic co-authorship within the US. National Bureau of Economic Research. NBER Working Paper No. 19905. http://www.nber.org/papers/w19905.

Friedland, R., and R. R. Alford. 1991. Bringing society back in: Symbols, practices, and institutional contradictions. In P. J. DiMaggio and W. W. Powell, eds., *The new institutionalism in organizational analysis,* 232–263. Chicago: University of Chicago Press.

Fu, Y. 2012. The effectiveness of traditional admissions criteria in predicting college and graduate success for American and international students. Unpublished

doctoral dissertation, Arizona State University. http://arizona.openrepository
.com/arizona/handle/10150/217056.

Furnham, A. 2001. Self-estimates of intelligence: Culture and gender difference in
self and other estimates of both general (g) and multiple intelligences. *Personality and Individual Differences* 31 (8): 1381–1405.

Garces, L. M. 2012. Necessary but not sufficient: The impact of Grutter v. Bollinger
on student of color enrollment in graduate and professional schools in Texas.
Journal of Higher Education 83 (4): 497–534.

———. 2014. Aligning diversity, quality, and equity: The implications of legal and
public policy developments for promoting racial diversity in graduate studies.
American Journal of Education 120 (4): 457–480.

Garfinkel, H. 1967. *Studies in ethnomethodology.* Malden, MA: Prentice Hall.

Gartner, J. D. 1986. Antireligious prejudice in admissions to doctoral programs in
clinical psychology. *Professional Psychology: Research and Practice* 17 (5):
473–475.

Geertz, C. 1973. Thick description: Toward an interpretive theory of culture.
In C. Geertz, ed., *The interpretation of culture: Selected essays,* 3–30. New
York: Basic Books.

———. 1982. The way we think now: Toward an ethnography of modern thought.
Bulletin of the American Academy of Arts and Sciences, 14–34.

Geiger, R. L. 1986. To advance knowledge. *Scientist* 1 (2): 24.

Gibney, E. 2012. So many aspirant doctors, so little time. *Times Higher Education,*
October 4. http://www.timeshighereducation.co.uk/news/so-many-aspirant
-doctors-so-little-time/421356.article.

Giddens, A. 1984. *The constitution of society: Outline of the theory of structuration.* Berkeley: University of California Press.

Gieryn, T. F. 2000. A space for place in sociology. *Annual Review of Sociology*
26:463–496.

Glaser, B. G., and Strauss, A. L. 1967. *The discovery of grounded theory: Strategies
for qualitative research.* New York: Aldine.

Goffman, E. 1959. *The presentation of self in everyday life.* New York: Overlook
Press.

———. 1974. *Frame analysis: An essay on the organization of experience.* New
York: Harper and Row.

Gold, R. 1958. Roles in sociological field observations. *Social Forces* 36 (3):
217–223.

Golden, D. 2011. China's test prep juggernaut. *Bloomberg Businessweek.* http://www
.bloomberg.com/bw/magazine/content/11_20/b4228058558042.htm

Gonzales, L. M., J. R. Allum, and R. S. Sowell. 2013. *Graduate enrollment and
degrees: 2002 to 2012.* Washington, DC: Council of Graduate Schools.
http://www.cgsnet.org/ckfinder/userfiles/files/GEDReport_2012.pdf.

Gonzales, L. M., J. R. Remington, and J. R. Allum. 2013. *Findings from the 2013
international graduate admissions survey.* Washington, DC: Council of Graduate Schools. https://www.cgsnet.org/ckfinder/userfiles/files/Intl_II_2013_report
_final.pdf.

Good, C., J. Aronson, and J. A. Harder. 2008. Problems in the pipeline: Stereotype threat and women's achievement in high-level math courses. *Journal of Applied Developmental Psychology* 29:17–28.

Gould, S. J. 1990. *Wonderful life: The Burgess Shale and the nature of history*. New York: W. W. Norton.

Graduate Employees and Student Organizations. 2005. *The (un)changing face of the Ivy League*. New Haven, CT: Yale University.

Gratz v. Bollinger. 2003. 539 U.S. 244.

Green, J., M. Franquiz, and C. Dixon. 1997. The myth of the objective transcript: Transcribing as a situated act. *TESOL Quarterly* 31:172–176.

Griffin, K. A., and M. M. Muñiz. 2011. The strategies and struggles of graduate diversity officers in the recruitment of doctoral students of color. *Equity & Excellence in Education* 44 (1): 57–76.

Grodsky, E. 2007. Compensatory scholarship in higher education. *American Journal of Sociology* 112 (6): 1662–1712.

Grodsky, E., J. R. Warren, and E. Felts. 2008. Testing and social stratification in American education. *Annual Review of Sociology* 34:385–404.

Grove, W. A., D. H. Dutkowsky, and A. Grodner. 2007. Survive then thrive: Determinants of success in the economics Ph.D. program. *Economic Inquiry* 45 (4): 864–871.

Grunig, S. D. 1997. Research, reputation, and resources: The effect of research activity on perceptions of undergraduate education and institutional resource acquisition. *Journal of Higher Education* 68 (1): 17–52.

Grutter [et al.] v. Bollinger [et al.]. 2003. 539 U.S. 306.

Guinier, L. 2003. Admissions rituals as political acts: Guardians at the gates of our democratic ideals. *Harvard Law Review* 117:113.

———. 2015. *The tyranny of the meritocracy: Democratizing higher education in America*. New York: Beacon Books.

Gumport, P. J. 1993. Graduate education and organized research in the United States and views from American campuses. In B. Clark, ed., *The research foundations of graduate education: Germany, Britain, France, United States, Japan*, 225–293. Berkeley: University of California Press.

———. 2002. *Academic pathfinders: Knowledge creation and feminist scholarship*. Westport, CT: Greenwood Press.

Gurin, P., E. Dey, S. Hurtado, and G. Gurin. 2002. Diversity and higher education: Theory and impact on educational outcomes. *Harvard Educational Review* 72 (3): 330–367.

Gurin, P., J. Lehman, E. Lewis, with E. Dey, G. Gurin, and S. Hurtado. 2004. *Defending diversity: Affirmative action at the University of Michigan*. Ann Arbor: University of Michigan Press.

Gutmann, A., and D. Thompson. 2004. *Why deliberative democracy?* Princeton, NJ: Princeton University Press.

Hagedorn, L. S., and A. Nora. 1996. Rethinking admissions criteria in graduate and professional programs. *New Directions for Institutional Research*, no. 92: 31–44.

Hagstrom, W. 1964. Anomy in scientific communities. *Social Problems* 12 (2): 186–195.

Hammersley, M., and P. Atkinson. 2003. *Ethnography: Principles in practice,* 3rd ed. New York: Routledge.

Hanassab, S. 2006. Diversity, international students, and perceived discrimination: Implications for educators and counselors. *Journal of Studies in International Education* 10 (2): 157–172.

Haro, Roberto. 1995. Held to a higher standard: Latino executive selection in higher education. In Walter Bennis, ed., *The leaning ivory tower: Latino professors in American universities,* 189–207. Albany: SUNY Press.

Harper, S. R. 2008. Realizing the intended outcomes of Brown: High-achieving African American male undergraduates and social capital. *American Behavioral Scientist* 51 (7): 1029–1052.

Harvey, C., and M. J. Allard. 2012. *Understanding and managing diversity: Readings, cases, and exercises.* Boston: Pearson Prentice Hall.

Harvey, J. T., and R. F. Garnett. 2006. *Future directions for heterodox economics.* Ann Arbor: University of Michigan Press.

Hatt, B. 2012. Smartness as cultural practice in schools. *American Educational Research Journal* 49 (3): 438–460.

Heimer, C. 2001. Cases and biographies: An essay on routinization and the nature of comparison. *Annual Review of Sociology* 27 (1): 47–76.

Hermanowicz, J. C. 2005. Classifying universities and their departments: A social world perspective. *Journal of Higher Education* 76 (1): 26–55.

Hersch, J. 2014. Catching up is hard to do: Undergraduate prestige, elite graduate programs, and the earnings premium. Vanderbilt Law and Economics Research Paper No. 14–23. http://papers.ssrn.com/sol3/papers.cfm?abstract_id =2473238.

Hess, D., and J. Posselt. 2002. How high school students experience and learn from the discussion of controversial public issues. *Journal of Curriculum and Supervision* 17 (4): 283–314.

Hibel, J., and D. M. Penn. 2014. An organizational perspective on the patterns and predictors of educator cheating on standardized accountability tests. Paper presented at the 2014 Sociology of Education Association Conference, Pacific Grove, CA, February.

Hiss, W., and P. Neupane. 2004. 20 years of optional SATs. *Bates News.* http://www .bates.edu/news/2004/10/01/sats-at-bates/.

Holsapple, M., and J. R. Posselt. 2010. The best in the country? High achieving rural students' enrollment in America's top-ranked colleges and universities. Paper presented at the annual meeting of the American Educational Research Association, Denver, April.

Howard, J. A. 2000. Social psychology of identities. *Annual Review of Sociology* 26: 367–393.

Hurtado, S. 2001. Linking diversity and educational purpose: How diversity affects the classroom environment and student development. In Gary Orfield, ed., *Diversity challenged: Evidence on the impact of affirmative action.* Cambridge, MA: Harvard Education Publishing Group.

Institute of International Education. 2013. *Open Doors Data*. http://www.iie.org /research-and-publications/open-doors/data.

Ioannides, S., and K. Nielsen. 2007. Economics and the social sciences: Synergies and trade-offs. In S. Ioannides and K. Nielsen, eds., *Economics and the social sciences*. Cheltenham, UK: Edward Elgar.

Iwamoto, D. K., and W. M. Liu. 2010. The impact of racial identity, ethnic identity, Asian values, and race-related stress on Asian Americans and Asian international college students' psychological well-being. *Journal of Counseling Psychology* 57 (1): 79.

Jackson, J. F. 2006. Hiring practices of African American males in academic leadership positions at American colleges and universities: An employment trends and disparate impact analysis. *Teachers College Record* 108 (2): 316–338.

James, W. 1903 The Ph.D. octopus. *Harvard Monthly*, March. http://www.des.emory .edu/mfp/octopus.html.

Jaquette, O., and B. R. Curs. 2015. Creating the Out-of-State University: Do Public Universities Increase Nonresident Freshman Enrollment in Response to Declining State Appropriations?. *Research in Higher Education*, 1–31. doi: 10.1007/s11162-015-9362-2.

Jaschik, S. 2008. Non-cognitive qualities join the GRE. *Inside Higher Ed,* May 22. http://www.insidehighered.com/news/ 2008/05/22/ets.

———. 2009. Ph.D. admissions shrinkage. *Inside Higher Ed,* March 30. https://www .insidehighered.com/news/2009/03/30/phd.

Jayakumar, U. M. 2008. Can higher education meet the needs of an increasingly diverse and global society? Campus diversity and cross-cultural workforce competencies. *Harvard Educational Review* 78 (4): 615–651.

Johnson, K. 2008. *Quantitative methods in linguistics*. Malden, MA: Blackwell.

Johnson, P. 1988. English language proficiency and academic performance of undergraduate international students. *TESOL Quarterly* 22 (1): 164–168.

Jones, E. 2003. Beyond supply and demand: Assessing the Ph.D. job market. *Occupational Outlook Quarterly*. Washington DC: Bureau of Labor Statistics.

Jorgensen, D. L. 1989. *Participant observation: A methodology for human studies*. Thousand Oaks, CA: Sage.

Kahlenberg, R. D. 1996. Class-based affirmative action. *California Law Review* 84 (4): 1037–1099.

Kahneman, D. 2011. *Thinking, fast and slow*. New York: Macmillan.

Kallingal, A. 1971. The prediction of grades for black and white students at Michigan State University. *Journal of Educational Measurement* 8 (4): 263–265.

Kant, I. 1951 [1790]. *Critique of judgment*. Translated by J. H. Bernard. New York: Hafner Press.

Kanter, R. M. 1977. Some effects of proportions on group life: Skewed sex ratios and responses to token women. *American Journal of Sociology* 82 (5): 965–990.

Karabel, J. 2005. *The chosen: The hidden history of admission and exclusion at Harvard, Yale, and Princeton*. New York: Houghton Mifflin.

Karen, D. 1990. Toward a political-organizational model of gatekeeping: The case of elite colleges. *Sociology of Education* 63: 227–240.

Kezar, A., and C. Sam. 2010. Special Issue: Understanding the New Majority of Non-Tenure-Track Faculty in Higher Education—Demographics, Experiences, and Plans of Action. *ASHE Higher Education Report* 36(4): 1–133.

Khan, S. R. 2011. *Privilege: The making of an adolescent elite at St. Paul's school.* Princeton, NJ: Princeton University Press.

Killgore, L. 2009. Merit and competition in selective college admissions. *Review of Higher Education* 32 (4): 469–488.

Klitgaard, R. 1985. *Choosing elites: Selecting the" best and brightest" at top universities and elsewhere.* New York: Basic Books.

Knorr-Cetina, K. 1999. *Epistemic cultures: How the sciences make knowledge.* Cambridge, MA: Harvard University Press.

Konrad, A. M., and J. Pfeffer. 1991. Understanding the hiring of women and minorities in educational institutions. *Sociology of Education* 64 (3): 141–157.

Kuhn, T. S. 1970. *The structure of scientific revolutions,* 2nd ed. Chicago: University of Chicago Press.

Kulis, S., Y. Chong, and H. Shaw. 1999. Discriminatory organizational contexts and black scientists on postsecondary faculties. *Research in Higher Education* 40 (2): 115–148.

Kuncel, N. R., and S. A. Hezlett. 2007. Standardized tests predict graduate students' performance. *Science* 315:1080–1081.

Kuncel, N. R., S. A. Hezlett, and D. S. Ones. 2001. A comprehensive meta-analysis of the predictive validity of the Graduate Record Examinations: Implications for graduate student selection and performance. *Psychological Bulletin* 127 (1): 162–181.

Kyllonen, P. C. 2008. The research behind the ETS® Personal Potential Index (PPI). Princeton, NJ: Educational Testing Service. http://www.ets.org/Media/Products/PPI/10411_PPI_bkgrd_report_RD4.pdf.

Labaree, D. F. 1997. *How to succeed in school without really learning: The credentials race in American education.* New Haven, CT: Yale University Press.

Lamont, M. 1992. *Money, morals, and manners: The culture of the French and American upper-middle class.* Chicago: University of Chicago Press.

———. 2009. *How professors think: Inside the curious world of academic judgment.* Cambridge, MA: Harvard University Press.

———. 2012. Toward a comparative sociology of valuation and evaluation. *Annual Review of Sociology* 38 (1): 201.

Lamont, M., and A. Lareau. 1988. Cultural capital: Allusions, gaps and glissandos in recent theoretical developments. *Sociological Theory* 6 (2): 153–168.

Lamont, M., and V. Molnar. 2002. The study of boundaries in the social sciences. *Annual Review of Sociology* 28 (1): 167–195.

Landrum, R. E., and M. A. Clump. 2004. Departmental search committees and the evaluation of faculty applicants. *Teaching of Psychology* 31 (1): 12–17.

Landrum, R. E., E. B. Jeglum, and J. R. Cashin. 1994. The decision-making processes of graduate admissions committees in psychology. *Journal of Social Behavior and Personality* 9:239–239.

Lannholm, G. V. 1968. Cooperative studies of predicting graduate school success. *Graduate Record Examinations Special Report Number 68–3.*

Lareau, A. 2010. Families, schools, and inequality: A reflection. Keynote address at the annual meeting of the Sociology of Education Association Conference. Pacific Grove, CA, February 19.

Larmer, B., and J. Lin-Liu. 2002. Diplomas for dollars: In China, education has always been sacred; Now, tainted by corruption, it's become big business, too. *Newsweek,* December 2.

Lattuca, L. R. 2001. *Creating interdisciplinarity: Interdisciplinary research and teaching among college and university faculty.* Nashville, TN: Vanderbilt University Press.

LeCompte, M. D., and J. J. Schensul. 1999. *Designing and conducting ethnographic research.* Lanham, MD: Altamira Press.

Lee, J. J., and C. Rice. 2007. Welcome to America? International student perceptions of discrimination. *Higher Education* 53 (3): 381–409.

Lee, S. J. 1994. Behind the model minority stereotype: Voices of high and low achieving Asian American students. *Anthropology & Education Quarterly* 25 (4): 413–429.

Lemann, N. 2000. *The big test: The secret history of the American meritocracy.* New York: Farrar, Straus and Giroux.

Leslie, S.-J., A. Cimpian, M. Meyer, and E. Freeland. 2015. Expectations of brilliance underlie gender distributions across academic disciplines. *Science* 347 (6219): 262–265.

Light, R. L., M. Xu, and J. Mossop. 1987. English proficiency and academic performance of international students. *TESOL Quarterly* 21 (2): 251–261.

Lincoln, Y. S., and E. G. Guba. 2000. Paradigmatic controversies, contradictions, and emerging confluences. *Handbook of Qualitative Research* 2:163–188.

Lodahl, J. B., and G. Gordon. 1972. The structure of scientific fields and the functioning of university graduate departments. *American Sociological Review* 37 (1): 57–72.

Logel, C. R., G. M. Walton, S. J. Spencer, J. Peach, and Z. P. Mark. 2012. Unleashing latent ability: Implications of stereotype threat for college admissions. *Educational Psychologist* 47 (1): 42–50.

Lounsbury, M. 2002. Institutional transformation and status mobility: The professionalization of the field of finance. *Academy of Management Journal* 45 (1): 255–266.

———. 2007. A tale of two cities: Competing logics and practice variation in the professionalizing of mutual funds. *Academy of Management Journal* 50 (2): 289.

Lundy-Wagner, V., J. Vultaggio, and M. Gasman. 2013. Preparing underrepresented students of color for doctoral success: The role of undergraduate institutions. *International Journal of Doctoral Studies* 8:151–172.

Madaus, G. F., and J. J. Walsh. 1965. Departmental differentials in the predictive validity of the Graduate Record Examination aptitude tests. *Educational and Psychological Measurement* 25 (4): 1105–1110.

Maddux, W. W., A. D. Galinsky, A. J. Cuddy, and M. Polifroni. 2008. When being a model minority is good . . . and bad: Realistic threat explains negativity toward Asian Americans. *Personality and Social Psychology Bulletin* 34 (1): 74–89.

Magnier, M. 2006. The world: The academic equation in China is making college a long shot. *Los Angeles Times,* June 18.

Maloney, P. 2014. Gaming or cheating? How teachers and administrators in low-income schools adapt to high stakes standardized tests. Paper presented at the 2014 Sociology of Education Association Conference, Pacific Grove, CA, February.

March, J. G. 1994. *A primer on decision making: How decisions happen.* New York: Free Press.

March, J. G., H. A. Simon, and H. Guetzkow. 1958. *Organizations.* Cambridge, MA: Blackwell.

Marichal, J. 2009. Frame evolution: A new approach to understanding changes in diversity reforms at public universities in the United States. *Social Science Journal* 46 (1): 171–191.

Marston, A. R. 1971. It is time to reconsider the Graduate Record Examination. *American Psychologist* 26 (7): 653–655.

Martin, J. 1992. *Cultures in organizations: Three perspectives.* Oxford: Oxford University Press.

Mason, M. A., M. Goulden, and K. Frasch. 2009. Why graduate students reject the fast track. *Academe* 95 (1): 11–16.

Maton, K. I., J. L. Kohout, M. Wicherski, G. E. Leary, and A. Vinokurov. 2006. Minority students of color and the psychology graduate pipeline: Disquieting and encouraging trends, 1989–2003. *American Psychologist* 61 (2): 117.

Mayhew, M. J., H. E. Grunwald, and E. L. Dey. 2005. Curriculum matters: Creating a positive climate for diversity from the student perspective. *Research in Higher Education* 46 (4): 389–412.

McAdam, D., S. G. Tarrow, and C. Tilly. 2001. *Dynamics of contention.* Cambridge: Cambridge University Press.

McDonough, P. M. 1997. *Choosing colleges: How social class and schools structure opportunity.* Albany: SUNY Press.

McPherson, M., L. Smith-Lovin, and J. M. Cook. 2001. Birds of a feather: Homophily in social networks. *Annual Review of Sociology* 27:415–444.

Melamed, D., and S. V. Savage. 2013. Status, numbers and influence. *Social Forces* 91 (3): 1085–1104.

Melcher, T. 2010. Busted: The top 5 ways that Chinese students cheat on their undergraduate applications to American schools (and what schools can do about it). In *The China conundrum: Insights for US schools.* White Paper No. 4, Zinch, Inc. http://www.aplu.org/document.doc?id=4004.

Merriam, S. B. 2009. *Qualitative research: A guide to design and implementation.* San Francisco: Jossey-Bass.

Meyer, H. D., and B. Rowan. 2006. *The new institutionalism in education.* Albany: SUNY Press.

Meyer, J., and B. Rowan. 1977. Institutionalized organizations: Formal structure as myth and ceremony. *American Journal of Sociology* 83 (2): 340–363.

Milem, J. F., M. J. Chang, and A. L. Antonio. 2005. *Making diversity work on campus: A research-based perspective.* Washington, DC: Association of American Colleges and Universities.

Miles, M. B., and A. M. Huberman. 1994. *Qualitative data analysis: An expanded sourcebook*. Thousand Oaks, CA: Sage.

Milkman, K. L., M. Akinola, and D. Chugh. 2014. What happens before? A field experiment exploring how pay and representation differentially shape bias on the pathway into organizations. *Social Science Research Network*. http://dx.doi.org/10.2139/ssrn.2063742.

Miller, C. 2013. Diversity in physics: Impact of using minimum acceptable GRE scores for graduate admissions. *Bulletin of the American Physical Society* 58. http://meetings.aps.org/Meeting/MAR13/Session/F38.3.

Miller, C., and K. Stassun. 2014. A test that fails. *Nature* 510:303–304. http://www.nature.com/naturejobs/science/articles/10.1038/nj7504-303a.

Montlake, S. 2006. High-tech cheating in Asia's high-stakes exams. *Christian Science Monitor*, June 9.

Mooney, P. 2005. Mercenaries of grammar. *Chronicle of Higher Education*, February 4.

Morphew, C., and M. Hartley. 2006. Mission statements: A thematic analysis of rhetoric across institutional type. *Journal of Higher Education* 77 (3): 456–471.

Morrison, K. 2006. *Marx, Durkheim, Weber: Formations of modern social thought*. Thousand Oaks, CA: Sage.

Morrison, T., and M. Morrison. 1995. A meta-analytic assessment of the predictive validity of the quantitative and verbal components of the GRE with graduate GPAs representing the criterion of graduate success. *Educational and Psychological Measurement* 55 (2): 309–316.

Morse, R., and S. Flanigan. 2013. Methodology: Best education schools. *U.S. News & World Report*, March 11. http://www.usnews.com/education/best-graduate-schools/articles/2013/03/11/methodology-best-education-schools-rankings.

Moss-Racusin, C. A., J. F. Dovidio, V. L. Brescoll, M. J. Graham, and J. Handelsman. 2012. Science faculty's subtle gender biases favor male students. *Proceedings of the National Academy of Sciences* 109 (41): 16474–16479.

Museus, S. D. 2008. The model minority and the inferior minority myths: Understanding stereotypes and their implications for student learning. *About Campus* 13 (3): 2–8.

Museus, S. D., and P. N. Kiang. 2009. Deconstructing the model minority myth and how it contributes to the invisible minority reality in higher education research. *New Directions for Institutional Research*, no. 142: 5–15.

Nadal, K. L., S. T. Pituc, M. P. Johnston, and T. Esparrago. 2010. Overcoming the model minority myth: Experiences of Filipino American graduate students. *Journal of College Student Development* 51 (6): 694–706.

Nagda, B. A., S. R. Gregerman, J. Jonides, W. vonHippel, and J. S. Lerner. 1998. Undergraduate student-faculty research partnerships affect student retention. *Review of Higher Education* 22 (1): 55–72.

National Center for Fair and Open Testing. 2014. Colleges and universities that do not use SAT/ACT Scores for admitting substantial numbers of students into bachelor degree programs. http://www.fairtest.org/schools-do-not-use-sat-or-act-scores-admitting-substantial-numbers-students-bachelor-degree-programs.

National Center for Institutional Diversity. 2011. Mission statement. http://www
.ncid.umich.edu/about/mission.shtml.

National Endowment for the Humanities. 2002. David McCullough interview with
Bruce Cole. http://www.neh.gov/about/awards/jefferson-lecture/david-mccull
ough-interview.

National Foundation for American Policy. 2013. *The importance of international
students to America*. Arlington, VA: National Foundation for American
Policy.

National Research Council. 2010. *A data-based assessment of research doctorate
programs in the United States*. Washington DC: National Academies Press.

National Science Foundation. 2004. *Women, minorities, and persons with disabili-
ties in science and engineering: 2004*. NSF 04–317. Arlington, VA: NSF Division of Science Resource Statistics.

———. 2010. *Doctorate recipients from U.S. universities: 2009*. Arlington, VA: NSF
Division of Science Resource Statistics.

———. 2013. *Doctorate recipients from U.S. universities: 2012*. Arlington, VA: NSF
Division of Science Resource Statistics. Tabulation engine at https://ncses.norc
.org/NSFTabEngine/#TABULATION.

Nee, V. 1998. Sources of the new institutionalism. In M. C. Brinton and V. Nee,
eds., *The new institutionalism in sociology*, 1–16. Stanford, CA: Stanford University Press.

Nettles, M. T., and C. M. Millett. 2006. *Three magic letters: Getting to Ph.D.* Baltimore: Johns Hopkins University Press.

Neumann, A. 1991. The thinking team: Toward a cognitive model of administrative
teamwork in higher education. *Journal of Higher Education* 62 (5): 485–513.

———. 2009. *Professing to learn: Creating tenured lives and careers in the American research university*. Baltimore: Johns Hopkins University Press.

Newman, R. I. 1968. GRE scores as predictors of GPA for psychology graduate
students. *Educational and Psychological Measurement* 28 (2): 433–436.

Ng, J. C., S. S. Lee, and Y. K. Pak. 2007. Contesting the model minority and perpetual foreigner stereotypes: A critical review of literature on Asian Americans
in education. *Review of Research in Education* 31 (1): 95–130.

Nivet, M. A. 2011. Commentary: Diversity 3.0: A necessary systems upgrade. *Academic Medicine* 86 (12): 1487.

Oakes, J., A. Wells, M. Jones, and A. Datnow. 1997. Detracking: The social construction of ability, cultural politics, and resistance to reform. *Teachers College Record* 98 (3): 482–510.

———. 2008. The social construction of ability, cultural politics, and resistance
to reform. In C. Grant and T. K. Chapman, eds., *History of Multicultural
Education*, 2:293–315. New York: Routledge.

Olivas, M. A. 1994. The education of Latino lawyers: An essay on crop cultivation.
Chicano-Latino Law Review 14:117–138.

———. 2009. What the "war on terror" has meant for U.S. colleges and universities. In R. G. Ehrenberg and C. V. Kuh, eds., *Doctoral education and the faculty of the future*, 249–258. Ithaca, NY: Cornell University Press.

Oltman, P. K., and R. T. Hartnett. 1984. *The role of GRE General and Subject test scores in graduate school admission*. GRE Board Research Report GREB. http://origin-www.ets.org/Media/Research/pdf/RR-84–14-Oltman.pdf.

Orfield, Gary, ed. 2001. *Diversity challenged: Legal crisis and new evidence*. Cambridge, MA: Harvard Education Publishing Group.

Ortiz, A. 2003. The ethnographic interview. In F. K. Stage and K. Manning, eds., *Research in the college context: Approaches and methods*, 35–48. New York: Brunner-Routledge.

Osajima, K. 2005. Asian Americans as the model minority: An analysis of the popular press image in the 1960s and 1980s. In K. Ono, ed., *A companion to Asian American studies*, 215–225. Malden, MA: Blackwell.

Osei-Kofi, N., L. E. Torres, and J. Lui. 2013. Practices of whiteness: Racialization in college admissions viewbooks. *Race Ethnicity and Education* 16 (3): 386–405.

Oyserman, D., K. Elmore, and G. Smith. 2012. Self, self-concept, and identity. In M. R. Leary and J. P. Tangney, eds., *Handbook of self and identity*, 2nd ed., 69–104. New York: Guilford Press.

Özturgut, O. 2011. Standardized testing in the case of China and the lessons to be learned for the U.S. *Journal of International Education Research* 7 (2).

Page, S. E. 2008. *The difference: How the power of diversity creates better groups, firms, schools, and societies*. Princeton, NJ: Princeton University Press.

Pallas, A. M. 2001. Preparing education doctoral students for epistemological diversity. *Educational Researcher* 30 (5): 6–11.

Pappano, L. 2011. The master's as the new bachelor's. *New York Times*, July 22.

Park, J. J. 2013. *When diversity drops: Race, religion, and affirmative action in higher education*. Newark, NJ: Rutgers University Press.

Patel, V. 2014. Why so few American Indians earn Ph.D.'s, and what can be done about it. *Chronicle of Higher Education*, May 27. http://chronicle.com/article /Why-So-Few-American-Indians/146715/.

Patton, E. and S. H. Appelbaum, S. H. 2003. The case for case studies in management research. *Management Research News* 26(5): 60–71.

Patton, M. Q. 2002. *Qualitative research and evaluation methods*. Thousand Oaks, CA: Sage.

Patton, S. 2013. At the Ivies, it's still white at the top. *Chronicle of Higher Education*, June 9.

Pennock-Roman, M. 1986. Fairness in the use of tests for selective admissions of Hispanics. In M. A. Olivas (Ed.), *Latino College Students* (pp. 246–280). NY: Teachers College Press.

Peterson, M. W., and M. G. Spencer. 1990. Assessing academic climates and cultures. *New Directions for Institutional Research*, no. 68: 3–18.

Pfeffer, J. 1993. Barriers to the advance of organizational science: Paradigm development as a dependent variable. *Academy of Management Review* 18 (4): 599–620.

Pfeffer, J., and G. R. Salancik. 1978. *The external control of organizations: A resource dependency perspective*. New York: Harper and Row.

Pfeifer Jr., C. M., and W. E. Sedlacek. 1971. The validity of academic predictors for black and white students at a predominantly white university. *Journal of Educational Measurement* 8 (4): 253–261.

Popper, S. K. 1959. *The logic of scientific discovery.* Fayetteville, AR: Hutchinson.

Porter, T. 1996. *Trust in numbers: Pursuit of objectivity in science and public life.* Princeton, NJ: Princeton University Press.

Portes, A. 2003. Social capital: Its origins and applications in modern sociology. *Annual Review of Sociology* 24:1–24.

Posselt, J. R. 2014. Toward inclusive excellence in graduate education: Constructing merit and diversity in Ph.D. admissions. *American Journal of Education* 120 (4): 481–514.

Posselt, J. R., and K. Black. 2012. Developing the research identities and aspirations of first generation college students: Evidence from the McNair Scholars Program. *International Journal of Researcher Development* 3 (1): 26–48.

Posselt, J. R., O. Jaquette, R. Bielby, and M. N. Bastedo. 2012. Access without equity: Longitudinal analyses of institutional stratification by race and ethnicity, 1972–2004. *American Educational Research Journal* 49 (6): 1074–1111.

Powell, K. 2013. Higher education: On the lookout for true grit. *Nature,* no. 504: 471–473. http://www.nature.com/naturejobs/science/articles/10.1038/nj7480 -471a.

Powell, W. W. 1985. *Getting into print: The decision-making process in scholarly publishing.* Chicago: University of Chicago Press.

Powers, D. E., and S. S. Swinton. 1981. Extending the measurement of graduate admission abilities beyond the verbal and quantitative domains. *Applied Psychological Measurement* 5 (2): 141–158.

Poyrazli, S., and M. D. Lopez. 2007. An exploratory study of perceived discrimination and homesickness: A comparison of international students and American students. *Journal of Psychology* 141 (3): 263–280.

Rao, H., and S. Giorgi. 2006. Code breaking: How entrepreneurs exploit cultural logics to generate institutional change. *Research in Organizational Behavior: An Annual Series of Analytical Essays and Critical Reviews* 27:269–304.

Rao, H., P. Monin, and R. Durand. 2005. Border crossing: Bricolage and the erosion of categorical boundaries in French gastronomy. *American Sociological Review* 70 (6): 968–991.

Redden, E. (2013, July 12). New report shows dependence of U.S. graduate programs on foreign students. *Inside Higher Ed.* http://www.insidehighered.com /news/2013/07/12/new-report-shows-dependence-us-graduate-programs-forei gn-students.

Regents of the University of California v. Bakke. 1978. 438 U.S. 265.

Rivera, L. A. 2011a. Go with your gut: A theory of emotion and inequality in hiring. In *Academy of Management Proceedings,* 1–2. http://proceedings.aom.org /content/2011/1/1.262.short.

———. 2011b. Ivies, extracurriculars, and exclusion: Elite employers' use of educational credentials. *Research in Social Stratification and Mobility* 29 (1): 71–90.

———. 2012a. Diversity within reach: Recruitment versus hiring in elite firms. *Annals of the American Academy of Political and Social Science* 639 (1): 71–90.

———. 2012b. Hiring as cultural matching: The case of elite professional service firms. *American Sociological Review* 77 (6): 999–1022.

Rizzo, M., and R. G. Ehrenberg. 2004. Resident and nonresident tuition and enrollment at flagship state universities. In C. M. Hoxby, ed., *College choices: The economics of where to go, when to go, and how to pay for it,* 303–354. Chicago: University of Chicago Press.

Roach, R. 2005. Affirmative action fallout. *Black Issues in Higher Education* 22 (11): 24–27.

———. 2013. U.S. international education enrollment reaches all-time high. *Diverse Issues in Higher Education,* November 11. http://diverseeducation.com/article /57394/#.

Robins, R. H. 1997. *A short history of linguistics,* 3rd ed. Harlow, UK: Longman.

Rogers, M. R., and L. E. Molina. 2006. Exemplary efforts in psychology to recruit and retain graduate students of color. *American Psychologist* 61 (2): 143.

Roithmayr, D. 2014. *Reproducing racism: How everyday choices lock in white advantage.* New York: NYU Press.

Rojas, F. 2007. *From black power to black studies: How a radical social movement became an academic discipline.* Baltimore: Johns Hopkins University Press.

Rojstaczer, S., and C. Healy. 2012. Where A is ordinary: The evolution of American college and university grading, 1940–2009. *Teachers College Record* 114 (7).

Room for debate: The fate of the humanities. 2013. *New York Times,* November 4, http://www.nytimes.com/roomfordebate/2013/11/04/the-fate-of-the -humanities.

Rubin, H. J., and I. Rubin. 2009. *Qualitative interviewing: The art of hearing data,* 2nd ed. Thousand Oaks, CA: Sage.

Ruscingno, G. 2006. Admission variables and academic success in a doctor of physical therapy program. Unpublished doctoral dissertation, Seton Hall University.

Russell, B. 1972. *The history of Western philosophy.* New York: Simon and Schuster.

Russell, S., M. Hancock, and J. McCullough. 2007. Benefits of undergraduate research experiences. *Science* 316:548–549.

Ryfe, D. M. 2002. The practice of deliberative democracy: A study of 16 deliberative organizations. *Political Communication* 19 (3): 359–377.

Salthouse, T., W. McKeachie, and Y. Lin. 1978. An experimental investigation of factors affecting university promotion decision: A brief report. *Journal of Higher Education* 49 (2): 177–183.

Sauder, M., F. Lynn, and J. M. Podolny. 2012. Status: Insights from organizational sociology. *Annual Review of Sociology* 38:267–283.

Scheurich, J. J. 1995. A postmodernist critique of research interviewing. *International Journal of Qualitative Studies in Education* 8 (3): 239–252.

Schillebeeckx, M., Maricque, B., & Lewis, C. 2013. The missing piece to changing the university culture. *Nature biotechnology* 31(10): 938–941.

Schmidt, F. L., and J. Hunter. 2004. General mental ability in the world of work: Occupational attainment and job performance. *Journal of Personality and Social Psychology* 86 (1): 162.

Schmidt, F. L., R. H. Johnson, and J. F. Gugel. 1978. Utility of policy capturing as an approach to graduate admissions decision making. *Applied Psychological Measurement* 2 (3): 347–359.

Schmidt, P. 2010. Graduate school applications spiked after economy's plunge. *Chronicle of Higher Education,* September 14. http://chronicle.com/article/Graduate-School-Applications/124387/.

Schmitt, M. T., R. Spears, and N. R. Branscombe. 2003. Constructing a minority group identity out of shared rejection: The case of international students. *European Journal of Social Psychology* 33 (1): 1–12.

Schoem, D. L., and S. Hurtado, eds. 2001. *Intergroup dialogue: Deliberative democracy in school, college, community, and workplace.* Ann Arbor: University of Michigan Press.

Schofer, E., and J. W. Meyer. 2005. The worldwide expansion of higher education in the twentieth century. *American Sociological Review* 70 (6): 898–920.

Scott, W. R. 2008. *Institutions and organizations: Ideas and interests.* Thousand Oaks, CA: Sage.

Sedlacek, W. E. 2004. *Beyond the big test.* San Francisco: Jossey-Bass.

Sellers, R. M., M. A. Smith, J. N. Shelton, S. A. J. Rowley, and T. M. Chavous. 1998. Multidimensional model of racial identity: A reconceptualization of African American racial identity. *Personality and Social Psychology Review* 2 (1): 18–39.

Skousen, M. 2009. *The making of modern economics,* vol. 2. Armonk, NY: M. E. Sharpe.

Smith v. City of Jackson. 2005. (03-1160) 544 U.S. 228.

Smith, D. G. 2009. *Diversity's promise for higher education: Making it work.* Baltimore: Johns Hopkins University Press.

Smith, D. G., L. E. Wolf, B. Busenberg, and Associates. 1996. *Achieving faculty diversity: Debunking the myths.* Washington, DC: Association of American Colleges and Universities.

Smith, L. M. 1978. An evolving logic of participant observation, educational ethnography, and other case studies. *Review of Research in Education* 6:316–377.

Snow, C. P. 1959. *The two cultures and the scientific revolution.* London: Cambridge University Press.

Spence, M. 1973. Job market signaling. *Quarterly Journal of Economics* 87 (3): 355–374.

Spillman, L. 2014. Mixed methods and the logic of qualitative inference. *Qualitative Sociology* 37(2): 189–205.

Stake, R. E. 2005. Qualitative case studies. In N. K. Denzin and Y. S. Lincoln, eds., *The Sage handbook of qualitative research,* 3rd ed., 443–466. Thousand Oaks, CA: Sage.

Stampnitzky, L. 2006. How does "culture" become "capital"? Cultural and institutional struggles over "character and personality" at Harvard. *Sociological Perspectives* 49 (4): 461–481.

Stanton-Salazar, R. D. 1997. A social capital framework for understanding the socialization of racial minority children and youths. *Harvard Educational Review* 67 (1): 1–40.

Steele, C. M. 2010. *Whistling Vivaldi: How stereotypes affect us and what we can do about it.* New York: Norton.

Steele, C. M., and J. Aronson. 1995. Stereotype threat and the intellectual test performance of African Americans. *Journal of Personality and Social Psychology* 69 (5): 797.

Stephens, N. M., S. A. Fryberg, H. R. Markus, C. S. Johnson, and R. Covarrubias. 2012. Unseen disadvantage: How American universities' focus on independence undermines the academic performance of first-generation college students. *Journal of Personality and Social Psychology* 102 (6): 1178.

Sternberg, R. J. 2003. *Wisdom, intelligence, and creativity synthesized.* Cambridge: Cambridge University Press.

Sternberg, R. J., and W. M. Williams. 1997. Does the Graduate Record Examination predict meaningful success in the graduate training of psychologists? A case study. *American Psychologist* 52 (6): 630–641.

Stevens, M. 2007. *Creating a class: College admissions and the education of elites.* Cambridge, MA: Harvard University Press.

Stevens, M. L., and J. Roksa. 2011. The diversity imperative in elite admissions. In L. M. Stulberg and S. L. Weinburg, eds., *Diversity in American higher education: Toward a more comprehensive approach,* 63–73. New York: Routledge.

Stock, W. A., A. T. Finnegan, and J. J. Siegfried. 2006. Attrition in economics Ph.D. programs. *American Economic Review* 96 (2): 458–466.

Strauss, A., and J. Corbin. 2008. *Basics of qualitative research: Techniques and procedures for developing grounded theory.* Thousand Oaks, CA: Sage.

Studley, R. E. 2004. Inequality, student achievement, and college admissions: A remedy for underrepresentation. In R. Zwick, ed., *Rethinking the SAT: The future of standardized testing in college admissions,* 321–344. New York: Routledge.

Suen, H. K., and L. Yu. 2006. Chronic consequences of high stakes testing? Lessons from the Chinese civil service exam. *Comparative Education Review* 50 (1): 46–65.

Suzuki, B. H. 2002. Revisiting the model minority stereotype: Implications for student affairs practice and higher education. *New Directions for Student Services,* no. 97: 21–32.

Swales, J. 2004. *Research genres: Explorations and applications.* Stuttgart: Ernst Klett Sprachen.

Sweitzer, K., and J. F. Volkwein. 2009. Prestige among graduate and professional schools: Comparing the US News' graduate school reputation ratings between disciplines. *Research in Higher Education* 50 (8): 812–836.

Swidler, A. 1986. Culture in action: Symbols and strategies. *American Sociological Review* 51 (2): 273–286.

Swidler, A., and J. Arditi. 1994. The new sociology of knowledge. *Annual Review of Sociology* 20 (1): 305–329.

Tajfel, H., ed. 2010. *Social identity and intergroup relations,* vol. 7. Cambridge: Cambridge University Press.

Tajfel, H., and J. Turner. 1986. The social identity theory of intergroup behavior. In J. T. Jest and J. Sidanius, eds., *Psychology of intergroup relations,* 7–24. Chicago: Nelson Hall.

Taylor, C. R., and B. B. Stern. 1997. Asian-Americans: Television advertising and the "model minority" stereotype. *Journal of Advertising* 26 (2): 47–61.

Temp, G. 1971. Validity of the SAT for blacks and whites in thirteen integrated institutions. *Journal of Educational Measurement* 8 (4): 245–251.

Teranishi, R. T., L. B. Behringer, E. A. Grey, and T. L. Parker. 2009. Critical race theory and research on Asian Americans and Pacific Islanders in higher education. *New Directions for Institutional Research,* no. 142: 57–68.

Thelin, J. R. 2004. *A history of American higher education.* Baltimore: Johns Hopkins University Press.

Thompson, J. 2013. *The changing demography of wealth: Demographics by wealth and wealth by demographics in the SCF.* Washington, DC: Federal Reserve Board of Governors.

Thorndike, R. L. 1949. *Personnel selection: Test and measurement techniques.* New York: Wiley.

Thornton, P. H. 2004. *Markets from culture: Institutional logics and organizational decisions in higher education publishing.* Stanford, CA: Stanford Business Books.

Thornton, P. H., and W. Ocasio. 1999. Institutional logics and the historical contingency of power in organizations. *American Journal of Sociology* 105 (3): 801–843.

———. 2008. Institutional logics. In R. Greenwood, C. Oliver, R. Suddaby, and K. Sahlin-Anderson, eds., *The Sage handbook of organizational institutionalism,* 99–129. Thousand Oaks, CA: Sage.

Thucydides. 1951. *The history of the Peloponnesian War.* Translated by R. Crawley. New York: Random House.

Thurgood, L., M. J. Golladay, and S. T. Hill. 2006. *U.S. doctorates in the 20th century: Special report.* NSF 06-319. http://www.nsf.gov/statistics/nsf06319/pdf/nsf06319.pdf.

Tienda, M. 2013. Diversity ≠ inclusion: Promoting integration in higher education. *Educational Researcher* 42 (9): 467–475.

Tierney, W. G. 1988. Organizational culture in higher education: Defining the essentials. *Journal of Higher Education* 59 (1): 2–21.

Tierney, W. G., and E. M. Bensimon. 1996. *Promotion and tenure: Culture and socialization in academe.* Albany: SUNY Press.

Tilly, C. 1998. *Durable inequality.* Berkeley: University of California Press.

———. 2005. *Social movements, 1768–2004.* Boulder: Paradigm.

Torche, F. 2011. Is a college degree still the great equalizer? Intergenerational mobility across levels of schooling in the United States. *American Journal of Sociology* 117 (3): 763–807.

Tough, P. 2012. *How children succeed: Grit, curiosity, and the hidden power of character.* New York: Houghton Mifflin.

Trice, A. G. 2004. Mixing it up: International graduate students' social interactions with American students. *Journal of College Student Development* 45 (6): 671–687.

Trower, C. A. 2009. Toward a greater understanding of the tenure track for minorities. *Change* 41 (5): 38–45.

Trower, C. A., and R. P. Chait. 2002. Faculty diversity: Too little for too long. *Harvard Magazine,* March/April.

Tumminia, D. 1992. Hard work, luck, and uncontrollable variables: A guide to getting into graduate school. *Sociological Practice Review* 3 (1): 37–41.

Twombly, S. 1992. The process of choosing a dean. *Journal of Higher Education* 63 (6): 653–683.

Urrieta, L. 2007. Orchestrating habitus and figured worlds: Chicana/o educational mobility and social class. In J. A. VanGalen and G. W. Noblit, eds., *Late to class: Social class and schooling in the new economy,* 113–140. Albany: SUNY Press.

U.S. Census Bureau. 2008. *2008 American Community Survey 1-year estimates.* Washington, DC: U.S. Census Bureau.

U.S. Department of Education, National Center for Education Statistics. 2012. *The condition of education 2012.* NCES 2012-045. Indicator 47. http://nces.ed.gov /fastfacts/display.asp?id=72.

Vaughan, D. 1992. Theory elaboration: The heuristics of case analysis. In C. C. Ragin and H. S. Becker, eds., *What is a case? Exploring the foundations of social inquiry,* 173–203. Cambridge: Cambridge University Press.

Wadsworth, B. C., M. L. Hecht, and E. Jung. 2008. The role of identity gaps, discrimination, and acculturation in international students' educational satisfaction in American classrooms. *Communication Education* 57 (1): 64–87.

Wait, I. W., and J. W. Gressel. 2009. Relationship between TOEFL score and academic success for international engineering students. *Journal of Engineering Education* 98 (4): 389–398.

Walker, G. E., C. M. Golde, L. Jones, A. C. Bueschel, and P. Hutchings. 2008. *The formation of scholars: Rethinking doctoral education for the twenty-first century.* San Francisco: Jossey-Bass.

Walters, A. M., S. Lee, and C. Trapani. 2004. *Stereotype threat, the test-center environment, and performance on the GRE General Test.* Princeton, NJ: Educational Testing Service.

Walton, G. M., and G. L. Cohen. 2003. Stereotype lift. *Journal of Experimental Social Psychology* 39 (5): 456–467.

Weber, M. 1978a. *Economy and society,* vol. 1. Berkeley: University of California Press.

———. 1978b. *Economy and society,* vol. 2. Berkeley: University of California Press.

Wechsler, H. S. 1977. *The qualified student.* New York: Wiley.

Wei, M., T. Y. Ku, D. W. Russell, B. Mallinckrodt, and K. Y. H. Liao. 2008. Moderating effects of three coping strategies and self-esteem on perceived discrimination and depressive symptoms: A minority stress model for Asian international students. *Journal of Counseling Psychology* 55 (4): 451.

Weick, K. E. 1979. Cognitive processes in organizations. *Research in Organizational Behavior* 1 (1): 41–74.

———. 1984. Small wins: Redefining the scale of social problems. *American Psychologist* 39 (1): 40.

———. 1998. Improvisation as a mindset for organizational analysis. *Organization Science* 9 (5): 543–555.

Weidman, J. C., and E. L. Stein. 2003. Socialization of doctoral students to academic norms. *Research in Higher Education* 44 (6): 641–656.

Weiss, R. S. 1995. *Learning from strangers: The art and method of qualitative interview studies.* New York: Free Press.

Weitzman, R. A. 1972. It is time to re-reconsider the GRE: A reply to Marston. *American Psychologist* 27 (3): 236–238.

Wendler, C., and B. Bridgeman, eds. 2014. *The Research Foundation for the GRE revised General Test: A compendium of studies.* Princeton, NJ: Educational Testing Service. http://www.ets.org/s/research/pdf/gre_compendium.pdf.

Wendler, C., B. Bridgeman, F. Cline, C. Millett, J. Rock, N. Bell, and P. McAllister. 2010. *The path forward: The future of graduate education in the United States.* Princeton, NJ: Educational Testing Service.

Wilkerson, T. 2007. The relationship between admissions credentials and the success of students admitted to a physics doctoral program. Unpublished doctoral dissertation, University of Central Florida.

Williams, J. D. 1969. Judgment analysis for assessing doctoral admission policies. *Journal of Experimental Education* 38 (2): 92–96.

Willingham, W. W. 1974. Predicting success in graduate education. *Science* 183 (4122): 273–278.

Winkle-Wagner, R., and A. M. Locks. 2013. *Diversity and inclusion on campus: Supporting racially and ethnically underrepresented students.* New York: Routledge.

Wilson, J. 1989. *Bureaucracy: What government agencies do and why they do it.* New York: Basic Books.

Wolfers, J. 2015. How economists came to dominate the conversation. *New York Times,* January 24. http://www.nytimes.com/2015/01/24/upshot/how-economists-came-to-dominate-the-conversation.html.

Worthington, R. L., R. L., Navarro, M. Loewy, and J. Hart. 2008. Color-blind racial attitudes, social dominance orientation, racial-ethnic group membership and college students' perceptions of campus climate. *Journal of Diversity in Higher Education* 1(1): 8–19.

Wulff, D. H., A. E. Austin, J. D. Nyquist, and J. Sprague. 2004. *Paths to the professoriate: Strategies for enriching the preparation of future faculty.* San Francisco: Jossey-Bass.

Xu, X. 2001. Chinese ETS test results doubted. *China Daily,* February 21.

Xueqin, J. 2011. Selecting the right Chinese students. *Chronicle of Higher Education,* November 3.

Yang, S. Y., and R. J. Sternberg. 1997. Taiwanese Chinese people's conceptions of intelligence. *Intelligence* 25 (1): 21–36.

Yin, R. K. 1994. *Case study research: Design and methods,* 4th ed. Thousand Oaks, CA: Sage.

Yosso, T. J. 2006. Whose culture has capital? A critical race theory discussion of community cultural wealth. *Race, Ethnicity, and Education* 8 (1): 69–91.

Young, J. W., and J. L. Kobrin. 2001. *Differential validity, differential prediction, and college admission testing: A comprehensive review and analysis.* College Board Research Report No. 2001-6. New York: College Entrance Examination Board.

Yule, G., and P. Hoffman. 1990. Predicting success for international teaching assistants in a US university. *TESOL Quarterly* 24 (2): 227–243.

Zald, M. N. 1971. *Occupations and organizations in American society: The organization-dominated man?* Cambridgeshire, UK: Markham.

Zerubavel, E. 1993. *The fine line.* New York: Free Press.

Zhang, L. 2009. Do foreign doctorate recipients displace U.S. doctorate recipients at U.S. universities? In R. G. Ehrenberg and C. V. Kuh, eds., *Doctoral education and the faculty of the future,* 209–223. Ithaca, NY: Cornell University Press.

Zhang, Q. 2010. Asian Americans beyond the model minority stereotype: The nerdy and the left out. *Journal of International and Intercultural Communication* 3 (1): 20–37.

Zhao, Y. 2001. Preparing early for the first of the all-important tests. *New York Times,* October 10.

Zimmerman, M. A., and G. J. Zeitz. 2002. Beyond survival: Achieving new venture growth by building legitimacy. *Academy of Management Review* 27 (3): 414–431.

Zucker, L. G. 1977. The role of institutionalization in cultural persistence. *American Sociological Review* 42 (5): 726–743.

Zwick, R. 2002. *Fair game? The use of standardized admissions tests in higher education.* New York: Routledge.

———. 2016. *Who gets in? Strategies for fair and effective college admissions.* Cambridge, MA: Harvard University Press.

Acknowledgments

The trust that enables prospective research participants to become forthcoming members of a study is a foundation of social inquiry, and I am grateful to the participants in this study for sharing with me their experience of admissions work and for helping me to see it from their perspectives. I extend special thanks to the department leaders and admissions committees who allowed me into the protected space of their admissions meetings. My observations of those meetings have added more richness to my findings than scores of additional interviews could have provided.

This project was also made possible through financial support from a few sources. The Center for Public Policy in Diverse Societies and the National Association of Graduate Admissions Professionals awarded grants that supported the fieldwork when the project was just an idea. I was thankful as well to receive a fellowship from the Rackham Graduate School, which afforded a level of focus that resulted in deeper analysis and better writing than would otherwise have been possible. I hope the quality of the outcome is commensurate with my gratitude for each of these groups' support.

I was delighted to connect with an academic press that shared my vision of disseminating this research to graduate education stakeholders outside the higher education and sociology circles for whom I usually write. Harvard University Press has been outstanding to work with from day one, and I am indebted in particular to Andrew Kinney and Elizabeth Knoll, who both served as editors. Elizabeth acquired the project, encouraged me to add the chapter on evaluation of international students, and provided sage guidance on each chapter in the manuscript. I looked forward to her manila envelopes, with official feedback accompanied by postcards with witty remarks. After she transitioned out of HUP, Andrew's editorial skill and eye for detail also contributed to the strength of the manuscript, and I'm grateful for his steady support through the publication process. I would be remiss not to acknowledge my appreciation to the two anonymous external reviewers, both of whom offered constructive and thoughtful advice that helped me improve the manuscript. Chapter 4 develops ideas originally treated in "Disciplinary Logics in Doctoral Admissions," published in the *Journal of Higher Education*.

Outstanding research and editorial assistance from University of Michigan doctoral students Kimberly Reyes, Kelly Slay, and Aurora Kamimura also supported the production of the book. I am particularly appreciative of Kim's dedicated editorial support with early chapter drafts. I also want to acknowledge my transcriptionist, Mary Ann Spitale, whose efficient, accurate work increases my research capacity.

I have been graced with several wise mentors whose counsel and support have been instrumental as I worked on this project. This book would not exist without Mike Bastedo's generous mentoring through the research and publication processes. I am deeply grateful to Deborah Carter for her wisdom, wit, and for all that I learned from her about qualitative research. Janet Lawrence and Janet Weiss offered astute interpretations of my early findings, and they helped me think about my data in new ways. I am also indebted to Annemarie Palincsar, Lisa Lattuca, Diana Hess, Chris Golde, Liliana Garces, and Tabbye Chavous for professional guidance and review of specific chapters.

For conversations and insights that strengthened the design, findings, and/or message of this work, I extend my sincere thanks to Elizabeth Armstrong, Ann Austin, Deborah Ball, Estela Bensimon, John Bound, Phil Bowman, Bryan Brayboy, Lenny Cassuto, Steve DesJardins, Kimberly Griffin, Eric Grodsky, Patti Gumport, Ozan Jaquette, Michèle Lamont, Anna Neumann, Gary Rhoades, Ed St. John, Mitchell Stevens, Barrett Taylor, and Rebecca Zwick.

Through the years I have conducted research on graduate admissions—the long haul of design, recruitment, fieldwork, analysis, writing, and revising—scholarly friendships with others who study higher education have been a great source of sustenance. I especially want to acknowledge Cassie Barnhardt, Nick Bowman, Julio Cardona Raya, Gloryvee Fonseca, Leslie Gonzales, Nathan Harris, Matt Holsapple, Ignacio Hernandez, Susana Hernandez, Marc Johnston, Anat Levtov, Chris Linder, Angela Locks, Johanna Masse, Matt Mayhew, Carmen McCallum, Genevieve Negron-Gonzales, Penny Pasque, Rosie Perez, Awilda Rodriguez, Shelley Strickland, and Kerri Wakefield.

Finally, my family. Blessings to each and every one of you. Special thanks to my parents, Janet and Gary Schmidt, and to Derek and Daniel Posselt, my dear husband and son. Thank you for being my foundation, and for your strong support of my work and its demands. Derek and Danny boy: I absolutely love our life together, and I dedicate this book to you.

Index